100 THINGS
AUBURN FANS
SHOULD KNOW & DO
BEFORE THEY DIE

100 THINGS
AUBURN FANS
SHOULD KNOW & DO
BEFORE THEY DIE

Evan Woodbery

TRIUMPH
B O O K S

No part of this publication may be reproduced, stored in a retrieval system, or transmitted in any form by any means, electronic, mechanical, photocopying, or otherwise, without the prior written permission of the publisher, Triumph Books, 542 South Dearborn Street, Suite 750, Chicago, Illinois 60605.

Triumph Books and colophon are registered trademarks of Random House, Inc.

Library of Congress Cataloging-in-Publication Data
Woodbery, Evan, 1980–
  100 things Auburn fans should know and do before they die / Evan Woodbery.
      p. cm.
  Includes bibliographical references.
  ISBN 978-1-60078-130-8
  1. Auburn University—Football—History. 2. Auburn Tigers (Football team)—History. I. Title. II. Title: One hundred things Auburn fans should know and do before they die.
  GV958.A92W66 2009
  796.332'630976155—dc22   2009012449

This book is available in quantity at special discounts for your group or organization. For further information, contact:

Triumph Books
542 South Dearborn Street
Suite 750
Chicago, Illinois 60605
(312) 939-3330
Fax (312) 663-3557
www.triumphbooks.com

Printed in U.S.A.
ISBN: 978-1-60078-130-8
Design by Patricia Frey
Page production by Prologue Publishing Services, LLC
All photos courtesy of Todd Van Emst unless otherwise specified

To the memory of my grandfather, Thomas S. Case

Contents

Acknowledgments

This book could have never been completed without the outstanding written work done by others over the last 50 years. Every book, article, and website used is cited in the back, and the writers have my gratitude for their research.

Two people who have so much knowledge of Auburn and Southern football that they could have written this book from memory in a week deserve special thanks. David Housel has written thousands of pages on Auburn football. His most recent publication, *Auburn University Football Vault*, is worth buying for any Auburn fan. Phillip Marshall, who is editor of AuburnUndercover.com, was gracious in sharing his work. His book, *The Auburn Experience*, is also a must-have.

My friends and colleagues on the Auburn beat helped me stay focused during the last eight months. Charles Goldberg, when he wasn't breaking down game film, offered valuable help. Internet associates Bryan Matthews and Jeffrey Lee were always an emailed question away. Jay G. Tate's blog was an important resource. Andrew Gribble, Andy Bitter, and Luke Brietzke insisted that I meet book deadlines before doing anything else. Friends Collin Mickle, Ross Dellenger, Josh Cooper, Kent Babb, Mike Szvetitz, Gary Thorne, and Bradley Handwerger also offered support.

Press-Register sports editor Randy Kennedy approved my work on this project and is a great boss.

Auburn's media relations department, especially Kirk Sampson and Brad Gust, produced outstanding media guides and notes that made my job easier.

The city of Auburn library and the Auburn University libraries were good resources and relaxing places to work.

My blog on AL.com is always a good sounding board and place for instant feedback, so thanks to my regular readers on there. Some readers are more avid than others; message-board poster "obtiger1" deserves special mention.

The people at Triumph Books extended enormous leeway and patience to a first-time book author.

Thanks to my parents, Alison Hollingsworth and Thomas Woodbery, and my brothers, Freddy and Will, for their support.

This book is dedicated to my grandfather, Thomas Case of Bay Village, Ohio, who passed away in 2007. He was a football fan and longtime Cleveland Browns season-ticket holder who brought me along with him to the old Municipal Stadium on more blustery days than I can count. He always supported my budding writing career, and I'm sure he would be excited about this book.

Introduction

I embarked on this project in July 2008 feeling somewhat under-qualified for the job. I have lived and worked in Auburn and covered the university's athletic programs since 2004, so I've been allowed to witness a fascinating chapter in Auburn's football history. But my institutional knowledge didn't reach as deep into history as this project demanded.

So I started reading. I checked out books, combed through archives, and spent eye-glazing hours in front of microfiche readers. Auburn's history goes much deeper than this decade, and I've tried to reflect that rich heritage in this book.

But it has been a fascinating decade.

I arrived from another newspaper job in Columbia, South Carolina, only a few days before Auburn was to kick off the 2004 season. I was without an apartment, a computer, or sources of any kind. Many said that I should be preparing to cover a coaching search within a matter of months. Instead, one of the most incredible seasons in Auburn's history happened. The 2004 season gets special attention in this book for two reasons. One, I was there to cover it firsthand. And two, the storylines from the season—the survival of Tommy Tuberville, the redemption of Jason Campbell, the brains of Al Borges, the brawn of Auburn's defense—were so plentiful and improbable that they were impossible to ignore.

The most challenging part of the book has been determining the 100 topics to include in the list and then ranking them appropriately.

I have no doubt that deserving chapters are left out. And I'm sure there will be disagreements about whether certain games, players, or feats were ranked too high or too low. I hope you'll take this book not as a definitive pronouncement about Auburn football, but as a jumping-off point for further discussion and debate.

Many of this book's readers will have lived through the games, the eras, the coaches, and the experiences that are written about here. That makes you a better judge than I of their relative importance. So if you want to move No. 32 to No. 17 and switch No. 5 and No. 6 or get rid of a couple chapters entirely and replace them with your own, be my guest. That's what this book is about.

It's been a privilege to learn more about the people, history, and traditions of one of the South's most storied football programs. I hope you enjoy it, too.

1 Ralph "Shug" Jordan

In 1950 Auburn's football team failed to win a game, an embarrassing low point that ended Earl Brown's three-year tenure. Georgia coaching legend Vince Dooley, then a freshman at Auburn, called it "probably the worst football team I've ever seen."

Auburn football was at a crucial juncture, and making the right hire was critically important. Auburn athletics director Jeff Beard knew who would turn the program around, and he wasted little time making it happen.

Ralph "Shug" Jordan, an Auburn man still stung by his snub three years earlier, sent a one-sentence application letter at Beard's urging. The search committee, stocked by Beard with Jordan partisans, had an easy choice. Newspapers said the Tigers were "starved for a winning ball team," and Jordan would waste little time satisfying fans and alumni.

Jordan was born on September 25, 1910, in Selma, Alabama. His dad worked for the railroads while "Shug," as he came to be known for his love of sugar cane, was deeply involved in youth sports at the local YMCA. Jordan enrolled at Auburn in 1928 and became a three-sport athlete—a center in football, a guard in basketball, and a left-handed pitcher in baseball. After college, his application to teach at one school was rebuffed because of his Catholic faith, so he returned to the Plains as an assistant coach for Chet Wynne.

During World War II, Jordan was a lieutenant who was part of invasions in North Africa, Sicily, Normandy, and Okinawa. Wounded during the D-Day invasion, he received a Purple Heart and Bronze Star. Returning from the war in 1946, Jordan coached

Ralph "Shug" Jordan won 176 games and a national championship during his 25 years as Auburn's head coach.

briefly for the Miami Seahawks of professional football before joining Wally Butts' staff at Georgia. Auburn picked Brown over Jordan in 1947, but corrected the mistake three seasons later.

Jordan turned things around in his first season. In his 25-year career, he won 176 games, an SEC championship, and a national championship. His teams played in 12 bowl games (missing another four due to NCAA probation) and featured 20 All-Americans, an Outland Trophy winner, and a Heisman Trophy winner. His teams finished in the top 20 of the Associated Press rankings 13 times, in the top 10 seven times, and in the top five four times. Twenty-two of his 25 teams finished with winning records.

Jordan planned to retire after his 25th season, and Doug Barfield was immediately tabbed as his successor. There were high expectations for the 1975 season (at least one preseason magazine picked Auburn to be national champions), but the Tigers struggled to a 4–6–1 record. Jordan went on to serve five years on Auburn's

Board of Trustees until he died of leukemia in July 1980 at the age of 69.

He was posthumously inducted into the National Football Foundation Hall of Fame in 1982. When fans selected Jordan as the coach for Auburn's 100-year team in 1992, he had been a part of 29 of those 100 seasons.

But Jordan was remembered for his character as much as his victories. "His record doesn't speak for him as a man," said Beard, one of his close friends. He cared deeply about his players. Lloyd Nix, quarterback of the 1957 championship team, remembered that "I never saw him when he didn't ask about my mother."

He commanded respect, not fear, from his subordinates.

"Coach Jordan coached by making his players and assistants feel good about themselves," said Buck Bradberry, a longtime assistant. "The way he did it, it was almost like his personality itself demanded respect, because he was so respectful of you."

David Langner, a former player who was the hero of the 1972 "Punt, 'Bama, Punt!" game, wrote a moving tribute to Jordan in recommending him for the NFF Hall of Fame.

"Everything I am and everything I hope to be, I owe to him," Langner said, "because he loved and cared about me as a person."

All-Time Coaching Victories

1. Ralph "Shug" Jordan (176–83–6, 25 seasons)
2. Mike Donahue (99–35–5, 18 seasons)
2. Pat Dye (99–39–4, 12 seasons)
4. Tommy Tuberville (85–40, 10 seasons)
5. Jack Meagher (48–37–10, nine seasons)
6. Terry Bowden (47–17–1, six seasons)
7. Doug Barfield (29–25–1, five seasons)
8. Chet Wynne (22–15–2, four seasons)
9. Carl Voyles (15–22, four seasons)
10. John Heisman (12–4–2, five seasons)

2 The 1957 National Championship Team

Fifty years later, their place in history is not only secure, it's celebrated. The players on Auburn's 1957 team mounted an incredible run to a perfect season, an SEC title, and the school's first and only national championship.

When they were honored in 2007, the roar of the fans let them know their magical season hadn't been lost to the history books.

Like many great seasons—including Auburn's perfect run in 2004—this one approached suddenly. There may have been mild optimism entering the season, but few were thinking in terms of championships.

"We had no idea," said defensive end Jimmy "Red" Phillips. "We expected to win. We were used to winning. But nobody was talking about national championships or even an SEC championship. We were just trying to do what our coaches wanted."

The Tigers were a respectable 7–3 in 1956, but the team's aspirations for 1957 took two big hits before the season even started. Auburn's starting quarterback and running back departed that summer, leaving coach Ralph "Shug" Jordan to search for solutions. He decided to hand the reins of the offense to Lloyd Nix, a left-handed halfback who hadn't played quarterback in years.

"I'm not worried about Lloyd's ability to get the job done," Jordan said at the time. "He's not flashy, but he gets that job done, and that's what counts."

Nix welcomed the move. "When Coach Jordan told me I was moving to quarterback," he said, "it wasn't that big a deal. I was getting to play, and that was all that mattered."

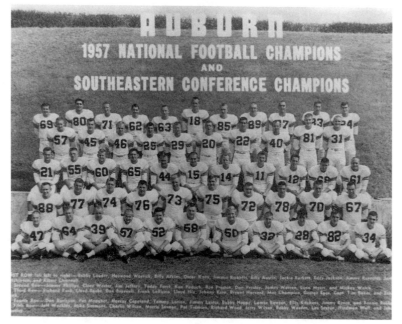

The 1957 Auburn Tigers are the only national champions in school history.

Although he would throw the ball only 60 times (completing 33) in 1957, Nix became one of the team's most valuable unsung heroes. Halfbacks Tommy Lorino and Bobby Hoppe combined with fullback Billy Atkins to lead the rushing attack.

When it was all said and done, Auburn had put together a 10–0 season and won the conference championship. It was the first time Auburn had gone undefeated since 1932 and the first perfect season since 1913. The Tigers led the nation in every defensive category in 1957, and some consider Auburn's defense one of the greatest in college football history. Led by nose guard Zeke Smith, linebacker Jackie Burkett, and ends Jerry Wilson and Phillips, the Tigers allowed an average of 2.8 points per game and shut out opponents six times. Of 28 points allowed all season, one touchdown was scored on an interception return and three touchdowns were said to be scored on the second-team defense.

5

After starting the season unranked, Auburn steadily moved up in the polls. A 7–0 win over Tennessee on a cold and rainy day in Knoxville jumped the Tigers to No. 7 and started them on the championship path. A win against Florida State moved them to No. 1.

Auburn's closest call came in the eighth game of the season against Georgia. Auburn led 6–0 at halftime, but the Tigers fumbled on their 10-yard line on the third play of the second half. Auburn held and got the ball back…only to fumble again! But the Bulldogs failed to score in eight plays (and had only three first downs the entire game), giving Auburn the narrow victory.

Auburn's rise to the top was aided by losses by Notre Dame, Oklahoma, and Texas A&M, and a poor performance by Michigan State.

The Iron Bowl provided a fitting exclamation point for the season. When the Tigers jumped out to a 34–0 lead at halftime, Auburn fans started to chant "56! 56!" in reference to the 1948 Iron Bowl that Alabama won 55–0. But Jordan declined to run up the score, and Auburn won by a still-impressive 40–0 margin.

Auburn still wasn't a shoo-in for the national title. The Tigers were prevented from playing in a postseason bowl game by NCAA sanctions (although the Associated Press poll was voted on before the bowls were actually played). And Ohio State coach Woody Hayes was adamant that the 9–1 Buckeyes deserved to climb over Auburn to No. 1.

Fortunately for Auburn, the Tigers had a plan to win the ballot. At this time, every AP subscriber was automatically given a vote in

Auburn's 10 Conference Championships
Southern Intercollegiate Athletic Association: 1913, 1914, 1919
Southern Conference: 1932
Southeastern Conference: 1957, 1983, 1987–1989, 2004

the poll. Auburn administrator Bill Beckwith contacted every paper and radio station in the Southeast—big and small—and lobbied them to vote for the Tigers. The plan worked, and Auburn finished atop the final AP poll for the school's first national championship. It was the first and only time that a school on bowl probation won the AP national title.

Today, memories of that season dot campus, from the murals in the stadium to the memorabilia at the athletic complex to even the phone number for ordering tickets (1-800-AUB-1957).

The landscape of college football has changed dramatically since then, but the season endures as one of the most significant moments in the program's history.

When Alabama Came to Auburn: The 1989 Iron Bowl

To the thousands of fans at Jordan-Hare Stadium, and the many thousands more outside who didn't have a ticket but merely wanted to soak in the atmosphere, it was more than a game.

The meeting between Auburn and Alabama on December 2, 1989, was a testament to Auburn's tenacity and a repudiation of those across the state who said it would never happen.

It happened. And those who witnessed the day will never forget it.

First, the background: since the resumption of the rivalry in 1948, Auburn and Alabama had met at Legion Field in Birmingham. The venue made sense because it was centrally located in the state and had a larger seating capacity than the campus stadiums in Auburn or Tuscaloosa. It wasn't uncommon for other schools to use off-campus stadiums for one or several games a year. But as times changed and on-campus stadiums grew and grew, off-campus sites fell out of favor.

Auburn felt it was time to bring the rivalry to its home stadium on the Plains. The move was complicated, though, because Legion Field was technically a "neutral" site. While each team was allotted an equal number of tickets, Alabama always seemed to have more fans, perhaps because of the tickets distributed locally in Birmingham.

Understandably, Auburn was ready to withdraw from an arrangement in which the Tigers effectively played a "road" game in Birmingham each year. Alabama was less eager to sacrifice the historic Birmingham location for which the Iron Bowl was named. It was Ray Perkins who reportedly said, "It won't happen," when asked about the chances of moving the game to Auburn. But in 1988 Alabama gave in and agreed to come the following year.

The anticipation started instantly. Auburn coach Pat Dye compared Alabama's visit to the fall of the Berlin Wall.

"Like the children of Israel entering the Promised Land, Auburn fans felt they had completed a journey they'd never imagined they would make—to Auburn to see the Alabama game," said longtime Auburn administrator David Housel. "The children of Israel had waited 40 years. Auburn fans had waited longer."

Ivan Maisel, then of the *Dallas Morning News*, opened his story this way: "Take a long look at that dateline. That this story is being written here, that 85,000 fans will congregate at Jordan-Hare Stadium on this particular Saturday, means more to Auburn University than any donation, any building, any academic achievement ever will."

The atmosphere surrounding the game would have been astronomical under any circumstance, but the game also had huge championship implications. The Tide came in with a perfect record and a No. 2 national ranking. Auburn was 8–2, but had only one SEC loss and was No. 11 in the country. (The records and rankings were remarkably similar to the 1972 "Punt, 'Bama, Punt!" game).

Alabama approached the trip to Auburn cautiously, with coach Bill Curry announcing that players had received death threats and that the FBI was investigating.

The game itself was wrapped in so much emotion that it may have taken players extra time to get focused. Auburn running back Stacy Danley was hammered on the first play of the game by Alabama nose guard Willie Wyatt, and a parade of trash-talking began. Players on both sides wanted badly to win.

"He was yelling and screaming and slobbering at the mouth," Danley said. "It looked like his head was coming through his helmet. He told me I wasn't getting anything that day. He was in my ear talking to me all that day."

Danley had 130 yards on 28 carries as Auburn built a 27–10 lead and held on for a 30–20 victory. The win gave the Tigers their third-consecutive SEC championship and fourth in seven years. The loss sent Curry (0–3 in Iron Bowls) packing to Kentucky. The Tigers went on to defeat Ohio State in the Hall of Fame Bowl in Tampa, Florida.

Believe it or not, Alabama eventually followed Auburn's lead. The Tide kept its home game in Birmingham for about a decade, but decided to move its games to Tuscaloosa in 2000.

With Bryant-Denny Stadium recently enlarged and Legion Field increasingly decrepit, few Alabama fans opposed the decision.

The first game back in Tuscaloosa had none of the fanfare of Auburn's first game. Auburn won 9–0 on a cold, dreary day.

4 George Petrie: Coach and University Leader

In one sense, it's appropriate that one man's name is synonymous both with the growth of Auburn University and the creation of its athletic program. "But in another way," writes Michael Glenn Jernigan in his biography of George Petrie, "it is unfortunate, for it

The father of Auburn football, George Petrie was the team's first head coach, arranged for its first game against Georgia in 1892, and chose orange and blue as the team's colors.

has overshadowed his many other contributions to the modern Auburn University."

Petrie arrived at Auburn in 1887, a recent graduate of the University of Virginia and a newly minted professor of history and language. He retired as dean of the graduate school and head of the department of history in 1942. In between, he became recognized as one of the nation's finest scholars and the most prominent in Alabama. He was the first Alabamian ever to hold a Ph.D. and the first Auburn faculty member to have an earned doctorate.

And yes, as Jernigan writes, "his name will be forever associated with that most popular and important of all Tiger athletic endeavors," football.

Petrie arranged the first intercollegiate football game between Auburn and Georgia and served as the team's first football coach.

He picked Auburn's colors of orange and blue (modeled on his alma mater, Virginia) and set up the school's first baseball game.

An avid sportsman, he was behind the construction of the college's first tennis courts and cycling path and the city's first golf course. He promoted the concept of university "extension," or spreading the knowledge of the college beyond the borders of its campus. He was a popular and prolific public speaker, giving talks on educational, historical, and international topics and promoting his university at every opportunity. He also wrote a newspaper column, hosted a regular radio show, gave frequent public lectures, and shared his enormous personal library with all students.

He was, wrote Jernigan, "a true Renaissance man—interested in almost everything and everyone around him."

Petrie was born in Montgomery, Alabama, on April 10, 1866. The Civil War had officially ended only a year and a day earlier, and Union troops still patrolled the city's streets.

His father was a Presbyterian pastor, and Petrie grew up in a religious and staunchly Southern home. But his parents were doting, and the young George was bright and precocious. He spent most of his childhood in Virginia but did spend one summer as a small child in Auburn as his father recovered from a bout of malaria. He would remember that summer when he was recommended for a professorship at Auburn after completing his master's degree at UVA.

He probably observed his first football game as a student at Virginia, but he got a firmer education in the sport at Johns Hopkins, where he went to get his Ph.D. When he returned to Auburn with the doctorate, he won respect in faculty circles. He was also ready to introduce football.

Football at Georgia and Auburn arrived at roughly the same time and in roughly the same way. Chemistry professor Charles Herty, who like Petrie had done graduate study at Johns Hopkins, introduced the game in Athens and was happy to accept a challenge from his old friend.

Auburn and Georgia agreed to meet February 20, 1892, at Piedmont Park in Atlanta. Petrie had ordered uniforms and a rule book and began drilling his team. "The huskiest men among the students and faculty were selected for the team, and practice was begun on the rough and stony drill ground in the rear of Samford Hall," according to an account by C.B. Glenn.

Before the game, fans and bands of both teams met at the Kimball Hotel for a pep rally. Quarterback Cliff Hare composed a simple but catchy cheer: "Rah-rah ree / Rah-rah ree / Ala-Bama / A-M-C" (Agriculture and Mechanical College). Georgia's mascot was a goat named Sir William who sported a red-and-black ribbon on its tail. Auburn's mascot was an African American boy named "Dabbie" who wore orange and blue with a white sash.

There are 22 players pictured on that first Auburn team. The average player was 5'10" and 163 pounds, with the largest being 215. They donned "rugby hats," but no helmets.

The game was played under the Walter Camp rule book. A touchdown was four points and a point-after kick two points. Teams had three downs to get five yards, and forward passes were illegal.

Petrie described the field as a "sea of mud." The first half was scoreless, but Auburn's Rufus "Dutch" Dorsey scored the first touchdown, and Jesse Culver added a fumble recovery returned 50 yards for a touchdown. Auburn won the first game of what would become the longest-running series in the South 10–0.

Auburn played three more games in November 1892, finishing 2–2 on the season. Petrie earned no pay and rejected (at the behest of the president) a gold-headed walking stick presented by appreciative students. He handed over the reins of the football team to a succession of coaches. None stuck for any length of time until John Heisman arrived in 1895.

Petrie continued his academic career until retiring in 1942. He was in ill health, and the country was at war. He died five years later of a massive heart attack, although not before penning the Auburn Creed, perhaps his most enduring gift to future generations.

5 The 2004 Undefeated Team

It would be easy to make the story of the 2004 season one of disappointment. After all, Auburn played flawless football and won every game but missed a chance at a national title. The 2004 Tigers might be the best team of the last decade not to win (or even play for) a national championship. They simply picked a bad year to be a great team.

But even if the 2004 team will only be a curious footnote in national college football history books, the unit will always be fondly remembered at Auburn. Emerging from turmoil at the end of the 2003 season, Auburn prospered in 2004. The defense was perhaps the best in the nation. The offense, under the direction of new coordinator Al Borges, finally reached its potential.

Auburn started behind Southern California (the eventual national champions) and Oklahoma (which would eventually be crushed by USC in the national championship game), and the pollsters and computers never gave the Tigers a chance to catch up. But rather than dwell on that, why not embrace the positive?

- Four first-round NFL picks: quarterback Jason Campbell, running backs Ronnie Brown and Carnell Williams, and defensive back Carlos Rogers
- Memorable wins over LSU, Tennessee, Georgia, and Alabama
- An SEC championship victory against the Volunteers and a Sugar Bowl win over Virginia Tech
- A season that few Auburn fans will ever forget

The story of 2004 starts at the end of 2003. Tommy Tuberville narrowly survived being fired after a season that failed to meet high expectations. (That saga is covered elsewhere in this book.) His job status was precarious at best heading into 2004. But Tuberville made some savvy decisions prior to the season. He demoted co-coordinators Hugh Nall and Steve Ensminger and hired Indiana offensive coordinator Al Borges. At the time, it seemed like a curious decision, and many fans were skeptical. However, Borges turned out to be the right choice at the right time. He found an efficient way to use the two-back tandem of Brown and Williams and helped lead Campbell to a career season that propelled him into the NFL.

The season itself had few close calls. Nonconference games against Louisiana-Monroe, The Citadel, and Louisiana Tech were all blowouts. (Some pollsters used Auburn's weak schedule as an excuse for voting the Tigers third, but it's not clear that even a tougher schedule would have made a difference.)

The only truly close SEC game was the Week 3 contest against LSU. The 10–9 game will go down as one of the most exciting in history (and is also recounted elsewhere in this book).

But one-sided routs were the norm. This team was dominant in all phases of the game, and it showed. The Tigers shellacked Tennessee at Knoxville, whipped Arkansas, and destroyed Ole Miss. But even after a memorable finish with wins against Georgia, Alabama, and Tennessee (in the SEC title game), the Tigers could never get higher than third in the BCS standings.

For that reason, the Sugar Bowl invitation was bittersweet.

"We feel like what we've done this year, no one can take away from us," said Jason Campbell when the final standings were announced. "We feel like champions—champions in our heart, champions of our conference."

Some feared that Auburn would come out flat a month later in New Orleans and lose its perfect season. It didn't happen. The

The 2004 Tigers rode a punishing defense to an undefeated season and an SEC championship, but they were left out of the BCS Championship Game.

Tigers beat back a solid effort from the ninth-ranked ACC champions to win the Sugar Bowl 16–13.

Auburn was 13–0 and No. 2 nationally in every major poll.

Tuberville had long said—both seriously and half-seriously—that he would accept a championship from anybody who would award it. So when an enterprising high school student set up a website called the People's Choice National Championship and voters awarded Auburn the honor, Tuberville accepted. *Golf Digest* made up a mock cover declaring Auburn No. 1 and sent it to Tuberville after the coach had mentioned the magazine.

There's some dispute among Auburn people about exactly how to commemorate the 2004 season. The 2008 media guide includes a mention of the "People's Choice" award, but most fans are content identifying 2004 as the "Perfect Season."

It's a fitting description for a flawless season.

6 "Punt, 'Bama, Punt!": The Story of the 1972 Iron Bowl

Auburn hadn't scored through three quarters, and Alabama's march to an undefeated season and a national title seemed inevitable. Then came one of the greatest and most incredible comebacks in Auburn's history. The game, its taunting nickname, and the final score would become part of the rich lore of the Iron Bowl.

"Punt, 'Bama, Punt!" may or may not have been the catcall that Auburn's fans yelled as the Tide self-destructed, but the phrase quickly developed a popular following after the game, and bumper stickers with that slogan were soon plastered on cars across the state. Today those three words are instantly recognizable to fans of either team as the moniker for the entire game.

Repeat the score "17–16" to any Auburn fan, and they'll instantly know what you're talking about (assuming they don't think you're referring to the popular bar on Magnolia Street that bears the same name). The Iron Bowl on December 2, 1972, was important for both sides. Alabama was 10–0 and gunning for a national title. The Auburn "Amazin's" had exceeded expectations in 1972, and took an 8–1 record into the regular season's final game.

The first three quarters were one-sided, and Alabama's lead seemed insurmountable. But Auburn added a field goal, and then the magic began.

The first sign of the shift in momentum came when Bill Newton blocked an Alabama punt. David Langner scooped it up, dashed for 25 yards, and scored.

Here's the first of two famous radio calls by Auburn play-by-play man Gary Sanders: "Johnny Simmons is going back as a single safety, Mitchell and Langner on the...uh...line of scrimmage coming from either side to try to block the kick. Auburn trying to go after it, here's the snap, they got it! Blocked kick! Ball's back to the 25, picked up on the bounce at the 25-yard line, and in for a touchdown is David Langner!"

A few minutes later, the Tide had to punt again. (Can you hear the chants?)

After Bill Newton blocked two Alabama punts in the 1972 Iron Bowl, perhaps the most famous phrase in the history of the rivalry was born.

Again, Bill Newton blocked the kick. Again, David Langner grabbed the ball and dashed into the end zone (this time from 20 yards out). Back to Sanders: "Greg Gantt standing on his own 30, Auburn will try to block it. Auburn going after it, here's the good snap…it is blocked! It is blocked! It's caught on the run! It's caught on the run and he's gonna score! David Langner! David Langner has scored, and Auburn has tied the game!"

Alabama had one final chance, but Langner intercepted his second pass of the game with 55 seconds remaining to seal the victory.

Newton, whose wife Sarah is a member of Auburn's Board of Trustees, said he's accepted that fans will never tire of talking about his role in those two plays. "That put my name in the books," Newton said. "It always humbles me when it comes about. It has really held on in the minds of Auburn people."

While the Tide missed a shot at the national title, Auburn went on to thump No. 13 Colorado in the Gator Bowl. Regrettably for Auburn fans, it would be 10 years before the Tigers won another Iron Bowl.

7 Jordan-Hare Stadium

Modern football stadiums in college and the NFL are built and designed with their eventual capacity in mind. But many of the historic stadiums of the SEC don't have that luxury. Seats are added, and the stadium is expanded, as interest in the program grows. Many schools are still adding capacity today.

Jordan-Hare Stadium is an aesthetic success because it manages to combine the history of its past with the practical needs of modern-day football.

Thanks to a renovation in 2004, Jordan-Hare Stadium is now the ninth-largest on-campus stadium in college football.

Many stadiums that have added capacity over the years don't look quite right. They are a mishmash of architectural styles or eras. Jordan-Hare fits together, perhaps because the foundation of the stadium itself—the lower seating bowl—has been around since the beginning.

Today, Auburn has the nation's ninth-largest on-campus stadium, with a seating capacity of 87,451. On Saturdays, it becomes the state's fifth-largest city.

Its history starts on November 30, 1939. Dick McGowen threw to Babe McGehee to score the first touchdown in what was then known as Auburn Stadium. McGowen, who later coached at Auburn under Ralph "Shug" Jordan, kicked the extra point, and Auburn's first game on its home field ended in a 7–7 tie.

The first stadium contained seats for 7,500 fans and consisted of what is now the bottom part of the lower stands on the stadium's west side.

In 1949 the stadium was renamed Cliff Hare Stadium in honor of the longtime Auburn professor and administrator who was a member of the school's first football team. About 14,000 seats were added in what is now the lower east section, making the capacity 21,500.

Jordan's tenure saw three stadium expansions that added 40,000 more seats to complete much of the modern lower bowl. In

1973 it became Jordan-Hare Stadium, making Auburn the first school in the country to be named for an active coach.

Auburn added upper decks on each side of the stadium in 1980 and 1987, becoming the largest venue in the state until the recent expansion of Bryant-Denny Stadium in Tuscaloosa. In 2005 the field was named in honor of Pat Dye, giving the stadium its official title of "Pat Dye Field at Jordan-Hare Stadium."

Entering 2009, Auburn had 264 wins, 67 losses, and seven ties in 338 games at Jordan-Hare, a winning percentage of nearly 80 percent.

There were small additions involving luxury boxes in 2000, 2001, and 2004. Today, most of the changes are cosmetic (although an expansion plan remains on the backburner). Auburn athletics director Jay Jacobs has committed to adding creature comforts to enhance the game-day experience. In 2007 Auburn installed a $3 million high-definition scoreboard to replace the old, fuzzy screen with bold, clear, and colorful video. A crew of HD videographers work out of a stadium studio to provide the 30-by-75-foot board with content. Auburn also added scoreboard display ribbons around the upper-deck facade. The ribbons flash scores, stats, and advertisements, and also encourage the crowd to "MAKE NOISE" at big moments in the game.

Pundits agree that Jordan-Hare can be a tough place to play, especially in big games. Tommy Tuberville credited the noise with putting Auburn over the top in a memorable victory against Florida in 2006. "Our fans won that game for us with how they got our players motivated and brought them back in the second half," he said.

Sporting News columnist Matt Hayes calls Jordan-Hare the eighth-most intimidating stadium in the country. Sportsline.com columnist Dennis Dodd rated the stadium ninth on his top 25, giving Jordan-Hare high marks for history and the passion of its fans.

That helps explain why Auburn wins about 80 percent of its games at home. With Jordan-Hare celebrating its 70th birthday in 2009, the Tigers want to keep the wins coming.

8 Bo Jackson

Any fan who watched an Auburn football game in the early 1980s also had the privilege of witnessing perhaps the greatest athlete in any sport in American history.

Many observers have made that assessment not based on Bo Jackson's impressive statistics in college or his regrettably brief career in two major professional sports leagues, but because he played two different sports so naturally, effortlessly, and dominantly.

"People in baseball often say that if Bo had just concentrated on the one sport…and people in football say much the same thing," Steve Wulf wrote in *Sports Illustrated* during the final days of Jackson's professional career. "But then Bo wouldn't have been Bo."

Vincent Edward Jackson was born into a large family in the Raimund community of Bessemer, Alabama, a gritty western suburb of Birmingham. His family had no indoor plumbing and eight and nine kids were crammed into a few rooms. They shared beds and slept on the floor.

His father was only an occasional presence in his life. It was his mother who ran the show in the household. Bo admits he was often a handful for her. He was an angry kid, a self-described bully and occasional hoodlum.

"Remember the Brady Bunch from television?" Jackson writes in the first words of his autobiography. "They were the perfect family. Everybody loved them. I hated them. I hated them because they had a mother and a father and enough food on the table for all of them."

Jackson was a bright kid but was held back in school because of a stuttering problem that afflicted him through college. He turned

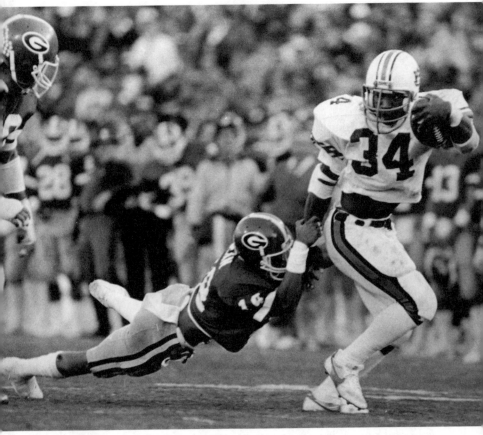

Bo Jackson was a spectacular multisport athlete during his years at Auburn, but he truly shined on the football field, racking up 4,303 career rushing yards.

a corner in high school, focusing his anger more constructively on the athletic fields at McAdory High School, where he was a good student and outstanding athlete in track, baseball, and football.

Baseball was his favorite sport, and not only could he crush the ball, he was also an intimidating pitcher with a blazing fastball. Football, he said, was almost a hobby, something to pass the time. As for basketball, he never had a knack for the sport.

He was coveted by many pro baseball teams and, even though he planned to go to college, the New York Yankees drafted him and offered him a $250,000 signing bonus. Jackson said no.

Seemingly every college in the country wanted Jackson, but as he had never even crossed the borders of the state of Alabama, the prospect of going too far from home daunted him. Thus it became a recruiting battle between Auburn and Alabama.

Jackson said he soured on Alabama when coaches made the mistake of hinting that the Tide's crowded depth chart at running back might mean that he had a faster path to playing time on the defensive side of the ball. Auburn assistant Bobby Wallace built a solid relationship with Jackson, who also liked what head coach Pat Dye had to say on a recruiting visit. So Jackson decided he was going to become an Auburn Tiger.

Almost immediately, stories started floating that Jackson was being paid handsomely for his decision. Surprisingly, he blamed not the spurned Alabama coaches for those rumors, but the New York Yankees, who were still bitter about his rejection of their contract offer.

Long after college was over, Jackson adamantly maintained that he never received a cent to play for Auburn, nor did he get a new car or any of the other gifts supposedly bestowed upon him. He did acknowledge that in the early days of his recruitment, many recruiters promised to "take care" of his mom and his family. But in the end, he picked Auburn to play sports and get an education. And that was that.

On the surface, Jackson had a great freshman year at Auburn, but he admits that he often battled depression and homesickness. His stuttering still made him anxious in front of groups, he still didn't like practice, and he clashed a time or two with some of Auburn's more old-school coaches.

At one point he sat at the Greyhound bus station in Opelika and watched the buses leave for Birmingham. He never bought a ticket. Finally, he called up Wallace because he knew the coach would talk him out of leaving. They sat at a picnic table outside Sewell Hall and talked until 4:00 AM.

Despite the strains of leaving home, Jackson was ambitious and confident from the start. Although he would later say that winning the Heisman Trophy never even entered his mind, he noticed Pat Sullivan's trophy early in his career and aspired to have one of his own.

His breakout game may have been his first Iron Bowl in 1982. That was the famous "Bo Over the Top" game in which he leaped for a touchdown on fourth-and-goal from the one-half-yard line to lead Auburn to a 23–22 win.

Jackson's mom was never a big football fan during his high school days and always feared that he would be injured. She never saw a game at McAdory, but quickly became hooked on the pageantry at Auburn and never missed a game during the rest of her son's college career.

In addition to football, Jackson also lettered in track and baseball, an accomplishment that would be almost impossible today and was extremely rare 25 years ago. Jackson became the first three-sport letter-winner in the SEC in 20 years.

He hit another milestone in his sophomore season when he ran for 256 yards in the 1983 Iron Bowl. Playing in a rainy downpour, Auburn won 23–20.

Meanwhile, after a taking a year off from baseball, Jackson returned to play for new coach Hal Baird. Once again, he could have been a high draft pick, but Jackson wanted to play his senior season.

Jackson fought through injuries in what would be his Heisman season, even playing through cracked ribs in his final Iron Bowl, a losing effort. (All four of Jackson's games against Alabama were decided by one, two, or three points. He finished his career 2–2.)

He rushed for 1,786 yards and an incredible 6.4-yards-per-carry average, but had stiff competition for the 1985 Heisman Trophy. The other finalists were quarterbacks Chuck Long (Iowa), Robbie Bosco (Brigham Young University), and Vinny Testaverde

(Miami, Florida) and running back Lorenzo White (Michigan State). Long, Bosco, and Jackson were seniors. Jackson edged Long in the closest vote in the award's history.

When he arrived back at Auburn, there was a huge crowd waiting for him outside Sewell Hall. The band was playing, thousands of people were cheering, standing on cars, and waving banners. That night Jackson went out to celebrate and got drunk for what he said was the last time in his life.

His college career ended with a loss to Texas A&M in the Cotton Bowl, the first and only bowl loss of his career.

But there was still baseball to think about, and he was determined to play his senior year. That's when he made a mistake by trusting someone he identified as a family friend or adviser, who had arranged for him to fly down to Tampa Bay to take a physical with the NFL's Buccaneers. Jackson said he was assured that the Bucs had cleared the visit with the NCAA and SEC. They hadn't, and Baird was forced to inform Jackson that he was ineligible to finish his senior baseball season.

Jackson was furious. He didn't want to play for the team that had cost him his last year of college baseball, although the Bucs

Bo Knows Class

As the Auburn women's basketball team prepared for the SEC basketball tournament in March 2009, Auburn's most legendary football figure wanted players to know he was thinking of them.

Bo Jackson sent Nell Fortner a bouquet of flowers (on her 50th birthday, no less) and sent red roses to each of the players on the women's basketball team. The accompanying note wished them good luck.

Fortner said the players were thrilled.

Fortner met Jackson for the first time in 2008 at a golf tournament. To her surprise, Jackson said he followed the women's team and knew all about the players. Fortner invited him to visit anytime. He did just that in 2009, giving an inspirational speech to the team that helped propel the Tigers to an SEC regular-season championship.

were convinced that monetary considerations would win out. Like the New York Yankees four years earlier, they would be wrong.

On June 21, 1986, Jackson said the words, "Let's play ball," as he announced his intention to sign with the Kansas City Royals of baseball rather than the Bucs. In the short-term, the Royals were offering much less money, but Jackson rarely took the conventional or predictable path. A year later, Los Angeles Raiders owner Al Davis decided to not only pick Jackson but embrace his baseball career.

Before injuries cut short his career, Jackson managed to excel in both sports. He was a solid contributor to the Raiders through parts of four seasons (1987 through 1990) and had the NFL's longest rush from scrimmage in three separate seasons (91 yards in 1987, 92 in 1989, and 88 in 1990).

In baseball, Jackson quickly established himself as a swing-for-the-fences corner outfielder. During his prime years, he was consistently among the league's best in at-bats-per-home-run.

Jackson's career as a superstar effectively ended on January 13, 1991, when he suffered a hip injury during a playoff game against the Cincinnati Bengals. However, his return to the Chicago White Sox more than two years later cemented his legacy as both an athlete and a sports and marketing icon.

In his first game back, he smacked a pinch-hit home run against the Yankees. He hit 16 homers in 1993 and 13 more in 1994. Then the players' strike hit, and Jackson decided to call it a career.

In 1992 Auburn retired Jackson's No. 34 uniform. He joined Sullivan (No. 7) and Terry Beasley (No. 88) as one of three numbers never to be worn again.

Was he the best athlete to ever wear an Auburn uniform, the greatest in any uniform?

"When people tell me I could be the best athlete there is, I just let it go in one ear and out the other," Jackson said in 1990. "There is always somebody out there who is better than you are."

9 Pat Dye

Officially, Patrick Fain Dye was hired to be Auburn's football coach from the University of Wyoming. More accurately, Dye was unemployed at the time.

After Doug Barfield was let go at the end of the 1980 season, Auburn was determined to hire Georgia coach Vince Dooley, an Auburn grad who had just won a national title for the Bulldogs. Dooley agonized over the choice, but decided to stay in Athens, forcing Auburn's search committee to start from scratch.

Dye was one of several candidates, and he was clearly the boldest. Pressed by Wyoming officials to sign a new contract and end his flirtation with Auburn, Dye decided to resign. If Auburn chose someone else, he would have no job. In the end, impressed with his commitment and zeal, Auburn chose Dye. He would repay their decision with an incredible decade of football.

Dye grew up in Blythe, Georgia, a small town about 20 miles southwest of Augusta. He was infused with a strong work ethic from childhood, working long hours picking cotton alongside laborers and sharecroppers on his family's large farming acreage.

"White families and black families lived on our farm," Dye remembered. "Those were the people I grew up with. When I got to be eight or nine years old, I started working in the field with them. My daddy demanded just as much from us—more from us, really—as he did any of the farmhands."

The youngest of three sons, Dye followed his brothers to the University of Georgia and its football team. All three boys were letter-winners, and Pat was able to parlay his success as a guard into a brief professional career in Canada. After a couple of seasons in

Pat Dye was the National Coach of the Year in 1983 and was inducted into the College Football Hall of Fame in 2005.

Edmonton, Dye joined the army and was one of the nation's top service ballplayers.

It was at a banquet in Washington, D.C., that Dye bumped into Alabama coach Paul "Bear" Bryant, who was being honored for his team's No. 1 ranking. Emboldened by the encounter, Dye penned a letter to the coach asking for a job. "To me the opportunity to coach under you at the University of Alabama would be the finest thing to happen to a young man who plans to coach football," Dye wrote.

Bryant's response was polite but noncommittal, and Dye thought his chances were slim. He made plans to return to Canada for another season. But a few days later, Bryant called to offer an interview. Dye had no civilian clothes, so he bought a new suit and drove excitedly to Tuscaloosa. The suit still had its tags as Dye walked through campus (fortunately, a couple of Alabama assistants noticed before Dye sat down with Bryant). The interview went well, and Dye left with a $6,000-a-year job coaching linebackers.

He would spend nine years at Alabama, coaching four All-Americans, picking up two national championship rings, and being a part of three unbeaten seasons, five SEC titles, and nine consecutive bowl games.

This Georgia graduate who built the foundation of his coaching career at Alabama would somehow end up at Auburn.

First, Dye left Bryant and the Tide in 1974 to be head coach at East Carolina. In his six-year tenure, Dye won 48 games and a Southern Conference championship. He left ECU for a brief, one-year stint at Wyoming, where he won six games.

Then Auburn called, and Dye returned to the SEC to compete against Bryant rather than wait for a chance to replace him. Bryant "genuinely liked and respected Dye and saw him as a possible successor," said Bryant biographer Keith Dunnavant. He also "desperately did not want to compete against the man who, in many ways, appeared to be a younger version of himself."

Dye lost his first Iron Bowl as Bryant earned his 315th victory and moved past Amos Alonzo Stagg as the game's winningest coach. But Auburn broke through in 1982, Bryant's last Iron Bowl. Freshman running back Bo Jackson's one-yard dive gave Auburn a 23–22 win. With Bryant's retirement and passing and Dye's elevation of the Auburn program, things were changing in the state of Alabama. The Tide may have been dominant in the 1970s, but the Tigers were poised to be the team of the '80s.

In a nine-year span beginning in 1982, Dye would lead Auburn to an 84–22–3 record and a .784 winning percentage, the third-best mark in country during that time.

Before retiring after the 1992 season, Dye would win 99 games, including four 10-win seasons and six bowl game victories in nine appearances. He was a three-time Coach of the Year and 1983 National Coach of the Year, and coached 21 All-Americans and 71 All-SEC players.

Dye had just turned 53 as his final season concluded, and he presumably would have had many years to coach. But he was forced to resign amid a major NCAA investigation that ended with Auburn receiving some of the most severe sanctions in history, including a two-year bowl ban, a one-year television ban, and the loss of scholarships.

To some, Dye's legacy was tainted by the way his tenure ended. But time has healed most of the wounds. In 2005 Auburn named its field in honor of Dye. The following year he was enshrined in the College Football Hall of Fame.

"This is such a fitting tribute to honor someone like Coach Dye," said Auburn athletics director Jay Jacobs as the field was named. "Coach Dye was instrumental in returning the Auburn football program back to respectability and prominence."

10 Pat Sullivan

When he was a prep star at John Carroll High School in Birmingham, Pat Sullivan was recruited by virtually every major program, but he grew up an Auburn fan and liked the easygoing nature of coach Ralph "Shug" Jordan.

Notable Auburn Passing Records

Pass attempts in a game: Stan White, 58 (September 29, 1990, against Tennessee)

Pass attempts in a season: Dameyune Craig, 403 (1997)

Pass attempts in a career: Stan White, 1,231 (1990–1993)

Completions in a game: Patrick Nix, 34 (October 28, 1995, against Arkansas)

Completions in a season: Dameyune Craig, 216 (1997)

Completions in a career: Stan White, 659 (1990–1993)

Yards gained in a game: Ben Leard, 416 (November 13, 1999, against Georgia)

Yards gained in a season: Dameyune Craig, 3,277 (1997)

Yards gained in a career: Stan White, 8,016 (1990–1993)

Touchdown passes in a game: Daniel Cobb, 5 (October 20, 2001, against Louisiana Tech)

Touchdown passes in a season: Jason Campbell, 20 (2004); Pat Sullivan (1971)

Touchdown passes in a career: Pat Sullivan, 53 (1969–1971)

Jordan took him to an NFL exhibition game at Legion Field one evening. Their car overheated, and Sullivan and Jordan had to get out and walk down Graymont Avenue with the other fans. As they walked to the stadium, a car escorted by police cars raced by. Inside was Alabama coach Paul "Bear" Bryant.

"Coach Jordan looked at me and said, 'Well, Pat, you can either go in the limelight with him or walk with me.'"

Sullivan chose Jordan and the Tigers and still managed to find a bit of the limelight, too. He finished his career with 6,284 passing yards, 53 touchdowns, two All-America honors, and a Heisman.

Sullivan's career coincided with another Auburn great, receiver Terry Beasley, and the two names are forever linked in the program's history. After a stint on the freshman team in 1968, Sullivan and Beasley graduated to the varsity roster in 1969. It's hard to imagine a more anticipated debut. The first play from scrimmage in the 1969 opener against Wake Forest was a bomb from Sullivan to a wide-open Beasley. Overwhelmed by adrenaline, Sullivan tossed the ball 20 yards too long. The crowd cheered, anyway.

Quarterback Pat Sullivan won the Heisman Trophy in 1971.

Auburn would go on to beat Wake Forest 57–0, but expectations for Sullivan's debut were quickly dampened by a 45–19 rout the next week at Tennessee. Sullivan threw five interceptions, but returned to practice unfazed. The Tigers went on to lose only one more regular-season game and capped the memorable year with a 49–26 win over Alabama that snapped a five-game losing streak in the series.

As a senior in 1971, Sullivan and the Tigers jumped out to an 8–0 start and were ranked sixth in the country. Their showdown with undefeated, seventh-ranked Georgia drew national media attention and was broadcast on ABC television. The media expected to see a great game, but they also were watching Sullivan's last audition for the Heisman Trophy. Auburn beat the Bulldogs handily in Athens, as Sullivan passed for 248 yards and four touchdowns in the 35–20 win.

"This is one of the greatest games that Auburn has played in its history," gushed coach Ralph "Shug" Jordan after the game. "It was as hostile as I've ever seen. You could feel it and hear it, and because of that maybe it was the greatest. Our team played like real champions."

Georgia coach Vince Dooley minced no words in his praise of Sullivan. "We were simply beaten by the best I've ever seen," he said. "Sullivan is the best I've ever seen. If Sullivan isn't the Heisman winner, I don't know who it would be."

On Thanksgiving night, Sullivan gathered with his wife and daughter to watch the Heisman Trophy announcement. Jubilation erupted as soon as his name was announced. Students gathered at Memorial Coliseum, and Sullivan was given a police escort to meet the cheering throngs. He deflected the credit and said all of his teammates deserved a piece of the award.

Unfortunately for Auburn fans, the tale of the 1971 season doesn't end there. The day after the Heisman announcement, Auburn boarded a bus for the Iron Bowl in Birmingham. An uncharacteristically flat Auburn team was routed 31–7 by the Tide, the first and only loss to Alabama in the Sullivan-Beasley era.

"I'm not saying [the Heisman announcement] is why we lost to Alabama, but I think it affected us," Sullivan said. "I'd be lying if I said I didn't want to show the people on national television that I deserved it, that we deserved it."

Undefeated Alabama went on to play (and lose to) Nebraska in the Orange Bowl, giving the Cornhuskers their second consecutive national championship. Auburn would lose to Oklahoma in the Sugar Bowl, ending a very successful three-year period on an unhappy note.

After college, Sullivan spent five seasons in the NFL with the Atlanta Falcons, Washington Redskins, and San Francisco 49ers. He spent a few years out of football but then jumped back into coaching. Sullivan served six years as an assistant coach under Pat Dye at Auburn, helping Auburn win three SEC championships (in 1987 through 1989). He was named head coach at Texas Christian in 1992, but made only one bowl appearance and was fired after a 1–10 season in 1997.

The opportunity to return to Auburn as head coach has never been in the cards, but Sullivan did the next best thing when he took a job in his hometown. After eight seasons as an assistant at UAB, Sullivan is now the head coach at Samford.

When he was given the prestigious Walter Gilbert Award by Auburn in 2008, he wasn't able to accept it in person because he was coaching the Bulldogs.

The award was a sign of the affinity Auburn people still hold for Sullivan.

"Pat is one of this institution's all-time greatest athletes," said athletics director Jay Jacobs, "yet more importantly he is an outstanding coach, husband, father, and friend."

11 The Iron Bowl

Purists will sometimes argue that the Iron Bowl shouldn't be called the Iron Bowl. Logically, they have a point. After all, the name refers to the roots of the series in Birmingham. The central Alabama city known as the "Pittsburgh of the South" has a long heritage in the iron

The annual Iron Bowl between Auburn and Alabama has become one of the fiercest rivalries in all of sports.

and steel industry. But Birmingham stopped being the annual home of the rivalry in 1989 and hasn't hosted an Alabama home game in the series since 1998. Even so, the name has stuck, and will probably be with us forever. And why not? A rivalry this great deserves a name.

The rivalry started slowly, but quickly became so intense that it was put on hold for four decades. Today it is played in front of packed campus stadiums in Tuscaloosa and Auburn and is considered by fans and media to be one of the most fiercely contested and historically significant rivalries in the nation.

The first game was played at Lakeview Park in Birmingham in 1893, where roughly 500 fans watched Auburn's 32–22 victory on a converted baseball field. Appropriately, the 1907 game ended in a 6–6 tie. The series then went on a 41-year hiatus.

Auburn historians have worked diligently to correct some of the common misconceptions about the reason for the long break. The most persistent myth is that there was a fight between the teams in 1907. In reality, the reason for the initial breakup was much more mundane, according to Auburn's history books. Auburn wanted to use an official from the North for the 1908 game; Alabama wanted a Southerner. The regional difference was important because football was still a young and evolving sport at the time, and the legality of unusual shifts and formations was still being debated. The teams also dickered over the appropriate roster size and how much should be allowed for expenses.

These seemingly minor issues festered until the two schools stopped playing each other in any sport.

In 1948 Auburn President Ralph B. Draughon and Alabama President John Gallalee decided to end the feud. Representatives from both schools buried a hatchet—literally—in Birmingham's Woodrow Wilson Park, and the rivalry was renewed. (There is no

Travis Tidwell

Tidwell was one of only two freshmen in college history ever to lead the nation in total offense. In 1946 he had a nation's-best 1,715 total yards. He repeated the feat again in 1949. Until Pat Sullivan's arrival about 20 years later, Tidwell was Auburn's offensive leader.

Playing quarterback out of the T formation, Tidwell almost single-handedly led the Tigers to an upset win against Alabama in 1949. He also played on defense and was a two-time All-American. After his college career, he played two years for the New York Giants and several seasons of Canadian ball. He died in 2004 in Trussville, Alabama, at the age of 79.

burial marker for the symbolic hatchet, and no one knows if it is still in the ground.)

After considering and rejecting Montgomery and Mobile, the schools chose Birmingham for the game site. Legion Field had room for 44,000 fans, making it the largest stadium in the state.

Alabama won the inaugural game 55–0, but Auburn returned with a stunning 14–13 upset the following year. The schools have traded jabs ever since.

Some eras are more one-sided than others. The Tide generally dominated the series for most of the 1960s and 1970s, but Pat Dye's teams answered back in the 1980s. The average margin of victory in the decade was only 6.4 points.

The end of the 1980s marked perhaps the most significant moment in modern Auburn history, when the game was played at Jordan-Hare Stadium for the first time ever. Alabama came into the game ranked No. 2 in the nation, but Auburn crushed the Tide's title hopes with a 30–20 victory.

The great games of the series are so intertwined with the football history of both teams that many of the greatest games get their own chapters in this book. But a few of the quirks of the series deserve special mention. For instance, until 2008, Auburn had won all six of the games played in Tuscaloosa, a streak that included victories in 1895, 1901, 2000, 2002, 2004, and 2006.

More nuggets:

- The game has been tied at halftime on seven occasions. Auburn has won only one of those.
- There have been 23 shutouts in the rivalry. Auburn has won eight, Alabama 15.
- Seventeen of the last 21 meetings have been decided by 10 points or fewer.
- The home team won 10 games in a row in a streak that extended through the 1980s. Entering 2008, the visiting team had won six of the last nine.

The 2008 installment was more memorable for Tide fans than Auburn partisans. The Tigers lost 36–0 in a game that unraveled rapidly after halftime. The victory gave Alabama an undefeated regular season and bragging rights for the next 364 days. That's a feeling that Auburn had savored for almost seven years.

"This game is different than any other game you play in," said former center Jason Bosley. "As soon as you step on the field for warmups, you can tell the atmosphere is different."

Fans live for the victories and take losses hard. So do players. But most of the trash-talking stays in the stands. Players on both sides say the rivalry is generally characterized by respect.

"From a fan's point of view, they probably think I just hate Alabama players, and Alabama players hate Auburn players," said cornerback Jerraud Powers, who grew up in Decatur, Alabama. "But from my experience, it hasn't been like that. I'm good friends with a lot of guys who play over there, and they're good friends with a lot of guys who play over here. But once we get on the field, it's all 'Bama for them and all Auburn for us."

12 Jimmy Hitchcock: Auburn's First All-American

The first All-America football player in Auburn's long history was also one of the best. Jimmy Hitchcock, known as the "Phantom of Union Springs," won the honor in 1932 as he helped Auburn win a Southern Conference championship and capped an illustrious athletic career on the Plains.

James Franklin Hitchcock Jr. was born on June 28, 1911, in Inverness, a small community in Bullock County, just south of Union Springs. He had six siblings—four brothers and two sisters.

Hitchcock was a superb athlete, but he gained most of the attention for his prowess in football at Union Springs High School. The back could run, throw, catch, and even punt. At Auburn, the Phantom played on both sides of the ball. He captained the 1932 championship team, which broke Tulane's four-year undefeated streak in the Southern Conference. In the crucial game against Tulane, Hitchcock returned an interception 60 yards and later returned an errant punt snap 63 yards for another touchdown. The 19–7 victory was a fitting finale to his career.

"Verily, it seems like old times," wrote Zipp Newman of the *Birmingham News*. "An Auburn team is back in the national grid spotlight for the first time in 13 years."

His selection as an All-American was no surprise.

"Hitchcock is the finest all-around back ever to play against one of my teams," raved Duke head coach Wallace Wade.

Hitchcock was also an All-American in baseball at Auburn, and he managed to get a cup of coffee in the big leagues. At the time, pro baseball offered more money and opportunities than football, so the decision was an easy one. He signed with the New York Yankees in May of 1933. The soft-gloved shortstop quickly moved up the minor league ladder, but hit a wall in Triple A. The stocked Yankees system pulled the plug on Hitchcock at that point, shipping him to the Chattanooga Lookouts of the Southern Association.

Joe Engle, the Bill Veeck–like owner of the Lookouts who loved promotions, thought the popular former Southern football player would be a great draw at the gate. He was right, especially since Jimmy's younger brother Billy was starring for Auburn at the time.

After a solid season with the Lookouts, Hitchcock was rewarded with a ticket to the big leagues when he was sold to the Boston Braves on August 18, 1938. His stay was brief. He played 24 games and managed only a .171 average on 13 singles.

Jimmy had a couple more solid seasons in the minors before deciding to call it a career in 1941. Meanwhile, Billy's career was on the ascension. William Clyde "Billy" Hitchcock, who passed away in Opelika in 2006, was associated with professional baseball for four decades. He played for nine years in the big leagues (though his career was interrupted by World War II) and later worked as a coach, manager, and scout. He also served as president of the Double A Southern League for a decade.

After his baseball career, the elder Jimmy returned to Auburn where he became head baseball coach and assistant football coach. His coaching career was interrupted by World War II. After service in the navy, he spent one year as a player-manager for a local low-level league and then returned to the university as a coach for one year under Ralph "Shug" Jordan.

In 1951 he served on the committee of Jordan partisans which were eager to bring the coach back home to Auburn. They succeeded. Three years later, Hitchcock was selected to the National Football Foundation Hall of Fame.

For most of the 1950s, Hitchcock stayed involved in the game by becoming a well-respected football official. He died of a heart attack in 1959 at the age of 48. Hitchcock is buried in Greenwood Cemetery in Montgomery.

13 Mike Donahue

Mike Donahue not only wanted to win, he wanted to win the right way. During an age in which college football was beginning to adopt the win-at-all costs mentality that is familiar today, Donahue was one of the voices speaking out for amateurism and advocating for student-athletes. He had no use for mercenaries or ringers, the quasi-professionals who cropped up in the 1910s. Instead, he won a lot of games at Auburn using regular students that he coached up his own way.

Most Auburn people were skeptical of Donahue when he first hopped off a train and arrived on campus in 1904. The Yale graduate was a slight man, perhaps 5'4", with red hair, blue eyes, and a bit of an Irish accent.

"They were the most disgusted bunch of people I've ever seen," Donahue reportedly said of the fans that greeted his arrival.

While Donahue didn't look like a football coach, he was an awful good one. He was also the university's first basketball coach. On top of that, he found time throughout his tenure to supervise baseball, track, and soccer, while serving as the faculty adviser for social affairs, overseeing the cafeteria, and teaching classes in English, math, history, and Latin. While he was certainly a Renaissance man of sorts, he was also trying to support his growing family financially.

Under Donahue, basketball practice was a contact sport. "He never bothered calling fouls—said it slowed up the game," said one of his players, Charles W. Woodruff, many years later.

Donahue learned football under Walter Camp at Yale and eventually led Auburn (or API, as it was then known) to a 99–35–5 record, including four one-loss seasons and three undefeated seasons. Donahue came to Auburn under the shadow of John Heisman, the king of coaches in the sport who had taken the Tigers to great heights during his brief stint on the Plains.

But Donahue and new Vanderbilt coach Dan McGugin would soon overshadow Heisman. McGugin was an offensive innovator, while Donahue had a more conservative, Eastern approach, but both men would become titans of football in the South. Heisman lost only 29 games in his 16 years at Georgia Tech, but 10 of those losses were to Donahue and Auburn.

Donahue had to be a good teacher, as high school football was virtually nonexistent at the time.

"No coach within memory of the writer ever did more with greener material," wrote Zipp Newman of the *Birmingham News*. "He took raw-boned boys, many of whom had never played high school football, and molded them into hard-charging, fierce blocking, and running teams."

Donahue's views were occasionally unorthodox, both for his times and ours. He felt so strongly about the intellectual development of his players that he hoped coaches would one day be banished from the sideline.

"My firm belief is that intercollegiate football will see a forward impulse toward a desirable goal when the coach is not permitted to sit on the sideline," Donahue said. "What is the theoretical aim of competitive college sports? Why, the encouragement of resource and initiative among those who participate. How is this aim accomplished when the coach from a vantage point on the sideline practically directs the play at important junctures, if not throughout?

"Personally, I had rather develop one man—I mean a rounded man who can use his brain as well as his muscles—than a dozen All-American stars who have learned to depend on the intellect of a non-participant."

Donahue stepped away from football for one season in 1907, but returned in 1908. Interestingly, the 1907 Auburn-Alabama game was the last time the teams met until 1948. Donahue claimed he tried many times to resume the rivalry, but terms could never be agreed upon.

It was also during his one-year absence that "ringers" began to be used by many Southern teams in an effort to catch McGugin and his Commodores, who were dominating the region. Donahue was known for abhorring that practice, and people took note. Auburn was honored by newspaper voters as the Southern champions in 1908 despite having one loss because the voters knew that Donahue "had been fighting a long, arduous, uphill battle for clean football. It was time he got some sort of reward for his earnestness of purpose."

Head coach Mike Donahue and the Tigers played 23 straight games without a loss between 1913 and 1915.

He continued to have success at Auburn, posting 23 consecutive games without a loss, starting with the 1913 opener and ending with the next-to-last game of 1915. Auburn outscored its opponents by an astounding 600–13 during that stretch. The streak was an Auburn record until broken by Ralph "Shug" Jordan in 1956 through 1958.

One of the greatest upsets of the era occurred under Donahue's watch in 1917. Southern football was generally regarded as inferior to the Northern variety, so Ohio State was a 30-point favorite when the Buckeyes met the Tigers on November 24 in Montgomery. But the teams fought to a scoreless tie, as Auburn stopped Ohio State inside its 10-yard line five times to preserve the shutout. The tie felt like a victory and gave Auburn—and the South—new respect.

Donahue was lured away from Auburn after the 1922 season by a generous $10,000-a-year offer from LSU. But he never had the same success with the other Tigers, resigning after a 23–19–3 record in five years at Baton Rouge.

In later years Donahue was a golf pro, head coach, and athletics director at Spring Hill College in Mobile. He eventually returned to LSU in 1937 as the director of intramurals, where he served until retiring 12 years later. He died in 1960 at the age of 84.

Donahue was a charter member of the National Football Foundation Hall of Fame in 1951 and was posthumously inducted with the first class of the Alabama Sports Hall of Fame in 1969.

14 Auburn-UGA in 1971

For all the pageantry of the Deep South's oldest rivalry, Auburn and Georgia have met only three times when both teams were ranked in the top 10—1971, 1983, and 2004.

The 1971 game came at a time when both teams looked nearly unbeatable and, were it not for a glut of undefeated teams atop the rankings, both could have contended for national championships.

Both squads were undefeated. Auburn was ranked sixth, Georgia seventh, and the showdown in Athens was anticipated nationally.

Georgia coach Vince Dooley, an Auburn alumnus, remembers his team as one of the best he had ever coached. The Bulldogs had an imposing defense led by Chip Wisdom, Chuck Heard, and

Mixon Robinson. They allowed 25 points to Oregon State in the opener, but allowed only four touchdowns in the next eight games combined.

The night before the game, students met on Auburn for the traditional "Burn the Bulldogs" pep rally and bonfire. About 13 bulldogs, most made of crepe paper and chicken wire, were sacrificed to the fire. A few students got creative with the fake dogs, constructing them out of graham cracker and marshmallow, potatoes, or ice cream cones.

The rally set the right tone for senior quarterback Pat Sullivan's second-to-last regular-season game. Sullivan threw four touchdown passes and set up a fifth as the Tigers beat the Bulldogs 35–20. The Sullivan-to–Terry Beasley combination was as strong as ever. Sullivan connected twice with Beasley for touchdowns of 31 and 70 yards. He hit Dick Schmalz for 15- and four-yard scores.

The long bomb to Beasley was the game's most important score. Auburn led 21–20 after Roger Mitchell blocked the extra-point attempt after Georgia's third touchdown. On the first play after Georgia's kickoff, Sullivan connected to Beasley, who broke free from two defenders and streaked down the field for the score. Auburn iced the game on Georgia's next drive when Dave Beck picked off a pass from Georgia quarterback James Ray, who had replaced starter Andy Johnson. Sullivan finished with 248 yards passing, while Beasley had four catches for 130.

For Dooley, the game was one of his "most bitter losses ever." He later said, "Sullivan was a superman having a super day, and Terry Beasley is a boy wonder."

Georgia went on to win the Gator Bowl over North Carolina, which was coached by Bill Dooley, Vince's brother.

Auburn, meanwhile, concluded Sullivan's magical senior season with disappointing losses. First, the Tigers were beaten by Alabama in the Iron Bowl. Then Auburn lost to Oklahoma in the Sugar Bowl.

15 The Auburn Creed

I believe that this is a practical world and that I can count only on what I earn. Therefore, I believe in work, hard work.

I believe in education, which gives me the knowledge to work wisely and trains my mind and my hands to work skillfully.

I believe in honesty and truthfulness, without which I cannot win the respect and confidence of my fellow men.

I believe in a sound mind, in a sound body and a spirit that is not afraid, and in clean sports that develop these qualities.

I believe in obedience to law because it protects the rights of all.

I believe in the human touch, which cultivates sympathy with my fellow men and mutual helpfulness and brings happiness for all.

I believe in my Country, because it is a land of freedom and because it is my own home, and that I can best serve that country by "doing justly, loving mercy, and walking humbly with my God."

And because Auburn men and women believe in these things, I believe in Auburn and love it.

George Petrie wrote thousands of pages of books, articles, speeches, and letters during the course of an illustrious academic career at Auburn University. But he's most remembered for the simple yet powerful list of Auburn values he jotted down in the final years of his life. By the time the Auburn Creed became a revered testament to the beliefs of Auburn people, Petrie had long since passed away. He died of a massive heart attack on September 5, 1947, but his legacy endures.

The story of the creed's creation isn't fully documented.

Petrie was retired, in ill health, and still mourning the death of his wife, Mary. Yet on November 12, 1943, Petrie sat down to handwrite a one-page document that summed up his philosophy and values.

There are two stories as to why the creed was written. According to a version that appeared in the *Montgomery Advertiser*, student leaders asked to put the Auburn spirit into words and were directed to Petrie for inspiration. The newspaper story has inaccuracies that make this version of the creed legend dubious.

A more likely version comes from Dean James E. Foy, a beloved Petrie-esque figure in his own right. This account was told to him by Marion W. Spidle, Auburn's dean of home economics from 1938 to 1966. According to Spidle, Auburn women were worried about their brothers, fathers, boyfriends, and husbands serving in World War II. Spidle invited Petrie to talk to the women, and in that setting the creed made its first appearance.

Whatever the creed's origin, it was first published on January 21, 1944, on the front page of the *Plainsman*. The newspaper's

What's in a Name?

For simplicity's sake, the Tigers are referred to as Auburn throughout this book. Indeed, for most of the university's history, Auburn was a colloquial name for the school, if not its official name.

But it was founded as the East Alabama Male College. When it came under state direction after the Civil War in 1872, it was renamed the Agricultural and Mechanical College of Alabama. In 1899, it became Alabama Polytechnic Institute, or API, a distinction it would hold until 1960 when it officially became Auburn University.

editors published the creed with no real explanation, other than a brief note that said the creed "speaks for itself, powerfully."

The original handwritten version did not include the final line: "And because Auburn men and women believe in these things, I believe in Auburn and love it." By the time of its publication, however, the final summation had been added. It didn't catch on immediately, only becoming popular some time later.

During Auburn's sesquicentennial celebration in 2006, 10 members of the Auburn family were selected to read a passage from the creed. Appropriately, Foy and longtime Auburn athletics figure David Housel jointly read the final line.

16 Backfield Built for Two: Ronnie Brown and Carnell Williams

Entering the 2004 season, Auburn's coaches had the type of "problem" that most can only dream about. The Tigers had two elite-level senior running backs on their roster. So what was the problem? Both players were unselfish, but both wanted to play.

Carnell Williams and Ronnie Brown had opportunities to turn pro after their junior seasons in 2003. But the lackluster season, and the opportunity to return with a senior-laden team in 2004, convinced them to stick around for one more year. The predicament for coaches then became how Auburn could maximize the value of the two backs, both of whom would be every-down rushers on virtually any other team.

"We want both of them to get as many carries as the other," said Auburn coach Tommy Tuberville shortly after their announcement that they would return. That was the goal in 2002 and 2003, as well, but it didn't always work out that way. Brown rushed for 1,008 yards in 2002 as Williams nursed injuries. But he averaged only 8.6 carries per game in 2003 and was outrushed by Williams 1,307 to 446.

"When you've got two guys like us, as talented as we both are, both of us want the ball, so I've got to accept the fact that I'm going to have to share time," Williams said. "I'm cool with that. I think, in the long run, it's going to keep me fresh and healthy." Williams was prophetic, and the one-two punch of Brown and Williams was one of the major reasons for the success of Auburn's ground game in the undefeated 2004 season.

Auburn avoided injuries and wear and tear by balancing the load between the two backs.

"We want to put them in situations where they can be successful," Tuberville said. "We don't want to go into games where one guy has to carry the ball 40 or 50 times. I think these guys understand that. I think we'll be a lot more successful when they're both playing well and healthy."

Williams played in every game. Brown missed only one. Their numbers weren't perfectly equal, but they were close. Williams finished with 1,165 yards on 239 carries and 12 touchdowns. Brown had 913 yards on 153 carries and eight touchdowns. Out of the backfield, they combined for 55 catches and almost 500 yards.

So exactly how and why did Auburn end up with two first-round backs in the same backfield? (That's not even counting another future NFL star, junior-college transfer Brandon Jacobs in 2003.)

"It's not over-recruiting," Tuberville said. "Since Ole Miss, we've built our philosophy around running the football. You've got to have a running game in order to be successful in college football.

"Having guys like that doesn't happen very often. When we got here we didn't have any, so we've been on both sides of the spectrum."

But the two-back partnership couldn't have worked with just anyone. Former Tampa Bay Buccaneers coach Jon Gruden, who coached Williams in the Senior Bowl and eventually drafted him in 2005, noticed that immediately.

The combined running attack of Ronnie Brown and Carnell Williams led Auburn to an undefeated season in 2004.

"These are the most unselfish guys I've seen in some time," Gruden said of Brown and Williams. "It's refreshing to be around them. They could have easily worked against each other and created a bad atmosphere [at Auburn]. But they chose to be team guys."

Then–offensive coordinator Al Borges said the system wouldn't work any other way.

"If that guy, Brown, decides, 'Heck with it, I'm not blocking for this guy, Carnell,' this whole thing does not work," Borges said of Auburn's offense. "The reason these two-tailback systems fail is one guy won't block for the other. They're jealous."

"If one of them had come back and said, 'I want to win the Heisman Trophy,' it would not have worked," added Tuberville.

They didn't win the big awards, but Williams and Brown won a lot of games.

"We knew coming back for our senior year we had to share the ball, and we were not going to win no kind of Heisman or make the All-America teams," Williams said. "We said, 'Let's go out and win for this team.' If we play a big role of staying unselfish, it was going to work."

It did.

17 An Era of Defense: Bill Oliver, Gene Chizik, Will Muschamp

In 2007 a brief clip on ESPN showed perhaps millions of viewers what Auburn players already knew. Will Muschamp was a loud, fiery, in-your-face defensive coordinator during his two years on the Plains.

"Is it fiery or crazy?" said head coach Tommy Tuberville with a smile. "I stay out of his way, especially when the team has done well and they're coming off the field, because he's jumping on everybody."

On one Saturday in Fayetteville, Arkansas, the ESPN field microphones caught just a bit of Muschamp's enthusiasm after Auburn had made a key stop in the third quarter.

"Boom! Yeah! That's what I'm talking about!" Muschamp yelled, as Auburn players ran off the field. Or at least those are the only words that can be put in print. Muschamp also unleashed a long string of celebratory obscenities that could be heard crystal-clear over the broadcast airwaves. An alert viewer posted the entire sequence on YouTube.com, the popular video-sharing website, complete with captions and commentary. Two years later, hundreds of thousands of people had downloaded versions of the tirade. At the time, Auburn players forwarded it throughout the team with knowing laughs.

"I think everybody's seen it," said nose guard Josh Thompson. "It's more funny than anything, because we know how he is. We see it every day. The public usually doesn't see how it is.

"We love that. He usually doesn't cuss that much. That just happened. He was just excited. That's how he is."

That enthusiasm translated itself into an Auburn defense that earned a reputation as one of the best in the country. It also got Muschamp a new job at Texas, where he is currently head coach–in-waiting for one of the richest and most successful college programs in the country.

Muschamp is one of a string of defensive coordinators who have helped Auburn build an elite defensive reputation over much of the last two decades. The heritage of great defenses, of course, goes back to Ralph "Shug" Jordan and Pat Dye, who were known for physical, no-frills football.

"My memories aren't very good of playing against Auburn," said current Auburn defensive coordinator Ted Roof, a former Georgia Tech linebacker. "They were the most physical football team that we played year in and year out. I made this comment to Coach Dye: 'When you got done playing Auburn, it felt like somebody had taken a rubber hose and just beat you with it.' As a football player, you always respect the physical teams, the teams that hit you in the mouth."

Coordinators like Bill "Brother" Oliver, Gene Chizik, and Will Muschamp have built on that heritage in more recent years.

Will Muschamp was one of several coordinators who helped build Auburn's defense into a national power over the last two decades.

A native of Rome, Georgia, Muschamp played football for the Georgia Bulldogs and spent two seasons with Oliver in 1995 and 1996 as a graduate assistant. Muschamp's career took off when he joined Nick Saban's LSU staff in 2001, eventually rising to defensive coordinator for the Tigers and then assistant head coach for defense with the NFL's Miami Dolphins.

Chizik, who was Auburn's defensive coordinator from 2002 to 2004 before becoming head coach more than four years later, also has ties to Oliver.

"They both worked with me as graduate assistants," Oliver said. "They have as much going for them as anybody, and they have both built a great foundation. I'd take them over anybody."

As a coach who has navigated both sides of the Auburn-Alabama rivalry, Oliver has an interesting story of his own.

Oliver played for coach Paul "Bear" Bryant at Alabama, then worked for five years as an assistant under Jordan before returning to Alabama in 1970. After Bryant retired, Oliver was head coach at Tennessee-Chattanooga and worked as a coordinator in the USFL and an assistant at Clemson. Gene Stallings called him back to Alabama in 1990, but Oliver defected to Auburn in 1996 in what was then a stunning switch and a major coup for then-coach Terry Bowden.

Trooperisms

When Trooper Taylor was hired from Oklahoma State to be Gene Chizik's assistant head coach and wide receivers coach, he brought with him both an impressive résumé and a gift for gab. Taylor is a favorite of reporters across the country because of his quick wit and knack for one-liners and great anecdotes.

Here are a sampling of Trooperisms from his very first meeting with the media:

On differences between the two coaching staffs: "Everybody cooks their dinner a different way."

On honesty: "Some people smile at your face but they're not your friend."

On Chizik as a taskmaster: "If you don't get it done, he'll go to the next one."

On DeAngelo Benton missing two years of football: "You don't go to sleep a circle and wake up a square."

On what happens if you don't succeed: "You'll be spraying fruit for a living really fast. I don't want to be on the grapes. I like doing the football, myself."

On how he knows a prospect is really good: "I like the ones that my wife can pick out. That's pretty good, you know, when she can put the tape on and say, 'Sign him, baby.'"

On effort and hard work: "One that won't is no better than that one who can't. They'll both get you beat."

After the departures of both Stallings in 1996 and Bowden a few years later, Oliver badly wanted the top job at both schools. When he didn't get it at Alabama, he moved to Auburn. When he didn't get it at Auburn, he retired from coaching.

But two of the coaches Oliver has mentored are still going strong. And Muschamp and Chizik aren't the only Auburn coaches who have used success as an Auburn defensive coordinator as a springboard to head-coaching gigs.

Paul Rhoads spent one season as the defensive coordinator in 2008. In 2009 he'll be on the sideline at Iowa State, replacing—you guessed it—Gene Chizik.

18 The 1983 Season: Shunned by the Poll

The proposition was considered so absurd that few even speculated about the possibility. If No. 5 Miami beat No. 1 Nebraska in the post-1983 Orange Bowl, who would win the national title?

The question itself almost provoked howls of laughter. Nebraska was considered one of the greatest teams in football history. Miami was the same team that got whipped by Florida. The game shouldn't have been close.

And yet it was. When Miami stunned the Cornhuskers 31–30, the Hurricanes ascended to the top spot in the Associated Press poll, costing Auburn a chance at a national title that many fans feel belonged to the Tigers.

But more on that later.

The 1983 season started with both sadness and anticipation. Greg Pratt, Auburn's first-team fullback, collapsed and died August 21 during a workout in 95-degree heat. The cause of death was ruled to be cardiac arrest, and his tragic passing cast a pall on the team. Head coach Pat Dye said that Pratt, a transfer from Tennessee State, was one of Auburn's most beloved players.

Yet there was optimism heading into the 1983 season. Auburn fans sensed that Dye was building a program that was primed for national recognition. And unlike some championship seasons that sneak up out of nowhere, this one was largely anticipated.

Auburn's lone slip-up was in Week 2. The Tigers lost to a very good Texas team 20–7 in what would be their only defeat of the year. It would also be the defeat that ultimately cost them the national title. Still, the SEC title was in sight, and Auburn's potent defense and Bo Jackson–led offense rolled through opponents. One of the biggest tests was November 12 at No. 5 Georgia. The Bulldogs were 33–1–1 in their last 35 SEC games (the tie and loss both coming to Auburn) and were trying to go undefeated for the fourth straight season. Auburn won the defensive struggle 13–7. The Tigers went on to defeat top 10–ranked teams in successive weeks (first Georgia, then Maryland and Alabama).

After winning the Iron Bowl and the SEC title, the Tigers were sent to the Sugar Bowl, where they were paired with No. 8 Michigan. Auburn beat the Wolverines 9–7 in another defensive war. The Hurricanes won their narrow victory over Nebraska when the Huskers failed a two-point conversion. (Many believed coach Tom Osborne should have kicked the extra point for the tie, perhaps preserving his team's national title.)

In any case, the shocking victory left the national title up in the air. Auburn fans thought the Tigers deserved the crown. Instead, voters picked Miami in a landslide. Auburn remained No. 3, just behind second-ranked Nebraska.

"I'm not bitter, just very disappointed," Dye said. "Stop with the bitter questions. Wouldn't you be disappointed if your football team had just survived a season like we have and accomplished what we have and then end up where we did? It's not exactly the greatest feeling in the world."

The Tigers did win a school-record 11 games, claim their first SEC title in 26 years, beat Alabama for the second year in a row, and finish with their highest national ranking since 1972.

"We deserve a better fate than third in the nation," Dye said. "If you'll check it out, go back and look at the teams that have won national championships over the years—no one has played a more difficult schedule than Auburn."

Dye was right and he offered the numbers to prove it.

But many memories of Auburn's snub have a ring of revisionist history. Days before the two bowl games, the *Miami Herald* solicited a poll asking who would win the national title if the Hurricanes shocked the Huskers. Overwhelmingly, Associated Press voters said it would be Miami. That survey may have gone unnoticed because the idea of a Miami upset was considered so unlikely.

Even after the season, many maintained that the best team was not Miami, Auburn, or Texas, but Nebraska.

"I will always wonder what the scoreboard would have said in Lincoln had the Cornhuskers played Miami on their home field— as Miami did with Nebraska," wrote Charles Hollis of the *Birmingham News*. "I think I know. I think we wouldn't be debating the everlasting pros and cons of the polls if Miami had played Nebraska in Lincoln."

Despite the disappointment from the near-miss at a title, there were encouraging signs from the 1983 season. Auburn was pulling away from Georgia, and indeed would win three more SEC titles by the end of the decade. Hollis said the season could be the "cornerstone that puts Auburn in the national spotlight from here on out."

In many ways, he was right. Auburn wouldn't win any national titles, but the rest of the 1980s would offer plenty of wins and plenty of memories.

19 The 10 Best Games of the 2000s: What the Fans Say

Take away a bumpy start and an unexpected finish, and the 10 years of the Tommy Tuberville era produced some pretty good football. It also produced a lot of thrilling football games. Tuberville had a knack for winning big games, whether pushing buttons as the Riverboat Gambler or buttoning up as the Gambler's more conservative alter ego.

In the summer of 2008, fans were asked to vote on the 10 best games of the last decade. From about two dozen nominations, fans pared down the most thrilling wins into a very convincing list. Some of the wins were meaningful. Others were just exciting. Some are in this book, while others didn't make the cut. Here's the top 10:

Number 10: November 24, 2007—Auburn 17, Alabama 10. Auburn won its sixth Iron Bowl in a row with a smothering defense that held the Tide to season lows in total offense.

Number 9: October 2, 2004—Auburn 34, Tennessee 10. The 2004 Tigers won their fifth consecutive game and began to be seen as a legitimate national title contender after this one-sided romp over the Volunteers. Auburn intercepted five passes and grabbed a fumble from two UT quarterbacks. Junior Rosegreen had four of the interceptions, setting a new Auburn record.

Number 8: September 16, 2006—Auburn 7, LSU 3. With two seconds left, LSU failed to score on a heart-stopping final play to give then-third-ranked Auburn a narrow win. Auburn safety Eric Brock crunched LSU's Craig Davis on the 4-yard line to end the game.

"Coach [Will] Muschamp told me to guard the end zone with my life," Brock said. "I had my heels on the end line and I [said] they weren't going to get past me no matter what."

Number 7: November 19, 2005—Auburn 28, Alabama 18. Still see any of those "Honk if you sacked Brodie" bumper stickers on cars around town? This was the game where the joke originated. No. 11 Auburn sacked Tide quarterback Brodie Croyle an astounding 11 times to beat the eighth-ranked Tide.

Number 6: November 23, 2002—Auburn 17, Alabama 7. With Auburn's top backs on the shelf, freshman Tre Smith came out of nowhere to rush for 126 yards in Auburn's upset of No. 9 Alabama in Tuscaloosa.

Number 5: November 12, 2005—Auburn 31, Georgia 30. Receiver Courtney Taylor pounced on Devin Aromashodu's fumble just before it skidded out of the end zone, giving John Vaughn an opportunity to make a game-winning 20-yard field goal in one of the zaniest games in the Deep South's oldest rivalry. Originally billed as a defensive battle, the game turned into a slugfest, with the teams combining for 952 yards and 45 first downs.

Number 4: October 14, 2006—Auburn 27, Florida 17. When Jerraud Powers and Tristan Davis blocked a punt, Tre Smith picked

Great Books

Dozens of books and hundreds of articles and websites were used in research for this book, but a few deserve special mention and belong on any Auburn fan's bookshelf. Phillip Marshall and David Housel have produced two impressive coffee-table books in recent years. Marshall's *The Auburn Experience* was published in 2004 and includes stories and vignettes from football and other sports. Housel's *The Auburn University Vault* is not only a collection of memories from Auburn's longtime athletics director, but also a gorgeously produced hardbound book filled with Auburn mementos and memorabilia.

Thom Gossom's recently published memoir is not only the story of the integration of Auburn football, but a fascinating picture of Auburn University during the integration era. In 2007 Mike Jernigan penned a well-researched and superbly written biography of George Petrie that doubles as an early history of the university itself.

Finally, Terry Beasley's 1999 autobiography written with Rich Donnell is a stirring account of Beasley's sometimes anguishing life and career.

up the loose ball and dove into the end zone, giving Auburn a lead that it never relinquished. The one-loss Tigers were coming off a perplexing blowout loss to Arkansas that damaged the squad's national title hopes. But the previous week's disappointment was forgotten after the stunning win over the undefeated and second-ranked Gators.

Number 3: September 29, 2007—Auburn 20, Florida 17. After early losses to South Florida and Mississippi State, Auburn's season seemed on the brink of unraveling. No one gave the Tigers a chance at No. 4 Florida. As time expired, Auburn's Wes Byrum kicked an apparent game-winning field goal, but the play was nullified because a timeout was called just before the snap. After the delay, Byrum coolly made the kick a second time for the win.

Number 2: September 18, 2004—Auburn 10, LSU 9. Courtney Taylor caught a 16-yard touchdown pass from Jason Campbell as Auburn beat No. 5 LSU and started on the path toward a perfect season.

Number 1: October 13, 2001—Auburn 23, Florida 20. The Tigers snapped a seven-game losing streak against Florida when Damon Duval hit his third consecutive game-winning field goal. Karlos Dansby picked off Rex Grossman with minutes left on the clock to set up Duval's 44-yard kick.

First Auburn-Alabama Game in 1893

Today the spectacle of the Auburn-Alabama football game trumps every other sporting event in the state. Surprisingly, the same was true more than 100 years ago when the first game was played.

In 1893, when the teams first met, the notion of spectator sports in America was still in its infancy. American-style football

The first football game between Auburn and Alabama took place in 1893.

was popular up North and was slowly and steadily making inroads in the South.

Auburn and Alabama were in their second year of football, and the teams—such as they were—were loosely organized. The game was set for February 22, 1893, at Birmingham's Lakeview Park. Because of the unusual timing, the game could be considered either a continuation of the 1892 season or the start of the 1893 season.

Auburn wanted to bring in a Yankee coach to help get the team ready for the big game. D.M. Balliet, a former center at Penn, was chosen for the job.

The game—and the sport itself—was not without controversy. Far from a gentleman's pursuit, football was considered by many to be a barbaric, unsafe game. Many faculty members opposed the sport. Auburn had no money to pay Balliet, which was both understandable and fortuitous, because the idea of a coach being paid would have sent the faculty into an uproar. (The 1894 game was controversial because of rumors that Alabama coach Eli Abbott was being paid a salary.)

Despite the sport's youth and dubious reputation, the game was a hot ticket. A yellow ticket stub proclaimed "Tuskaloosa vs. Auburn" and sold for 25¢. A train from Auburn brought 226 fans, including 100 students. A train from Tuscaloosa arrived with 320 fans and 150 students. Auburn's headquarters at the Florence Hotel was adorned with orange and blue, while Alabama stayed at the Caldwell.

The *Birmingham Daily News* noted: "Every private vehicle, stable turn out, and public hack was filled with people on the way to Lakeview Park. The dummies and electric cars were crowded with lovers of the manly sport of football. Men and women who heretofore have jeered at such exhibitions of brawn and muscle were eager to see the contest."

Sportswriting was in its infancy, as well. Wayne Hester amusingly noted in his book *Where Tradition Began* that the reporter proceeded to "say something nice about every player in the game," but never got around to describing the scores or any of the game's action.

In any event, about 4,500 people saw Balliet win his first and only game as Auburn's coach, 32–22.

The nation's most fearsome rivalry had begun.

21 Experience Tiger Walk

I have never covered a riot. I have never covered the police beat.
The mayhem I witness is contained between the white lines.

I have covered the Super Bowl, the World Series, the NBA Finals, and the Final Four. I have covered the Olympics, Summer and Winter; the Opens, U.S. and British; the Bowls, Rose, Sugar, Fiesta, Orange, Gator, and GMAC.
I have covered nearly every major college football rivalry. And on nearly 90 campuses, from Hawaii to Boston College, Washington to Miami; in six different countries, from Russia to Texas (It's Like a Whole Other Country), only once have I genuinely feared for my safety.
That was at Tiger Walk in 1989.

So begins reporter Ivan Maisel's account of the Tiger Walk before the Auburn-Alabama game in 1989.

Don't worry. That was a one-time deal. But as Maisel writes, Tiger Walk is a bit of a misnomer. It's not a walk in the sense of a leisurely stroll or jaunt. It is an intensity-packed pregame tradition that is one of the staples of fall Saturdays at Auburn University.

Tiger Walk began some time in the 1960s. The origin of the walk was merely informal. Players would walk down Donahue Drive from their Sewell Hall dorm rooms to the football stadium. Fans—mainly kids—would run and watch and cheer.

Since then, it's become "the most copied tradition in all of college football," former athletics director David Housel likes to joke. "We had a cool Bruin walk we did at UCLA, but nothing like this," said former Auburn offensive coordinator Al Borges.

Tiger Walk remained a sort of spontaneous and unorganized celebration until the late 1970s, when Doug Barfield began actively encouraging fans to join in—although Barfield disclaims any ownership over the concept.

The most passionate, intense, fan-packed Tiger Walk was in 1989, when Alabama came to Jordan-Hare Stadium for the first time.

Maisel witnessed the scene with a writer from the *Atlanta Journal-Constitution*: "The Auburn fans roared, their eyes glazed

Few traditions in college sports can match the pageantry and excitement of Tiger Walk.

with a mixture of fervor, pride, passion, and perhaps a touch of the Jack Daniels. We were five or six deep and couldn't get any closer to the street. We were also hemmed in, and didn't have the zeal-fueled adrenaline to ward off the elbows and other parts of the bouncing, heaving, deafening masses. I no longer had any interest in taking notes, which was just as well, because the noise and the lack of space made it impossible. My own adrenaline kicked in, and I worked my way into open space.… The height of emotion [during Tiger Walk] reached in 1989 will be a watermark for years to come."

Today Tiger Walk is no longer spontaneous. In recent years, there have been upgrades in security, and barricades have been added to keep the friskier fans away from players. Some controversial "safety measures" were added in 2006, although most fans came to accept that the changes were needed to preserve what has become an impressive tradition.

Players appreciate the support. Walt McFadden, asked to name his favorite Auburn experience, doesn't hesitate.

"The Tiger Walk," he replied. "When I first got here, we played Alabama here. I hadn't seen that many fans, the support. It's like the state shut down just for that game."

Can't make it to Jordan-Hare Stadium? Tiger Walk goes on the road. A scaled-down but equally passionate version of Tiger Walk usually occurs as the Tigers troop from their buses into the visiting stadium. It's not the same as Donahue Drive, but it's a worthy attempt at approximating the original.

22 Media Watch

Once upon a time, the Internet didn't exist, the modern concept of "beat writer" was still in its infancy, and coaches might deal with only a handful of reporters on a weekly basis. Today no detail of Auburn's football program is too insignificant to chronicle on websites and blogs. Dozens of reporters cover the Tigers on a daily basis, and managing the media horde is a full-time occupation for several professionals in the athletic department.

Occupying several offices on the second floor of Auburn's athletic complex, media relations staff members (sometimes called "sports information directors") set up interviews, handle press conferences, distribute stats and notes, create media guides, and do a million other things that might not necessarily fall under their job description.

Across the hall is the media room—playfully nicknamed "the Bunker"—where scribes for print publications and websites bang out stories and blogs, post photos and videos, and sometimes kill time between practices and interviews.

The immediacy of the Internet dramatically affects how reporters do their job. Three full-time, nationally affiliated websites cover Auburn, often with two or three reporters at a time. At least a half-dozen newspapers are present just about every day. Each writer updates a blog or website immediately. Several television stations—from Birmingham, Huntsville, Montgomery, Mobile, and elsewhere—are usually represented on media days.

Feedback—whether through message boards, blog comments, or emails—is immediate.

Football is, of course, the most-covered sport at Auburn, and the season increasingly seems to last 12 months out of the year. From August through December, the focus is on the actual football season. Auburn has a weekly media day that features player interviews and a formal press conference with the head coach. But the rest of the week can be just as busy for players and coaches, who must learn to be savvy in front of a mic or a tape recorder. Most reporters churn out two dispatches—a story and notebook—every day of the football season. By midseason, finding a fresh topic can seem almost impossible.

In January and February the focus turns to recruiting. In fairness, the focus is recruiting just about every month of the season for some of the websites. Player visits are scrutinized and commitment lists are compiled. On National Signing Day, websites report each signed letter of intent as it arrives via fax in the athletic complex.

In March and April the focus is on spring football. Storylines and position battles to watch in August are developed and introduced, and younger players often get a chance to get some media time.

The summer is increasingly a time to follow camps, where the next crop of young players gets to impress college coaches.

With all these reporters, all these stories, and all this scrutiny, conflicts inevitably occur. Reporters and sports information personnel have different goals. Sometimes those goals overlap; sometimes they don't.

A media-friendly or even just media-savvy coach can keep things running smoothly. Tommy Tuberville was both understanding of the importance of the media in modern college football and genuinely friendly to the people who worked in the business. That was a valuable—and increasingly rare—combination.

But even under Tuberville, things weren't always easy for scribes. When things went south during the 2008 season and soon-to-be-ousted coordinator Tony Franklin became increasingly frustrated and frank with reporters, Tuberville barred media from speaking to assistant coaches. New head coach Gene Chizik is still fleshing out his media policy, although it seems likely he'll be less of a backslapper than Tuberville was.

Assistants can be just as valuable—and often more useful—to media than head coaches. Former defensive coordinator Paul Rhoads, who was hired to replace Chizik at Iowa State, was a great quote and a genuinely nice guy. Former offensive coordinator Al Borges rarely had an off-day when it came to filling up notebooks with notes and quotes.

Players are interesting to cover because they grow so much in the four or five years that they are in school. As freshmen, they're often anxious or shy in interviews. By their senior year, they might be confident and polished, although sometimes they become jaded and boring because they are understandably sick of the same parade of questions.

Star players are forced to handle the brunt of the media requests, and the good ones are the most appreciated. Three-year starting quarterback Brandon Cox was never a spectacular quote, but he was unfailingly polite, professional, and friendly in good times and bad. The players who do that deserve special praise. It's easy to face the media after winning a big game; it's much more difficult after a poor performance.

23 The History of Auburn's Uniforms

When Auburn donned "throwback" uniforms in 2007 to honor the 50th anniversary of the 1957 championship team, the difference was subtle.

"There's not a lot of 'throwback' in the uniform," then-coach Tommy Tuberville said plainly.

Part of the reason was that it was difficult to construct a modern homage to an old-school uniform. But it was also an indication that Auburn's uniforms, colors, helmets, and history have remained remarkably consistent over the years.

For the 50-year throwback game, Auburn donned its white jerseys and pants, removed the interlocking AU logo from the helmet, and replaced the blue face masks with gray bars. It wasn't a perfect match for the 1957 team, but it was close enough.

"I think we wear throwback uniforms every week," Tuberville said. "We haven't changed things much in years, which is good. You need to have tradition."

A real throwback might seem a bit garish for fans accustomed to the orange and blue. Auburn wore tan pants and black jerseys from 1893 until the 1930s, before switching to tan pants and blue and white jerseys. In the late 1930s and early 1940s the Tigers wore green jerseys and blue pants to honor its coaching ties to Notre Dame. Then the team used black pants with blue or white jerseys until the late 1940s. The traditional colors found their home with the hiring of Ralph "Shug" Jordan in 1951, and blue and white jerseys have been used almost exclusively since 1955.

The Helmet Project website, an incredible database of helmets for every college and professional football team that ever existed, shows few changes in Auburn's helmet over the years. The Tigers added the AU logo in 1966. Since then, the face-mask colors have changed, but the basic look of the helmet has remained the same.

Auburn's boldest apparel move may have had nothing to do with the team's colors. In 2005 the Tigers ended a 55-year relationship with Russell Athletic to sign a $10.6 million deal with Under Armour. Russell was born in nearby Alexander City, Alabama, and still maintains a strong presence there, but Auburn opted for the young, hip, Baltimore-based Under Armour apparel company to make its uniforms, cleats, and accessories.

"Russell was a great partner for us," Auburn athletics director Jay Jacobs said at the time. "It was a great relationship, and we appreciate all they did. At the end of the day, when you look at it, this [deal] is so much better. Being the steward and doing business in this department, a $54 million business, it was a very objective decision."

It's not the first time Auburn has made a switch. The Tigers switched to Nike in 1995, but fans' support for the homegrown company prompted Auburn to return to Russell when there were delays in signing the new contract.

Ten years later, there was no such backlash. Money wasn't the only factor in the decision. Auburn wanted to align itself with what was seen as a progressive company with savvy marketing and a nationwide following among young people.

"You sit at an Auburn junior high game, and those football players in the eighth grade come onto the field [mimicking] the Under Armour commercial," Jacobs said. "Those are our future recruits. What they're doing nationally is going to be a great story to tie us with them to get that national exposure. From that standpoint, it's invaluable."

The biggest hurdle for the new deal was the football cleats, an area in which Under Armour didn't have as much expertise. Auburn had previously used New Balance, and getting players to switch shoes proved to be difficult.

Some players taped over the New Balance logo in an effort to avoid having to give up their favorite shoes. Running back Tristan Davis, who was plagued with chronic foot and toe problems for much of his career, had to battle Under Armour to wear his preferred New Balance shoes. Davis eventually got his wish, and the Tigers got their new uniforms.

24 Terry Beasley

Terry Beasley's story is one of triumph on the football field and trials off the field. And it wasn't until relatively late in his life that the legendary Auburn receiver determined that the two areas intersected in ways he never thought possible.

Beasley struggled with depression and various mental health issues after his career and went through aggressive and arduous rounds of treatment than included more than a dozen sessions of electro-shock treatment, or electro-convulsive therapy. But when a doctor marveled at the "swiss cheese" that his brain had become, Beasley realized that he was paying a price for the fearlessness he displayed on the football field.

He has suffered 16 concussions of varying degrees throughout the course of his life (including one as a small child and one as an adult in a car accident). And he struggles with memory loss and sometimes has trouble putting his thoughts into words.

"In the middle of talking about something, I suddenly go blank and forget what I was talking about," Beasley wrote in his memoir, *God's Receiver.* "I also repeat myself. I may tell you something right now, and tell you the exact same thing in five minutes."

Beasley bears no ill will toward the sport of football, which defined much of his life.

He was born February 5, 1950, in Montgomery, Alabama. His dad struggled with alcohol and was often abusive to his wife and kids. Beasley's dad was a firefighter, but he spent much of the money on booze. Terry helped out with his family's part-time sawdust business to help make ends meet. He often went to school on an empty stomach but had too much pride to accept food from classmates.

The Beasley boys were all great athletes, and Terry starred at Montgomery's Robert E. Lee High School. He credits athletics and a loving mother for keeping him on the right path.

"Growing up with an alcoholic father, not knowing if we'd be sleeping in our own bed or on the run, us boys could have easily taken the wrong road, gotten into alcohol ourselves, or drugs and robbery," Beasley wrote. "But we didn't do that. We went out and became athletes instead of thieves. My mama, the goodness that was inside her, had a lot to do with us keeping between the lines."

Beasley was a top prospect and was recruited heavily by both Auburn and Alabama. Alabama's Paul "Bear" Bryant wanted him badly. Beasley visited Bryant's home three times and was once even invited to climb up Bryant's fabled tower while the coach watched practice.

Beasley admitted candidly in his autobiography that both schools offered illegal, under-the-table inducements, although Alabama was more "generous" in that regard. His father pushed him heavily to attend Alabama, eager for "gifts" and perhaps a way to ingratiate himself with city officials. But Beasley said he felt intimidated and self-conscious around rich kids at Alabama fraternity parties, while he sensed a more "down-to-earth and friendly" atmosphere at Auburn. It didn't hurt that he also knew that another prep phenom, Pat Sullivan, would be throwing passes for the

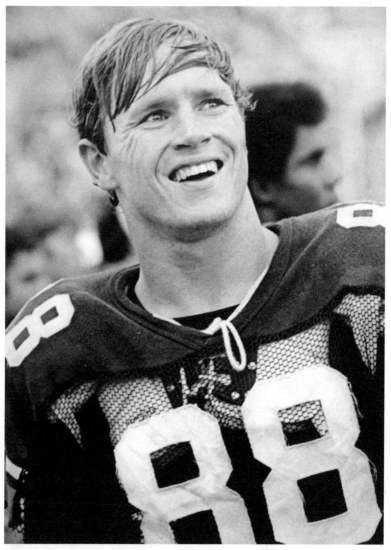

Wide receiver Terry Beasley struggled with personal issues after his career at Auburn.

Tigers. His mom knew he wanted to attend Auburn, and provided a counterweight against his father's influence, saying "the Beasleys are not for sale."

People who saw Beasley play swear he was the best receiver ever to play the college game.

"I have never seen his equal as a pass receiver," Bryant once said.

The "boy wonder," as Georgia coach Vince Dooley called him, caught 141 passes for 2,507 yards and 29 touchdowns in his three-year playing career.

Beasley took some vicious hits in college and has memories of blackouts and other fuzziness, especially on hard surfaces like the University of Tennessee's old artificial turf. But Beasley believes much of the damage occurred during his four-year NFL career with the San Francisco 49ers.

He described receiving "very fierce blows that knock you dumbfounded, paralyze you on the ground, that when you finally come around, everything is in slow motion; you get to the sideline and you're slobbering on yourself; you see these little fireflies, thousands of them, all around you.... You're totally incapacitated." The next day there would be large blank spots in his memory instead of recollections of the game.

After his football career was over, Beasley built a successful business but began to be derailed by personal problems in the mid-1980s. He went through a divorce, his business went under, and his health suffered.

He later picked up a sales job and was thriving in his position until the old football injuries began to return. He was driving to a golf course he had gone to dozens of times when he suddenly forgot how to get there. He started forgetting simple things routinely. His stress, anxiety, and depression began to overtake him.

He wrote candidly of these dark times in his life in his memoir. His struggles were daunting, but Beasley said he hasn't lost faith in God or felt sorry for himself.

His life story is a powerful one, and his perseverance is inspiring. It's a story that anyone who cheered his exploits on the football field should know.

The SEC: How the League as We Know It Came to Be

Today the Southeastern Conference is an economic and competitive powerhouse, generating millions of bucks and winning championships in all sports. But football is the cash cow, and football is behind the story of the league's formation.

The origin of the SEC stems from two precursor leagues—the Southern Intercollegiate Athletic Association (SIAA) and the Southern Conference. The SIAA was formed in 1894 at the urging of Vanderbilt chemistry professor William Dudley, who thought the growing sport needed some sort of organizing body. It became the first conference in the nation with an original membership of Alabama, Auburn, Georgia, Georgia Tech, North Carolina, the University of the South (Sewanee), and Vanderbilt.

By 1920, the conference's membership had swelled to an unwieldy 30, and rifts started to develop. When the SIAA refused to ban players from playing summer baseball for money or restrict freshman football eligibility, several of the larger programs voted to break away.

The new league was the Southern Conference. Alabama, Auburn, Clemson, Georgia, Georgia Tech, Maryland, Mississippi State, North Carolina, Tennessee, Virginia, and Virginia Tech were the original members. They were quickly joined by Washington and Lee and North Carolina State. In 1922 Florida, LSU, Ole Miss, South Carolina, Tulane, Vandy, and the Virginia Military Institute joined. A year later, Sewanee came on board. Duke joined in 1929.

The league thrived—and, indeed, is still in existence today—but once again became too large for its own good.

On December 9, 1932, the 13 members west and south of the Appalachian Mountains reorganized as the Southeastern Conference.

The league's composition has changed remarkably little since then. Sewanee left in 1940, withdrawing from big-time athletics. Today the school plays Division III sports, and the chapter of its history played against schools like Alabama, Auburn, and Tennessee is remembered curiously but fondly. Georgia Tech left in 1964, eventually joining the Atlantic Coast Conference, where many former Southern Conference schools now reside. Tulane departed in 1966 and, after a long stint of independence in football, joined Conference USA in 1995.

Only two members have joined. South Carolina and Arkansas were added to the league for the 1992 season, and the conference used the opportunity to create East and West Divisions and start a championship football game.

In September of 1933 Kentucky beat Sewanee in the first SEC football game ever played. But the early days of the league offered more than football. In its inaugural year, the SEC featured championship competitions in basketball, boxing, baseball, and track and field.

The SEC had a president, but not actually a "commissioner" until former Mississippi governor Martin S. Conner took office in 1940. Eight years later, the conference office moved to its current home in Birmingham under new commissioner Bernie Moore, a former LSU coach.

The lucrative television era of the SEC began in 1951, when the Alabama-Tennessee game became the first televised event in the league's history. More television agreements followed. Turner Broadcasting System started airing a game of the week in 1984. In 1992 Jefferson Pilot Sports started airing a weekly football game syndicated in the Southeast. The conference's mega-deal with CBS came in 1994 and pushed the SEC to national network audiences every week. Most recently, the conference signed a massive deal with ESPN that will increase exposure for football and other sports.

In 2002 Mike Slive became the league's current commissioner. He took the reins from Roy Kramer, who served 12 years and ushered the conference through explosive growth in the 1990s. Slive has plenty of challenges on his plate, including navigating the future of the bowl system. But the cash registers are still ringing for SEC members.

Slive distributed a record $122 million in revenue-sharing money in 2007.

26 The "Wreck Tech" Tradition and Auburn's 1955 Win

In 2005 Auburn fans rekindled a tradition that had been dormant for years, renewing a rivalry with Georgia Tech and evoking memories of great games from the past. On September 2, 2005, the day before Auburn's season opener against Tech, students and fans held a "Wreck Tech" Pajama Parade that marched from campus to downtown.

The Auburn-Tech series, and its accompanying parade, was a staple of college football in the South for most of the last century. The Tigers played the Yellow Jackets every season from 1906 through 1987, breaking only in 1943 for World War II.

So why were students parading around in their pajamas?

According to legend, the origin of the tradition dates to Auburn's first home football game, which was played against Georgia Tech in 1896. Tech was scheduled to arrive by train at the Auburn station near College Street early on November 7. Some

Auburn fans broke out their pajamas for the "Wreck Tech" parade in 1955.

mischievous pajama-clad Auburn cadets woke up in the middle of the night, scampered to the station, and greased the rails with lard. When Tech's train tried to brake a few hours later, it skidded halfway to Loachapoka. The Tech players supposedly had to hike back into Auburn, where they were routed 45–0.

Although that was the first game played on the Plains, it was actually the 18th football game played by the fledgling team. Auburn had played 17 games in six cities, going 9–6–2, before that first game in Auburn.

The facilities, such as they were, left a lot to be desired. The game was played before a "couple thousand fans" on a hard, clay field behind Samford Hall. Auburn quarterback Walter Holcombe

Joe Childress

Childress helped his team as both a fullback and a kicker from 1953 to 1955. As a junior, he had a team-best 836 yards on 148 carries, including a 164-yard performance in a win against fifth-ranked Miami (Florida). He was an All-American in 1955 and a first-round draft pick of the Chicago Cardinals. Some of his best seasons came late in his career when he was among the league's top rushers for the St. Louis Cardinals in 1963 and 1964.

directed the offense and returned punts. L.E. Byrum blocked a Tech punt and returned it for a touchdown. Auburn led 22–0 at halftime, and the game was never in doubt.

Tech was understandably hesitant about playing again the next year, and only agreed when Auburn officials warned students that they would be expelled for any further hijinks. Thus, the pep rally remained, a pajama parade eventually emerged, and the rail-greasing was retired permanently.

Auburn leads the all-time series with Georgia Tech 47–41–4, and although there are no current plans to renew the annual rivalry, the series remains one of the most tradition-rich in the history of both schools.

Perhaps the most memorable game was in 1955. The Tigers were in the midst of a 15-year losing streak in the series and the Yellow Jackets were heavily favored, playing at Grant Field in Atlanta.

But the Tigers ended the "long famine," as the headline in the *Atlanta Journal* read the next day, with a 14–12 victory.

The *Journal's* Ed Danforth described it this way: "'War Eagle' was the mating call of destiny at Grant Field Saturday. Two placement kicks after touchdown by fullback Joe Childress of Robertsdale, Alabama, etched graceful arcs over the goal posts in the crisp autumn air. That was the increment that gave Auburn its first football victory over Georgia Tech since 1940 and sent the

Plainsmen on their way toward a conference championship that they can hardly miss. It spilled the Engineers from the undefeated list after four victories over major opponents."

The game was played in front of a raucous crowd of 40,000 and the teams were "so closely matched…that the game turned on small plays here and there."

The two smallest—and biggest—plays of the game were Tech's missed extra points. The first one sailed wide, while the second fell victim to a bad snap.

27 David Housel

David Housel has written books, papers, pamphlets, introductions, articles, program features, and more about Auburn. He's lived, breathed, and talked more about Auburn University and its athletic programs than just about any person alive. He knows more people, more players, more coaches, more numbers than probably anyone.

But that won't give you the full picture of David Housel. You'd have to meet him in person for that. Fortunately, since he's spent 35 years at Auburn, most people have already done that. And most know that Housel is as friendly and generous as they come, an embodiment of everything Auburn wants its values to be.

In a recent memoir, longtime friend Bill Hancock aptly describes Housel as "Auburn's resident historian, raconteur, and keeper of the faith.… He could walk no more than a few steps without greeting an Auburn admirer. Yet he was the same humble, quietly brilliant person I had known for 20 years. It was a privilege to watch such a gentle person doing what he loved. To stand with him at Toomer's Corner…was like visiting Frontierland with Walt Disney."

David Housel has been an Auburn man for more than three decades. The university named the press box at Jordan-Hare Stadium after him in 2005.

Housel retired in 2004, but he's still a familiar presence around town, whether at sporting events or his regular breakfast seat at Chappy's Deli.

He grew up in the small town of Gordo, Alabama, in Pickens County, not far from Tuscaloosa. It was Crimson Tide country, without a doubt, but Housel's been in love with Auburn since he was a kid.

He worked as an editor at the *Plainsman* student newspaper and graduated from Auburn in 1969 with a degree in journalism. After a brief stint in the newspaper business, he returned to Auburn for good. He worked in the ticket office from 1970 to

1972, taught journalism from 1972 to 1980, and then rejoined the athletic department in the sports information department. Housel became sports information director (today it's sometimes called media relations or communications) in 1981, acquired the assistant athletics director title in 1985, and was elevated to athletics director in 1994.

In 2005 Housel decided to forgo a plane trip to Arkansas and missed his first Auburn game—home or away—in 35 years, breaking a streak that started an incredible 412 games earlier against Clemson in 1970. The streak still didn't touch the one maintained by former assistant athletics director Buddy Davidson, who certainly is worthy of a book chapter himself.

Later that year, Auburn named the press box at Jordan-Hare Stadium for Housel, a fitting tribute to a man who was a nationally respected sports information director before he ever moved into the big office.

"Coach Ralph Jordan taught me what it means to be an Auburn Man, and Pat Dye taught me what it means to be a competitor," Housel said. "That my name is being added to the press box in a facility bearing their names is more humbling than I can say. I am blessed, truly blessed and honored."

Some worry that the first sentence in Housel's life story will inevitably include a reference to his role in the clandestine attempt to hire Bobby Petrino at the end of the 2003 football season. Housel was a participant in the now-infamous plane trip to meet with Petrino days before the Iron Bowl. The flight was revealed, fans rallied around coach Tommy Tuberville, and Housel and Auburn President William Walker were forced into retirement.

But much of the criticism of Housel is dependent on selective memory. Many fans were eager to unload Tuberville earlier in the 2003 season, and had Auburn lost the Iron Bowl finale, many would have wondered not why Auburn officials were searching for a new coach, but why they had waited so long? Strangely, current

Auburn athletics director Jay Jacobs was criticized by some for conducting a by-the-book search, eschewing the techniques that landed Auburn in so much hot water in 2003.

Although Housel wasn't the impetus for the secret flight, he has admitted it was bad judgment to accompany other university officials—including the president and two trustees—on the trip. It's hardly rare for universities to use backhanded channels to pursue coaching candidates. If anything, Auburn's attempt was almost comically ham-handed and probably doomed from the start. Had they been a bit savvier, no one might have discovered it.

One ill-advised decision surely isn't enough to discount a career of service.

"The things that you can't always see are the countless lives David has touched, his love for Auburn and his leadership which has impacted us in such a positive way," said current athletics director Jay Jacobs. "It is fitting that the press box at Jordan-Hare Stadium bears his name."

28 Recruiting Players to the Plains

Auburn defensive back Walter McFadden had a lot of recruiters come to his house in south Florida, but few compared to Gene Chizik, who was intense and personable without being patronizing.

"He was honest," McFadden said. "From what I remember, I had a lot of guys that came to the house, and they were just telling me anything I wanted to hear."

McFadden developed a test.

"I'd just put out a question. I'd be like, 'I want to be No. 20.' Twenty minutes later, I'd be like, 'Can I be No. 6?' They were like, 'Sure, sure, sure.' I tried to get [Chizik] with it. He was like, 'I don't care what number you are. I just want you to play ball.' I was kind of hyped about that."

Chizik's efforts on the recruiting trail will play a big part in his success or failure as a newly minted SEC head coach.

The state of Alabama churns out a ton of Division I football prospects, but there are two big programs and an assortment of smaller ones that have to fight over all of them. That means Auburn frequently has to go out of state to assemble an SEC-level signing class. Auburn's geographic location is both a blessing and a curse when it comes to recruiting, but coaches have a found a way to maximize its value. In 10 years under Tommy Tuberville, the Tigers built on their traditional strength in Georgia and metro Atlanta. Tuberville also exploited the wealth of talent in south Florida, scooping up several valuable prospects that were overlooked by the Hurricanes, Gators, and Seminoles.

In state, the Tigers have generally held their own, although Alabama has emerged as a fierce competitor since the hiring of Nick Saban. Other programs like Troy, UAB, and now South Alabama pick up the players that Alabama and Auburn miss or don't have room for. Non-SEC programs like Louisville and West Virginia often chase the higher-tier athletes that don't have SEC offers. Mobile is a particularly fierce battleground, not only because of the Auburn-Alabama fight, but also because of the emergence of nearby LSU as a national power in the last several years.

Chizik grew up in Clearwater, Florida, played for Florida, and coached at Central Florida. So it seems likely that the Sunshine State will remain an integral part of Auburn's recruiting strategy. But recruiting Florida may be more difficult than it was just a decade ago.

Not only do out-of-state programs have to compete with the big boys—Florida, Florida State, and Miami—but other schools like Central Florida and South Florida have emerged as serious threats.

Head coaches are now a major part of the recruiting game, thanks to the aggressive attitude of coaches like Saban and Florida's Urban Meyer. Chizik has a reputation as an intense and persistent recruiter. Although none of the players on Auburn's current roster played for Chizik in 2004, his last season on the Plains, several were recruited by him.

McFadden said the last time he saw Chizik before a team meeting in 2008 was a recruiting visit in 2004.

"Last thing I remember, he was in my house telling me he was here for the next five years," McFadden recalled with a laugh. "Next thing I see a short guy—scrawny, smaller than me—called David Gibbs [Chizik's replacement]. It was kind of weird."

Even so, Chizik was a persuasive recruiter before he left.

"He's the one who got me here," McFadden said. "He's the one who [made me] comfortable coming to Auburn."

29 Pumping Iron: Auburn's Strength Program

At the end of football practice, you'll sometimes catch a glimpse of a poor, unlucky soul who has crossed Kevin Yoxall. Maybe he was late for a meeting or he skipped a weight-lifting session. Whatever the case, the punishment is often 100 yards worth of "up-downs," or an equally arduous task, under the glaring visage of Coach Yox.

Yox is Auburn's head strength and conditioning coach, and he's the coach who players love to hate. Or hate to love. Or something. He makes many of their freshman seasons miserable. The summer workouts he conducts are notoriously tough, but ultimately many of the players come to appreciate his work by the time their careers are done.

Success on the field begins inside Auburn's state-of-the-art weight-training room.

"I kind of see him as the co-head coach," said former running back Brad Lester says. "He's real hard on us, but we really appreciate him at the end of the day. He's the one that makes us what we are and pushes us past our limits."

Yoxall joined Tommy Tuberville's staff at Auburn in 1999 after four seasons as the top strength coach at UCLA. Before that, he served in a similar position at Minnesota. Yoxall got his start at Texas Christian, where he earned a master's degree and spent six years on the Horned Frogs' staff.

His background is in power-lifting. He was a collegiate regional record-holder for power-lifting in 1982 and a collegiate All-American in 1983 at East Texas State. In 2002 he was certified as a master strength and conditioning coach by the Collegiate Strength and Conditioning Coaches Association. Three years later he was named Collegiate Strength Coach of the Year by the Professional Football Strength and Conditioning Coaches Society.

Yoxall puts as much or more emphasis on conditioning as he does on strength.

"This does not diminish the importance of the weight room, but there always needs to be a certain level of fitness for each player," he wrote in a column for *American Football Monthly*. "You can't overemphasize the importance of conditioning, especially in this day and age. No matter how great the player is in the weight room, if he can't run, he can't play. This not only applies to straight-ahead running but the ability to move athletically, to change direction, and to react to movement."

Rather than focus on brute force, the former power-lifter stresses things like sprinting, flexibility, and the importance of lower-body strength.

"We have a 2:1 ratio in lower-body to upper-body training," he said. "I may have a guy who can bench press 500 pounds, but if he can't squat 500, he's not taking a lot onto the field with him. If he can't change directions and be explosive, he's not going to get into position to use his upper-body strength."

Yoxall doesn't play favorites. He has the same rules for everyone, and he spends as much time working with kickers as he does with linemen.

"They have to be able to trust me," Yoxall said, "but I have to be able to trust them, too. It's a little bit of a tightrope sometimes. There will be kids that do everything you ask them to do, but let's say they show up late one day or they screw up and miss a day. I have to do the same thing to them I do to anybody else. I tell the kids all the time I'll be as fair as they let me be. If a kid screws up, I have to deal with it."

When Tuberville resigned, Yoxall became the de facto leader of the team. Players were going through off-season workouts at the time, so it was logical that Yoxall and his staff be in charge. Two weeks after his hiring, Gene Chizik announced that he would retain Yoxall for an 11th season at Auburn.

Yoxall is often around the athletic complex from sunup to sundown. He's at every practice, meeting, and team function. In many ways, he has more contact with players than the actual position coaches because his staff is allowed under NCAA rules to conduct off-season workouts.

For as much as Yoxall demands out of players, he puts in a lot of time himself.

"The players respect him for his work ethic," Tuberville said. "Some strength coaches don't even go to practice. He never misses one. He's involved with those players' lives."

30 On the Air: Auburn Radio Broadcasters

Jim Fyffe was raised in the hills of northeastern Kentucky. He was such an ardent Kentucky Wildcats fan as a child that even one regular-season loss could move him to tears.

So how did he end up becoming a beloved Auburn radio broadcaster? As Fyffe told it, he was simply in the right place at the right time.

Fyffe passed away in 2003 from a brain aneurysm. He was only 57. In his 22 years as the voice of Auburn football and men's basketball, he won over initially skeptical fans and presided over some of the most exciting games in Auburn history.

"In a very real sense, the voice of Auburn has been silenced," then–athletics director David Housel said upon Fyffe's passing. "There will be other voices, but no one else will carry the excitement and enthusiasm Jim did. He had a special talent and he used that talent in a special way for the glory of Auburn. As long as people remember what has happened here in the last 20 years, 20 of the best years in Auburn history, they will remember Jim. He will forever more be a very special part of it. I've lost a friend; Auburn has lost a patriot."

Fyffe's signature was his touchdown call. There was no clever, ESPN-hip phrase that he used. It was a merely a statement of fact—Auburn had scored a touchdown—delivered in an enthusiastic manner.

"It does my heart good to be outside on my patio grilling steaks while a bunch of youngsters play football in a neighbor's yard, and then to hear them scream TOUCHDOWWWN AUBURRRN," Fyffe wrote. "Here is the most basic call in football, the same thing that many other announcers say, only with their schools inserted, and it has become an abbreviated anthem of sorts for Auburn University and Auburn football."

When Fyffe's wife, Rose, suggested that the call's notoriety took away from his other attributes as an announcer, he disagreed.

"I'd rather have a signature than not have one," he wrote. "What more can an announcer ask for? 'Touchdown Auburn' is my small contribution to mankind."

Fyffe grew up in Keaton, Kentucky. He attended UK and majored in broadcasting. Afterward, he was drafted and served in the army, but was never sent to Vietnam. He worked for three years at his brother's radio station in Paintsville, broadcasting games and doing just about everything else. In 1971, eager to leave home, he took a job sight-unseen at a Birmingham, Alabama, radio station. He did some news reporting and some Samford football before getting an opportunity to move to Montgomery and work in television.

On television, Fyffe would play up his Kentucky roots and his love of the Wildcats. In one burst of showmanship, he burned two tickets to an Auburn-Kentucky basketball game because the Wildcats were struggling and he couldn't bear to see them lose. The stunt prompted waves of complaints from Auburn fans, who felt they were being mocked. Fyffe said that wasn't the case, but the controversy may have helped derail his chance at the Auburn job in 1979.

WAUD won the rights to broadcast games for the 1979 and 1980 seasons, and Paul Ellen was named the lead broadcaster. In retrospect, Fyffe wrote, it may have been a blessing that he missed the job that year, as he might have been swept out when Auburn changed stations again.

Two years later, Auburn awarded the rights to WLWI, a station owned by Montgomery banking magnate and soon-to-be-trustee Robert "Bobby" Lowder, who wanted Fyffe to do the broadcasts. Fyffe said it was a stroke of opportunity: he was in the right place at the right time.

Then-coach Pat Dye didn't hit it off with Fyffe from the start. But eventually they came to like and respect each other and made for an entertaining duo on radio shows. The same could be said for Auburn fans who were initially hesitant about embracing the folksy announcer from Kentucky. Fyffe soon won them over with his passion and professionalism.

After Fyffe's death, Auburn didn't have to search far for a new top announcer. Rod Bramblett, an Auburn graduate and native of Valley, Alabama, assumed the role of lead play-by-play man for football and men's basketball. He had already been a part of Auburn's broadcast team by doing baseball games and the weekly call-in show, *Tiger Talk*.

On football games, he's assisted by partner Stan White, a former Auburn quarterback, and sideline reporter Quentin Riggins, a former Auburn player and current Montgomery lobbyist.

"I told Rod that it won't be easy replacing a legend like Jim Fyffe and he knows that there will be comparisons and that there will also be criticism," said Auburn Network president Mike Hubbard when he selected Bramblett out of 100 applicants. "That was going to be the case no matter who we selected for the job.

I told Rod that he will need to develop an extra layer of skin. I think he understands that."

Bramblett hasn't tried to replace Fyffe, but instead has followed his own style.

"It is important to not try to be like Jim or to copy Jim, because he was one of a kind," Bramblett said.

31 A Modern Rivalry: Auburn-LSU

Fans of a tradition-rich league like the Southeastern Conference often view rivalries as permanent and unbending, rooted in history and continuing in perpetuity. Alabama-Auburn, Tennessee-Alabama, and Auburn-Georgia are all games that fit the bill. But a fresh crop of rivalries have popped up right under our noses. It's hard to imagine any series with a greater string of exciting and meaningful games than Auburn-LSU.

The Auburn-LSU game certainly isn't new, but it has taken on added importance in the last decade. Six of the last nine SEC championships have featured either Auburn or LSU. The last five games in the series have been decided by an average of 3.8 points. And several of the games have produced their own bit of folklore that helps a rivalry build.

The last four seasons have been especially noteworthy and unusual. In 2007 LSU coach Les Miles stunned everyone—perhaps even his own team—when he called for a pass to be launched into the end zone in the game's waning seconds rather than attempt a field goal. The ploy worked, as Demetrius Byrd caught the touchdown pass from Matt Flynn to give LSU the 30–24 win. A year earlier, Auburn quarterback Brandon Cox scored the game's only touchdown and Eric Brock made a touchdown-saving tackle on the

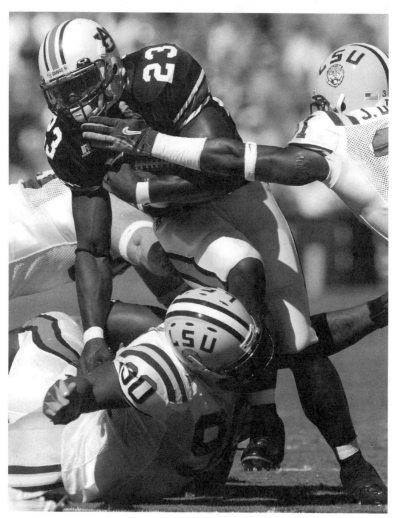

Auburn-LSU has become one of the hottest rivalries in the SEC. The conference championship game has featured at least one team in six of the last nine years.

final play in Auburn's 7–3 victory. In 2005 John Vaughn missed five field goals, including potential game-winning and game-tying kicks, in Auburn's 20–17 defeat. And Auburn's 10–9 win in the 2004 game was so significant that it gets its own chapter in this book.

Even games with no SEC championship implications have managed to have a little sizzle.

In 1999, Tommy Tuberville's first year at Auburn, the Tigers routed LSU 41–7 in Baton Rouge. After the game, Tuberville and some players puffed on cigars on the field outside the stadium tunnel. The smoking inflamed LSU fans and earned Tuberville a reprimand from the NCAA, which forced players to sit through an anti-tobacco session.

Two years later, some Auburn players hopped on the LSU logo at midfield, drawing a 15-yard penalty. Later, kicker Damon Duval had a notorious run-in with the LSU marching band at halftime and nearly came to blows with a tuba player.

Weather has also played havoc with the game. It was nearly canceled in 2004 due to the landfall of Hurricane Ivan. In 2003 the game was delayed for thunderstorms. When it started, LSU jumped out to a 21–0 lead and went on to win 31–7.

The atmosphere at Baton Rouge—with surly, booze-addled fans—makes for a memorable bus ride into the stadium and an intense game. In fact, the tense atmosphere has enhanced the rivalry by creating some less-than-pleasant memories for players and fans.

"I remember the bus shaking, and fans bringing up our loss to Georgia Tech that year," said Brock, who traveled to LSU in 2005 and 2007. "Their fans are intense. They are in your face, yelling, saying everything, talking about your coaches, talking about you. But you have to block that out and really focus on the game because in the end that's what it's going to come down to."

32 Family Traditions

Auburn people talk often about family, but in some cases the term is literal.

The first signing class of coach Gene Chizik in 2009 was helped by players with family ties. Linebacker Jonathan Evans followed his older brother Chris, also a linebacker, by signing with the Tigers. The nephew of star defensive end Antonio Coleman, Terrance Coleman, did the same. Both Colemans went to Williamson High School in Mobile, Alabama, while the Evans brothers both attended Blount High in Prichard, Alabama.

The elder Evans was known as an outstanding student and an overachiever who got the most out of his athletic ability. He was a lightly recruited prospect who became a solid four-year contributor at Auburn.

"I have learned a lot from him," said his younger brother. "We work out together. We do a lot together.... My mind is the strength of my game. You have to think things through and make the play. I think me and Chris are similar in that respect. He likes the game as much as I do. We have the same goals."

Chizik got two treats from the Coleman family when Antonio announced he would return for his senior year rather than enter the NFL Draft and Terrance picked the Tigers over a host of other suitors. Terrance was actually Tommy Tuberville's first recruit of the 2009 class, way back on Junior Day in the spring of 2008. He shopped around a bit in the intervening months but ultimately stayed with the Tigers.

"I'm looking forward to playing on one end at the strong side, and [Antonio] will be on the other end on the weak side," Terrance Coleman said. "I felt Auburn was home for me."

Auburn has a long line of fathers, sons, and brothers through the years.

Liston Eddins was cocaptain of the 1975 Auburn football team and sent two sons to the Plains. Bret Eddins was a senior starter at defensive end on Auburn's undefeated team. Bart is a reserve offensive lineman on the 2009 team.

Lee Gross was an All-SEC center for the Tigers who later played three seasons with the NFL's New Orleans Saints and one year for the Baltimore Colts. His son Gabe was a three-sport star at Dothan's Northview High School who came to Auburn planning to play football and baseball. An incredible athlete, he managed to win the starting quarterback job as a true freshman in 1998 and hit .363 on the baseball field. But he lost his job the next season, Tuberville's first, and decided to stick with baseball. The choice was rewarded when he was selected by the Toronto Blue Jays with the 15th overall pick in the 2001 Major League Baseball amateur draft after his junior year.

"I wouldn't trade the memories I have for any amount of money in the world," Gross said. "Playing in probably the last Auburn-Alabama game ever at Legion Field, playing Florida down in the Swamp, playing Georgia here in a night game with all that fog rolling in, I'll always have that."

33 John Heisman

One of the fathers of college football spent five of his early seasons at Auburn, leaving an important imprint on the young sport at the university.

John Heisman, an iconic figure for whom college football's most prestigious trophy is named, coached at Auburn from 1895 to 1899, going 12–4–2. He led the Tigers in their first on-campus game, a win against Georgia Tech.

He was Auburn's fifth head coach, but the first who stayed for any significant length of time. The Pennsylvania native earned an undergraduate degree at Brown and a law degree from Penn, though he never used it. He coached at Oberlin and Akron before coming to Auburn, and later spent time at Clemson, Georgia Tech, Penn, Washington and Jefferson, and Rice. Overall, he compiled a 185–68–18 record.

Heisman thought of himself as a sophisticated and cosmopolitan world traveler, so moving from larger Midwestern cities to a small village in the South was quite a change for him.

But moving to Auburn provided the opportunity to, as biographer Wiley Lee Umphlett wrote, "spread the gospel of football in what was then virgin territory." Heisman had been around for the early years of the sport in the East, helped it grow in the Midwest, and saw an opportunity to do the same in the South, where the sport's popularity was on the verge of exploding.

Heisman was always an innovator, pushing the boundaries of the rules, which were ill-defined and constantly changing at the time. In his first game with the Tigers, Heisman executed a flawless hidden-ball trick. In a game against Vanderbilt, Auburn quarterback Reynolds Tichenor "stuffed the ball under the front of his jersey" in the midst of a revolving wedge. While Vandy was trying to break up the wedge, Tichenor was seemingly out of the play, bending down to tie his shoe. Then he nonchalantly galloped into the end zone.

The play was eventually outlawed, but it resulted in Auburn's only touchdown. Auburn had the ball on the 2-yard line when the game was called on account of darkness (despite the sun not having set). The decision predictably infuriated Heisman and illustrated the arbitrary nature of the game's rules in the sport's early days.

Heisman quickly became popular in Auburn, teaching classes on oratory and acting in a local play. He was an intellectual who loved football strategy, yet knew the game was "violent and brutish." He quickly saw the forward pass as a way to expand the game's appeal and lessen the physical pounding on players.

Early in his Auburn tenure, Heisman first witnessed a forward pass while "scouting" a game between North Carolina and Georgia.

College football's most famous award is named after John Heisman, who coached at Auburn from 1895 to 1899.

(Heisman was one of the first coaches to actively scout opponents.) Getting the rules committee to allow forward passes became a "personal obsession," although the rule wouldn't be changed until 1906.

Heisman's last year at Auburn promised to be his best, as the team was stocked with veterans in 1899. But conflicts with officials marred the final two games. Auburn was leading Georgia 11–6 in the second-to-last game when the official suspended play on account of darkness. He then declared that the game should end in a 0–0 tie. The Southern Intercollegiate Athletic Association took the rare step of overruling the official on appeal and reinstating Auburn's win.

Auburn then faced the legendary Sewanee team of 1899, which had barnstormed the country and beaten five big schools in six days. The Tigers controlled most of the game, and Sewanee seemed fatigued and overwhelmed. Auburn appeared to recover its own fumble late in the game, but the official awarded possession to the Purple at the 1-yard line. Sewanee promptly scored the game-winning touchdown. Heisman was furious, and wrote a long letter to a Birmingham newspaper eviscerating the official. Umpire William P. Taylor responded with a lengthy diatribe of his own, poking fun at Heisman's fledgling acting career (he was not a coach but a "would-be actor of character parts") and calling him a "failure."

"Is it not most likely that he must keep in Auburn's good graces by ascribing his defeats to the officials?" Taylor asked.

The disputes over officiating during this era are difficult to evaluate because there are few unbiased, contemporary accounts. But few dispute that officiating was often inconsistent, if not totally incompetent much of the time. In any case, Taylor was clearly out of his league in trying to win a debate against Heisman, who responded with yet another lengthy rebuttal.

"What on earth has my capacity or incapacity as an actor have to do with Mr. Taylor's rank football decisions?" he wrote. "I have coached for eight years in succession, and the last five of them at Auburn. People don't usually re-engage failures."

Heisman seemed to enjoy Auburn, and in later years he would always write fondly of his experiences there. But the disputes with officials left a sour taste in his mouth and gave him something to prove. Plus, he had found a comfortable destination that could offer an even bigger salary. Former Auburn professor Walter Merritt Riggs was now president at Clemson. He loved football and had even brought along Auburn's name and colors to his new college. For Heisman, it seemed like a sensible move.

In five years, Heisman had put Auburn football on the map. And he would continue to wield significant influence in the development of the sport.

Many of Heisman's half-humorous adages persist today. He described tackling this way: "Thrust your projections into their

The Heisman Connection

Auburn is the only school at which John Heisman has coached that has had a Heisman Trophy winner. Quarterback Pat Sullivan and running back Bo Jackson have won the Heisman for the Tigers. The same can't be said for Oberlin, Akron, Clemson, Georgia Tech, Pennsylvania, Washington and Jefferson, and Rice, Heisman's other coaching stops.

cavities, grasping them about the knees and depriving them of their means of propulsion. They must come to earth, locomotion being denied."

Then there's the speech he supposedly gave to players before the season began. Heisman would face his team holding a football. "What is it?" he would ask. "A football is a prolate spheroid, an elongated sphere—in which the outer leather casing is drawn up tightly over a somewhat small rubber tubing." Then, after a dramatic pause, he would intone, "Better to have died as a small boy than to have fumbled this football." Versions of the story differ, and Heisman apparently got a kick out of repeating it in public speaking engagements.

Of football, Heisman said it took "25 percent talent, 20 percent aggressiveness, 20 percent mentality, 20 percent speed, and 15 percent weight." The role of the coach, he said, "should be masterful and commanding, even dictatorial. He has no time to say 'please' or 'mister.' At times he must be severe, arbitrary, and a little short of a czar."

Heisman could be self-promotional and far from modest about his success. Only a few years after leaving Auburn, he put together a pamphlet extolling "Heisman football" that said successful coaches were so "few and far between" that it's no wonder "they command salaries virtually without limit."

The legendary coach, who died in 1936, would probably fit in just fine today.

34 Jeff Beard

To honor and recognize Jeff Beard's career, Auburn inscribed his name on one of the university's most prominent athletic buildings—Beard-Eaves-Memorial Coliseum—15 years ago. It was a fitting tribute to someone who had spent his career as a builder.

Beard spent 40 years in Auburn's athletic department, and 21 years as athletics director, ushering Auburn through one of its most successful eras, returning the department to solid financial footing and upgrading the program's faltering sports facilities.

"To understand Jeff Beard's impact on the Auburn athletic program, consider this fact," soon-to-be–athletics director David Housel wrote in 1994. "With but two exceptions—the athletic complex built in 1989 and the swim center opened [in 1994]—each and every facility used by the Auburn athletic department was built or dramatically altered during his tenure as athletics director."

Garland Washington "Jeff" Beard grew up in Greensboro, Alabama, and came to Auburn in 1928, following the path of his older brother Percy. To make ends meet during those Depression-era years, Beard took a job at a local boarding house, waiting tables and washing dishes. He still found time to compete in track and field, and his record in the discus throw stood for 30 years.

He graduated in 1932 and joined the athletic staff a year later. He would serve as assistant track coach, football program manager, cameraman, business manager, and any other position at which he was needed.

In 1951 President Ralph Draughon turned the entire department over to Beard. Eleven days later, Beard hired Ralph "Shug"

Jordan as Auburn's new head football coach, which he later said was the best decision he ever made.

Beard would stay in the position for 21 years, bringing much-needed stability to Auburn's then-struggling department. When he started, the facilities were aging and the department was in financial crisis. "Had it not been for the good graces of the local banks, the department might have ceased to exist," Housel wrote.

Improving facilities and firming up the finances went hand in hand. Beard and Jordan wanted to improve their home schedule, rather than be forced to rent home games at stadiums in Birmingham, Columbus, Montgomery, and elsewhere. By 1970 the stadium had 64,000 seats and home games against teams like Maryland and Miami (Florida) were possible. Then rivals started to play at Auburn: Georgia in 1960, Georgia Tech in 1970, and Tennessee in 1974.

He wasn't athletics director in 1989, when Alabama finally played at Jordan-Hare Stadium, but his efforts laid the groundwork for that eventuality.

Wrote Housel, "The Auburn athletic program as we know it would not exist had it not been for Jeff Beard, his love, his devotion, his loyalty, his wisdom, and his foresight."

35 Zeke Smith

When Auburn's 1957 national championship started preseason camp, coach Ralph "Shug" Jordan expected to field a good defensive team. But if he never expected one of the best defensive teams in college football history, it's probably because he didn't know that he had one of the best defensive linemen in the game's history right under his nose.

Defensive lineman Zeke Smith won the Outland Trophy in 1958.

Zeke Smith was a native of Uniontown, a small city in Alabama's Black Belt, who worked his way from relative obscurity to the top of his sport. He arrived on the Plains in 1955, unsure whether he really belonged on a top-level college football team.

"I got discouraged several times and started to quit," Smith said in the 2004 book *Auburn Experience*. "I'd get up the next day and say, 'If this guy can stay, I can, too.' I just kept hanging in there. Practice was really rough."

Smith did more than just hang in there. He was part of Auburn's national title team in 1957 and won the Outland Trophy for the nation's top interior lineman in 1958 (Tracy Rocker would repeat the feat for Auburn 30 years later). In 1982 he was inducted into the Alabama Sports Hall of Fame.

He started as a fullback at Uniontown, but didn't attract much interest from college teams. Born Roger Smith, he acquired the nickname "Zeke" when his high school coach compared him to Georgia quarterback Zeke Bratkowski. The nickname stuck.

He played several positions, but excelled most in the backfield.

"If they wanted to run the ball, they left me at fullback," he said. "If they wanted to throw the ball, they put me at end. It didn't matter to me."

Smith came to Auburn through a family connection. His father, Morgan, worked for Southern Railroad with Jordan's father.

"I wasn't recruited much," Smith said. "People said they weren't taking players from little schools. I just wanted to go somewhere they would give me a scholarship. Coach Jordan's daddy and my daddy talked about it. Coach Jordan's daddy talked to Coach Jordan. That's how I ended up at Auburn."

His time at fullback didn't last long at Auburn. Coaches saw him as a more valuable defensive player, and practice observation quickly confirmed it. "They let me run a couple of plays," he said. "I think I fumbled one time, and they told me to go to the line. That was fine with me. That's what they recruited me for, anyway."

Coming from a small town and lacking a blue-chip pedigree, Smith had to conquer his own doubts before he could excel on the field. "I'd never seen so many good players in one place," he said. "At Uniontown, some of the guys that were playing should have been managers or cheerleaders.

"[Auburn] had so many players they had to run some of them off. I knew I was going to have to give everything I had. I wanted to do it really bad. I didn't want to go back to Uniontown."

He didn't. The 1957 championship season was his breakout year, as Auburn led the nation in every defensive category. The Tigers allowed an average of 2.8 points per game and shut out opponents six times. The national stage helped set up Smith to win the Outland Trophy the following season.

After college, Smith played two seasons with the Baltimore Colts, two seasons with the New York Giants, and one season in the Canadian Football League.

"I don't have any complaints," he said. "I've been successful and I've enjoyed myself. Those days at Auburn were some of the greatest days of my life. The national championship was great. That was about as big as it gets. That's something to strut about."

36 Gene Chizik

The news was stunning, and the first reaction from Auburn fans reflected that shock. On Saturday afternoon, December 13, 2008, word leaked out that Gene Chizik, the struggling head coach at Iowa State, would become Auburn's 26th head football coach.

Up until about 24 hours earlier, when Chizik first emerged as a candidate, few had even considered him as an option. His 5–19 record and 10-game losing streak at Iowa State seemed to be a disqualifying mark against his résumé. But Auburn athletics director Jay Jacobs had Chizik on his list from the start. And after an interview in Texas and a follow-up in Memphis, Chizik was offered the job.

Gene Chizik took over as the 26th head coach in Auburn history in December 2008, following a 5–19 run at Iowa State.

Since then, passions have cooled and most fans have rallied around the coach—some cautiously, others enthusiastically.

No one disputes his sterling track record as a defensive coordinator. In 2004 Chizik directed Auburn's dominant defense in the Tigers' perfect season. A year later, after jumping to Texas, he was part of the Longhorns' national championship.

But he may have made a misstep on his carefully planned career path when he accepted the head-coaching job at Iowa State, long a bottom-dweller in the Big 12. He inherited a four-win team, and things only got worse. The Cyclones sunk to 3–9 in 2007 and 2–10 in 2008. His once-bright career prospects had fizzled.

But Jacobs took a chance—and faced the ire of some Auburn fans—when he decided to give Chizik an opportunity to coach in an environment more hospitable to winning. Chizik promised he wouldn't let Jacobs down, even turning to the athletics director at one point during his introductory press conference and saying, "Jay, you've got the right guy."

Only time will tell if that turns out to be true. Chizik got off to a fast start, hitting the road to woo recruits only minutes after wrapping up his introductory press conference. Chizik's backers maintain he won't be outworked. Not by Nick Saban. Not by anyone.

"Don't let his record fool you," said Boots Donnelly, who gave Chizik his first full-time college coaching position at Middle Tennessee in 1990. "Whatever he's done wrong, he won't repeat it. That first experience as a head football coach is always the toughest."

Chizik grew up in Clearwater, Florida, the son of Gene Sr., a World War II veteran, Bronze Star recipient, and head coach at Tarpon Springs High. The younger Chizik was a player and eventual captain at Clearwater High. His coach, John Nicely, would later become Chizik's father-in-law.

After an injury-shortened career at Florida, Chizik decided to follow in his father's footsteps and become a coach. After a stint in high school, stops at Clemson, Middle Tennessee, Stephen F. Austin, Central Florida, Auburn, and Texas followed.

While a graduate assistant at Clemson, Chizik met Bill "Brother" Oliver, the future Alabama and Auburn defensive coordinator whose support helped Chizik land full-time gigs elsewhere.

"It didn't take very long to see Gene had all the qualities to be a head coach," Donnelly said. "He was an extremely tireless worker. He was a very, very solid recruiter. He had a maturity level that was a little bit different than most young coaches. Hours meant nothing to him. He had a great feel for the game and he learned things very quickly."

When Chizik's plane landed in Auburn, hecklers from the previous day had been replaced by a cheering crowd.

"I am very, very overwhelmed," Chizik said after he stepped off the plane with his family. "I'm back home. What can I say? I'm back home. I feel very blessed. My family, myself—this is a dream come true for us. I'll tell you this—these people of Auburn University and the Auburn family is what I got into coaching for. And I left it with a dream to one day come back to it, and today I'm living that dream and I want to thank you guys."

Former players under Chizik helped pitch the hire to a skeptical fan base. "He's a players' coach and a hard worker," said Carlos Rogers, a 2004 Jim Thorpe Award winner under Chizik. "If you're not committed to working hard and trying to be your best, you're not going to be a fit for him. I think that's what we did [in 2004]. We had a coach that loved players and loved football. You have to take that same enthusiasm and passion he has for the game and tie it into your game.

"I have a real tight relationship with him. I think it was real important to come down here and just see him again. He's like a father to me."

Former Auburn linebacker Antarrious Williams was so elated by the hire that he showed up at the airport to greet his old coach.

"He was my No. 1 choice before they even mentioned him," Williams said. "I think Jay Jacobs got this right. A lot of people are underestimating Gene Chizik's coaching ability. He's a fiery guy. I couldn't tell you one time I can remember him cussing players out, but he got on to us. He coached us hard. When

Chizik left, it hurt us more to lose the guy than the coach. He's a really good coach, but players were sad to lose Gene Chizik as a person as well."

The Sacrifices of James Owen and the First Black Players

Auburn University accepted the racial integration of its student body grudgingly but peacefully. The latter was important in that tumultuous era, when every modest step of civil rights progress in the South was challenged by fear and intimidation.

But when it became inevitable that Harold Franklin would enroll in graduate school, and that the courts and the federal justice system would see to it, Auburn declined to put up a fight. Students and faculty were gathered in the stadium and told that any attempts to circumvent the law would be handled harshly.

"[President Ralph Draughon] told everyone that we are not in favor of integration, but we are going to do it," recalled Dean James E. Foy. "We follow the law. We follow the Auburn Creed. Next fall, if you can't do that, you need to transfer now."

Even if the students and local residents remained under control, Auburn officials feared that the state's unpredictable governor, George Wallace, would make a grandstanding gesture like the infamous "Stand in the Schoolhouse Door" at the University of Alabama in 1963.

The process was thankfully violence-free, although Franklin's college experience was less than ideal. Isolated on an empty wing of a residence hall, he eventually transferred to another school.

Four years later, Auburn athletics took a much bolder step into integration. In 1968 Henry Harris became the school's first black student-athlete when he was given a scholarship to play basketball.

Then James Owens became the first African American on the football team.

Thom Gossom soon joined him. Gossom was different in that he was not a recruited athlete, but a student from Birmingham's integrated Catholic high school, John Carroll. He came from a hardworking family that stressed educational achievement. He had offers from top schools up North.

But Gossom wanted to be one of the first pioneering black students at Auburn University. And he wanted to play football. He hadn't talked to any coaches beforehand, but when he walked into the football offices, he was given a locker and a jersey and a chance to compete. He impressed coaches immediately, eventually winning a scholarship and playing in games as a receiver.

Fans probably remember him most for his role in the so-called Gossom incident in the 1974 Iron Bowl. An official ruled that Gossom stepped out of bounds on a touchdown run, possibly costing Auburn the game. Gossom says he's still asked about that play today.

His recent memoir, *Walk On: My Reluctant Journey to Integration at Auburn University*, is a fascinating portrait of Auburn University during the history-changing years of the early 1970s. Like many of the early black pioneers, Gossom had ambivalent feelings about his Auburn experience. A return trip to campus in 2002 for the 30th anniversary of the 1972 "Amazin's" teams gave him a chance to reflect on those times.

"I realized something that night," he wrote. "All of us had lived through a time of change in our society. It was not just James and I that had to live in and through a painful era. We all had."

It's difficult for Gossom to say whether he would live through that experience again.

"It can't be wrapped up in a neat, meaningless sound bite. It's complicated. Very complicated," he wrote.

But he doesn't dispute the important place in history occupied by the first black students and student-athletes.

James Owens broke the Auburn football team's color barrier in 1970.

"The evolutionary change of the civil rights movement needed to come to that small segment of the world," he wrote. "The less than 100 blacks that journeyed there in the first 10 years of Auburn integration and graduated became the vessels of that change. The

five black athletes, who played for Coach Jordan, made it possible
for those who followed."

Jason Campbell

Prior to 2004, Jason Campbell's career had not exactly been the
stuff of storybooks. Sure, he had won plenty of games and had
played very well at times, but he'd also been booed for losses,
unfairly blamed for offensive failures, and forced to juggle a revolving door of offensive coordinators.

Before the season, Auburn coach Tommy Tuberville even talked
of Campbell being pushed for the starting quarterback job. Would
2004 be just the final, unhappy chapter in Campbell's underachiev-
ing career?

Not a chance.

In 2004 the football gods finally reversed Campbell's karma
and gave him the resources to excel—a loaded backfield, veteran
receivers, and a new coordinator who believed that he could
succeed. The result was a perfect season that vaulted Campbell into
the first round of the NFL Draft and a lucrative NFL career.

Campbell was a *Parade* All-American and an elite quarterback
from Taylorsville, Mississippi. He was also a top-notch student
from a solid family and an avid churchgoer with unquestioned
character. In short, he was the type of player and person that
coaches drool over.

Campbell's decision to attend Auburn—announced in front of
the congregation at his church—was a mild surprise, but Campbell
felt comfortable with Tuberville and his relatively new staff at
Auburn. Little did he know how rapidly his coaches would change
throughout his five-year Auburn career.

He started with Noel Mazzone, who was replaced with Bobby Petrino. When Petrino went to Louisville, Tuberville promoted Hugh Nall and Steve Ensminger to run the offense in 2003. It was in that disappointing season that Campbell suffered through some of the worst abuse from fans, who couldn't understand how an offense with so much talent could be so ineffective.

But the 2004 season was one of redemption for Campbell, who was named the SEC's Offensive Player of the Year after throwing for 2,700 yards and 20 touchdowns in the 13–0 season.

He left Auburn as the school's second-leading passer in total yards, passing touchdowns, pass attempts, and pass completions, and first in completion percentage and passing efficiency.

For most of his career, Campbell was stoic in the face of criticism. But he admitted later that he took some of the slights personally. Late in the season, Campbell brought up a preseason poll of the nation's top 30 quarterbacks. It appeared in some preseason magazine—he's not sure where—and Campbell wasn't anywhere to be found on the list.

"I was in the SEC for four years, doing positive things, and no one seemed to take notice," Campbell said. "I was like, 'What's really going on?' That really motivated me."

Campbell eventually stopped worrying about the critics.

"You've got to understand that you can never please those people," he said. "Some people are not going to like you no matter what."

Campbell's career has continued on an uncomfortably familiar path in the pros, as the Washington Redskins have cycled through coordinator after coordinator. In that sense, the rough years at Auburn were good preparation.

"People don't understand how difficult it is to learn a different offense every year," he said.

There was actually a bit of intrigue surrounding Campbell's selection in the 2005 NFL Draft. The usual predraft cycle of misinformation was even more confusing than usual, as teams pursuing

Quarterback Jason Campbell was named the SEC's Offensive Player of the Year after the Tigers' undefeated season in 2004.

Campbell tried to throw others off the scent. Then–Redskins coach Joe Gibbs visited Auburn to conduct a private workout with Campbell, and the Redskins traded up to acquire the 25th pick. But when word leaked out about Washington's interest in Campbell, Redskins officials were frantic and tried to douse the credibility of the reports.

Between the rumors and false stories, it was difficult to know what to believe. ESPN analyst Chris Mortensen said he believed the Redskins' concern about the leak was genuine, and not merely a predraft ruse. In the end, it didn't matter, as Campbell was still around for the Redskins. Campbell was the fourth Auburn player picked in the first round, and Tuberville described the first draft day as a six-hour infomercial for Auburn.

"We couldn't come close to putting the price tag for what it would cost us to have this much publicity nationwide," Tuberville said. "Every time you turned around, they were talking about Auburn."

Tommy Tuberville

When news broke Wednesday, December 3, 2008, that Tommy Tuberville's 10-year tenure on the Plains had come to an end, the initial reaction was shock. Then it turned to appreciation.

The *Plainsman*, Auburn's student newspaper, rushed out a special edition listing Tuberville's accomplishments under the headline, "Thanks, Tommy!" Signs of support started popping up around town. A pro-Tuberville group of students even led a march to Auburn president Jay Gogue's home.

Officially, Tuberville resigned. Athletics director Jay Jacobs maintained adamantly in the days to come that Tuberville could have remained as head coach if he had wanted to do so. The $5.08 million buyout was paid, Jacobs said, because it was the right thing to do.

Tuberville largely chose to stay silent in the weeks that followed. For the first time in decades, he spent his January relaxing and vacationing—not agonizing over the decisions of high school recruits.

His departure, however it came about, occurred after a miserable 2008 season. Tuberville candidly admitted that many of the season's wounds were self-inflicted. The hiring and subsequent midseason firing of offensive coordinator Tony Franklin doomed the Tigers to offensive struggles throughout the year. Even if Franklin's offense had eventually worked, it was quickly clear that he was a bad fit for Tuberville and his staff.

Despite the sour season that ended his Auburn tenure, Tuberville's legacy on the Plains seems fairly secure, judging by the fans' outpouring of support.

The pinnacle of the Tuberville era at Auburn will be remembered as the perfect season of 2004. But there were other equally important accomplishments. The Tigers won 50 games in a five-season stretch from 2003 to 2007. They played in bowls in every season except Tuberville's first and his last. They played in the SEC Championship Game twice, and won once. They beat rival Alabama six times in a row from 2002 to 2007.

But Tuberville's Auburn teams were equally notable for their good citizenship. Players rarely graced the police blotter, the team's academic standing was solid, and there was never a whiff of NCAA trouble on the recruiting trail.

Tuberville's values were shaped growing up in Camden, Arkansas, where his father worked at the Grapette soft drink factory and was a well-known youth sports coach and official. Tommy loved the outdoors and playing sports and was a tenacious, if not terrific, athlete.

Tuberville Back Overseas

When he returned from an overseas trip visiting American troops in 2008, Tommy Tuberville could scarcely stop talking about what a life-changing experience it had been and how impressed he was with the young soldiers.

So even though he's no longer an active coach (at least for the moment), Tuberville took the trip again.

In the summer of 2009, Tuberville joined Mack Brown of Texas, Jim Tressel of Ohio State, Troy Calhoun of Air Force, Rick Neuheisel of UCLA, and Houston Nutt of Ole Miss on Round 2 of the coaches' goodwill tour.

"I felt good about this country and what we're doing," Tuberville said after returning from his trip in 2008. "The courage these young people have is just amazing."

Tuberville said what he enjoyed most was the casual interaction with the troops, whether eating in mess halls or signing autographs.

"They're the same age as a lot of our players, but they're so mature," Tuberville said. "They really know what they're doing. I feel even better now—though I felt really good before—about what our military does for us."

He walked on as a safety at Southern Arkansas University, where he planned to major in business and find some sort of career. Instead, he ended up embarking on a long and ultimately rewarding coaching career.

When Tuberville was hired as Auburn's head coach after the 1998 season, it was hard to imagine that only a decade earlier he had been pinching pennies as a volunteer assistant at Miami. Or that only a few years before that, he had dropped out of coaching entirely to help run a catfish restaurant in Tennessee.

But Tuberville said the time he spent laboring in obscurity helped prepare him for the time in the spotlight—and gave him an appreciation of the assorted band of graduate assistants, volunteers, and administrative staff members who help a program function.

"I think it's helped me that I kind of remember where I came from," Tuberville said. "When I go into these small schools, I know how important it is. I sign autographs and take pictures. You don't forget where you came from. It helps me remember that my job is important, but it's not nearly as important as I think it is sometimes."

Tuberville's career started humbly at Hermitage High School, where he spent two years as an assistant and two years as a head coach. "Since Hermitage was more of a basketball-oriented school, everyone had to be educated about football," Tuberville said. "We went around to the booster club groups and talked about the sport and what they could look forward to on Friday nights.

"I became the head football coach in my third season. That was a lot of responsibility for a young person. But I really enjoyed it. The community embraced me, and we had a successful season and beat our crosstown rivals for the first time."

In 1980 he started a five-year stint as an assistant at Arkansas State in Jonesboro. Unsure about his future in the coaching business, Tuberville left Jonesboro to help own and manage a catfish restaurant with his sister in Tennessee.

It was during his time in the restaurant industry that he heard of an available position on Jimmy Johnson's staff at the University of Miami. Tuberville spent the next eight years of his life in south Florida—three years as a humble unpaid assistant, four years as linebackers coach, and one as defensive coordinator. A one-year stint at Texas A&M positioned him for a head-coaching move. He took NCAA probation–saddled Ole Miss to a 25–20 record in four years before jumping to the Plains to replace Terry Bowden.

While the start of Bowden's tenure was filled with wins and optimism, the ending was not pretty. Under the impression that he would not survive past the end of the year, Bowden quit in the middle of 1998.

But Tuberville rebuilt the program more quickly than anyone could have imagined. In 1999, his second year, the Tigers bounced back from a blowout loss at Florida to finish the regular season with

Head coach Tommy Tuberville left Auburn in 2008 after compiling an 85–40 record, including a 7–3 mark against Alabama.

four consecutive wins, including narrow victories against Georgia and Alabama. Auburn went on to lose handily in the SEC Championship Game, but it was clear to fans that the progress was real.

In 2008 Tuberville was inducted into the Arkansas Sports Hall of Fame, a fitting tribute for a coach who never forgot his roots.

"I'm still an ol' country boy at heart," Tuberville said.

40 Shake Hands with the Coach at an Auburn Club Meeting

Most of what fans hear from a head coach is through a filter. The coach sanitizes his speech for the television cameras and makes it diplomatic enough for the sports pages. But there are a few chances to meet the coach in person, and local booster clubs provide the perfect opportunity.

New Auburn head coach Gene Chizik hit the circuit in 2009 after a whirlwind first few months of recruiting and practice. Chizik is professional but very guarded when talking to reporters. He's more apt to loosen up in different settings.

He's not the only coach who can shine in front of different crowds. Even coaches known for being prickly with the media can be engaging and personable in front of a friendly audience. Alabama coach Nick Saban has attracted adoring throngs on the off-season speaking circuit.

Long before "Jetgate" or his controversial departure from the Atlanta Falcons, Bobby Petrino impressed fans during a visit to Mobile in 2002 when he was the Tigers' offensive coordinator. Today, he is head coach at Arkansas.

"In a crowd that was friendly and that he felt comfortable with, he was very personable and very funny," said Laura Megginson, the president of the Mobile Auburn Club.

Former Auburn coach Tommy Tuberville was an avid back-slapper who thrived in settings with lots of fans. "I think it's important in today's time with so much information out there that coaches be heard directly," Tuberville said.

Most SEC coaches have a summer schedule packed with charity events, golf tournaments, and booster club meetings, and

Megginson said Tuberville seemed to earnestly enjoy visiting with fans. "He'll stay two hours just to make sure everyone standing in line gets an autograph or picture made with him," Megginson said.

During Tuberville's first year with Auburn, he went from table to table and shook hands with every person in attendance. "You expect that in the beginning, but for that to go on throughout his coaching tenure is really commendable," Megginson said.

What makes a good speaker on the rubber-chicken circuit? Mostly, fans are easy to please, especially if the team is doing well.

"I'm very open with them," Tuberville said. "I let them ask questions. I want them to ask what they want to know. I try to be as honest as I can be."

41 Jimmy "Red" Phillips

Most think of Jimmy "Red" Phillips as a receiver. The old-school, trading-card-style image used at the time shows Phillips slanted at a 45-degree angle while a football soars toward his hands. But Phillips also made valuable contributions on defense at Auburn. On the 1957 Auburn national champions, it was on defense—not the relatively pass-free offense—where he made his biggest impact.

Why was Auburn so dominant on that side of the ball during the title season? Phillips said it came down to coaching and the way defensive coordinator Joel Eaves focused so intently on the details.

"The coaches had us prepared," Phillips said. "It was really that simple. They freed us up to go get the ball. Coach Eaves had a big part of that. He was a perfectionist and didn't play around during meeting times, especially. There would be a clock on the wall behind him, and if he ever saw your eyes wander to it, you were in big trouble."

Phillips grew up in Alexander City, just down the road from Auburn, where he picked up his nickname because of his red mane of hair.

At Auburn, Phillips admits he was soft-spoken and shy, even as he became a consensus All-American and helped lead the Tigers to the national championship.

"I didn't know how to get up and speak in public," Phillips said. "Half the time, I didn't even know what kind of award I was getting. I was so naïve. A microphone scared me to death. They'd stick that microphone in my face, and my mind would shut down."

Although he was uncomfortable in the spotlight, he was respected by teammates.

"He was a heck of a football player," said center and linebacker Jackie Burkett. "He was a great receiver, but he was probably even better on defense."

Said quarterback Lloyd Nix, "He was a real thinker. He had great hands and great speed."

Phillips caught 23 passes for 383 yards and four touchdowns as a junior in 1956, and had 357 yards on 15 catches in 1957. Even so, he said, "I think defense was the strongest part of my game in college. They listed me at, like, 6'2", 215. I was actually 188 or 190, but you have to remember we had guards that weighed 165. I was one of our bigger players."

Phillips quickly found success in the NFL as a receiver. He was drafted in the first round—the fifth overall selection—of the 1958 draft by the Los Angeles Rams. He played seven seasons for the Rams and three for the Minnesota Vikings. His best season was in 1961, when he led the league in receiving with 78 receptions for 1,092 yards.

"It was a good experience playing in the NFL," Phillips said. "I just never did take it as that big of a deal. Never having much confidence, I never knew if I was going to make it to the next year."

Jimmy "Red" Phillips played on both sides of the ball for Auburn's 1957 national championship team.

Phillips said he always waited until the last players were cut from camp before telling his wife to bring the family west for the season. The one exception was his final year in Los Angeles.

"George Allen was named coach in L.A., and it was down to the final cut, and I asked Roman [Gabriel] to find out if I was in or not," Phillips said. "He said, 'Don't worry Red, Coach is going to keep you.' So I called my wife and said for her to come out. Then I got cut the next day. She was in Texas somewhere, and I couldn't get in touch with her. George Allen was a defensive-minded coach, so they kept one receiver that punted also—he wasn't worth a darn, either. They might have won the championship if they had another receiver, because everyone got hurt and that guy had to play. Heck, he was a bad punter, too."

42 Auburn's History in the Bowls

There was something strange about December of 2008. For the first time in almost a decade, while bowl games were on television and SEC teams were jetting around the country, Auburn fans were sitting at home.

Fortunately for fans, bowl-less seasons don't happy very often. The SEC has a long lineup of bowl affiliations, so any team that manages to win six games is virtually guaranteed a slot.

The Tigers have played games from coast to coast. They even can boast the unusual distinction of being one of the only two teams to a play a bowl game outside North America—the 1936 Bacardi Bowl in Havana, Cuba.

When Auburn defeated Clemson in the Chick-Fil-A Bowl on December 31, 2007, it marked the Tigers' 34th overall bowl appearance, the 16th-highest total of any team.

The Tigers would be higher on that list, but they got off to a slow start. Before Shug Jordan's arrival on the Plains, the Tigers had only participated in two bowls—a tie against Villanova in Cuba and a win over Michigan State in the Orange Bowl one year later.

But Jordan broke that 16-year dry spell by accepting an invitation to the Gator Bowl after the 1953 season, the first of three consecutive postseason trips. More recently, Auburn has made bowl games in 20 of the last 27 years. Pat Dye had a nine-year streak of bowl appearances from 1982 to 1990, while Tommy Tuberville had eight in a row from 2000 to 2007.

Overall, Auburn is 19–13–2 in bowl games. But since the 1974 Gator Bowl, the Tigers are 14–6–1.

A quick look at some of the more memorable moments in Auburn bowl history:

• Auburn went to two Gator Bowls in 1954, becoming the first team to play the same bowl game twice in the same calendar year. Auburn lost to Texas Tech 35–13 on January 1, 1954, and beat Baylor 33–13 on December 31, 1954. The first game came after a long bowl-free slump and was the first bowl game under Jordan. The starting backfield included a future governor of Alabama, Fob James, and a future coaching legend, Vince Dooley.

In Game 2, Auburn had a better time in Jacksonville, Florida. The Tigers recovered a Baylor fumble on the opening kickoff and controlled the game the rest of the way. "Joltin'" Joe Childress was named the game's most valuable player, finishing with 134 yards on 20 carries.

• Auburn's first trip back to the Orange Bowl in 26 years was a letdown, as Nebraska beat Auburn 13–7 on January 1, 1964, in Miami.

The Tigers used an option offense with quarterback Jimmy Sidle and halfback Tucker Frederickson. But a defensive gaffe on Nebraska's second play from scrimmage gave the Cornhuskers a 68-yard touchdown run and an early lead. Auburn had a chance to win in the final minutes, but two costly penalties doomed the Tigers' chances deep in Nebraska territory.

Auburn's season, highlighted by a 10–8 win over Alabama, would end 9–2.

• Auburn made the first of two trips to the Sun Bowl in El Paso, Texas, on December 28, 1968, and won an impressive 34–10 victory over Arizona. The game was actually tied at halftime, but the Tigers dominated the second half. The most notable play occurred when the Wildcats blocked Connie Frederick's punt and seemed poised to score a touchdown. But Frederick managed to wrest control of the ball and punt the ball a second time.

Arizona was its own worst enemy in the game. Auburn's defense combined for eight interceptions, a Sun Bowl record.

• After an eight-year bowl gap, Auburn wanted to show it was back on the national stage in the December 18, 1982, Tangerine Bowl in Orlando, Florida. The Tigers beat Boston College and quarterback Doug Flutie 33–26. Auburn quarterback Randy Campbell was named the game's most valuable player. Ten Auburn backs carried the football, led by Lionel James (101 yards on 18 carries) and Bo Jackson (two touchdowns).

• Bo Jackson finished his injury-shortened senior year with an MVP performance in the Liberty Bowl on December 27, 1984. Jackson had 88 yards on 18 carries and scored two touchdowns, the last of which made the difference in Auburn's 21–15 win over Arkansas. The game marked the last time Auburn appeared in the Memphis bowl game.

• Auburn's 28–14 win over Wisconsin in the Music City Bowl after the 2003 season won't be remembered as the most thrilling in history, but it did set the tone for Auburn's memorable 2004 season.

The game was the first since the attempted firing of Tommy Tuberville a few weeks earlier, but Auburn managed to overcome the distraction and play a solid game in Nashville, Tennessee.

Quarterback Jason Campbell was named the bowl MVP, and the defense contributed six sacks.

The Tigers didn't know it at the time, but they would keep winning games until the start of 2005.

43 In the Classroom: Great Student-Athletes

No one can deny that there are glamorous moments in the life of a college football player. Surely the attention, fame, and recognition can be gratifying to players. But many fans gloss over just how rigorous the daily life of a student-athlete in a major football program can be.

Think back to your college career, when you fretted about papers, exams, and midterms. Now throw in 20 hours a week of practice, film study, meetings, weight lifting, and the added stress of preparing mentally to play a game in front of 80,000 people on Saturday. Somewhere, in the midst of all that, student-athletes have to find room for classes.

That's why the athletes who not only survive but excel are all the more remarkable.

Since 1957, Auburn has had 14 academic All-Americans and four National Football Foundation Scholar-Athlete award winners. Many are mentioned elsewhere in the book for their on-field exploits. Consider this section a hat tip for their time in the classroom.

The All-Americans: Jimmy "Red" Phillips (1957), Jackie Burkett (1959), Ed Dyas (1960), Bill Cody (1965), Buddy McClinton (1969), Pat Sullivan (1971), Chuck Fletcher (1975), Chris Vacarella (1976), Jim Skuthan (1980), Gregg Carr (1984), Matt Hawkins (1994 and 1995), Dontarrious Thomas (2003), and

Kody Bliss (2006). Dyas, Carr, Thomas, and John Cochran (1963) also won the prestigious NFF honors.

Carr presents one of the most compelling example of academic success because he traveled such an unusual path to his ultimate destination—an orthopedist in his hometown of Birmingham, Alabama.

Carr was both a top-notch linebacker and an award-winning engineering student at Auburn in the early 1980s. He was an All-American in his senior year of 1984 and was a late-round draft pick by the Pittsburgh Steelers. At some point in his four-year professional career, Carr started kicking around the idea of becoming a doctor. He took premed courses at Auburn during the offseason. When he was accepted to the UAB medical school, he decided to hang up his cleats for good.

"What I'm doing now is something I strived for and wanted to do," Carr said. "Just like everything else, it was kind of a goal people thought I'd never accomplish. I certainly didn't get a lot of support from my teammates, who thought I'd flipped my lid."

Win Lyle, a kicker for the Tigers' championship teams of the late 1980s, grew up in Auburn and graduated from Auburn High School. After his playing career, he earned a medical degree from the Chicago Medical School and completed a residency in orthopedic surgery at Wright State.

Now he's back in Auburn, working as an orthopedist in a sports medicine fellowship that seeks to prepare future athletic trainers for their careers.

Another kicker, Scott Etheridge, who succeeded Lyle and kicked from 1989 to 1993, was a finalist for the Auburn athletics director spot that went to Jay Jacobs in 2004. Etheridge was a former senior vice president for NBC Universal and now works as a vice president at Liz Claiborne.

Thomas, a linebacker who played five seasons for the Minnesota Vikings after his college career was done, was another celebrated scholar who was just as impressive on the field. He left Auburn with a degree in management information systems and was awarded an $18,000 postgraduate scholarship by the NFF. He took part in the NFL's Business Management and Entrepreneurial Program at the University of Pennsylvania's Wharton School of Business during the 2007 off-season.

There are many more examples, far too many to name, including several academic achievers on Auburn's current roster. That's worth remembering the next time a player is booed or cheered for something he does on the field. The game of football is just a portion of his day.

44 The Eric Ramsey Case and Other Run-Ins with the NCAA

Auburn has had seven major infractions cases before the NCAA, but perhaps none was more sordid or brought more ugly publicity to the university than the Eric Ramsey case.

The details of the entire affair are complex, but the basic version is this: in 1991 a former Auburn defensive back named Eric Ramsey alleged that he had tape recordings of conversations that proved he was given food, cash, and other illegal benefits during his time as a player at Auburn.

The news broke in state newspapers like the *Montgomery Advertiser* and *Birmingham News*, and the transcripts of conversations between Ramsey and booster Bill "Corky" Frost appeared incriminating.

Frost: "Eric…I'm going to send you enough steaks to last you about a month at a time, two months at a time."

Ramsey: "What about the bonus [money] you paid last year? Are you going to cut me out?"

Frost: "No, sir! That's still good."

Ramsey: "That's cool."

Frost: "You'll get your bonus from me…with the meat. But I don't want to even hear about it. It would hurt Auburn."

Ramsey: "You won't."

Frost: "Don't ever hurt Auburn. Auburn is a great place and I love it. I'll be your friend until the day I die. Auburn's been mighty good to you, whether you realize it or not."

Frost appeared genuine and perhaps even meant well, but was clearly violating NCAA rules in a flagrant manner. Ramsey and his wife, Twilitta, were just as if not more unsavory. Before the news broke in statewide newspapers, Twilitta shopped the story to *Sports Illustrated* while identifying herself as Dawn Webb, Ramsey's agent. The Ramseys' attorney, Donald Watkins, began parceling out the secret tapes to news organizations one at time, trying to maximize the news effect.

As more tapes were released, the news got worse. Auburn assistant coaches appeared to be implicated in the payment scheme. Even head coach Pat Dye was forced to acknowledge that he should have done a better job as head coach and athletics director.

"If the tapes are true, and the allegations are true," Dye said, "then what I'm guilty of is doing a damn poor job of management."

The NCAA came down with severe penalties just before the kickoff of the 1993 season, the first for new coach Terry Bowden. Auburn was docked 11 initial scholarship offers—from 25 to 14—for three seasons. The Tigers were prohibited from appearing on television for one season and prohibited from playing in the postseason for two seasons. The NCAA had stern words for Auburn.

"This case is a very unfortunate one," the final report read. "The violations of NCAA rules that were committed at Auburn University are indicative of what can occur when, in the minds of members of a university's athletics department staff and representatives of its athletics interests, the athletics program becomes more important than the university of which it is a part. As a result of this case, Auburn University has become one of only three universities that have been placed on probation six or more times by the NCAA. (Auburn added a seventh major infractions case in 2004 in men's basketball.) Since 1956 and prior to this case, Auburn University's athletics program has been placed on probation for a total of 10 years."

The probation spoiled Auburn's undefeated season in 1993. The Tigers' undefeated championship season in 1957 also came just after the NCAA handed down sanctions in Auburn's first run-in with the infractions committee. Auburn was also found guilty of major infractions in 1958, 1979, 1980, and 1991.

But the wounds of the Ramsey case are still raw. And the aftermath left no winners. Rick Telander summed up the case in a 1991 *Sports Illustrated* piece:

> Still, Ramsey is a victim, no matter how mercenary he may be. He was not the one with power. He took, but the system gave. Ramsey may not have a logical explanation for his deeds, but sometimes being in the midst of a disorienting ordeal—and college football can be just that—can throw off one's ethical compass. Whistle-blowers and star witnesses are not always pleasant or virtuous people. Sometimes they are criminals and informants trying to beat a rap. Sometimes they are deluded fanatics. Often, though, their stories bring about change, even when the tellers do not benefit from the telling, and it's hard to see what Ramsey stands to gain from his disclosures. College football, however, could benefit. The message should not be diminished by the messenger.
>
> When Ramsey asked for money while playing at Auburn, somebody—some adult—should have said no and sent him to the woodshed. But someone, perhaps many people, said yes, and the demons were let loose. Above all

else, one is left saddened by this ugly affair, which when reduced to its essence is little more than a circle of people using one another.

Vince Dooley

When Vince Dooley was hired to be Georgia's head football coach in 1963, the reaction from fans ranged from concern to alarm.

How could this green coach of freshmen players from archrival Auburn possibly be ready for the biggest job in the state of Georgia? And who did Georgia athletics director Joel Eaves think he was, hiring a crony from his old school?

"Looking back, it amazes me that somebody would hire a 31-year-old coach, and only a freshman coach at that, to be the head coach at a rival school," Dooley said. "I was young enough to think it was a good decision, and I was probably the only one who did."

Eaves' decision, of course, paid off richly for the Bulldogs. Dooley led Georgia to 201 wins and six SEC championships. He was named SEC Coach of the Year seven times and National Coach of the Year twice. After he retired from coaching, he continued to serve as a popular athletics director until 2004.

But if history had turned out just a little bit differently, he might have been coaching at Auburn.

Dooley grew up in Mobile, Alabama, where he served as an altar boy and was a star athlete at McGill Catholic High School. According to one biography, Dooley was a "short-tempered, irascible youngster who early on recognized athletics might be the only thing keeping him from a life toiling in the shipyards of his hometown."

He was a two-sport star at McGill, excelling at both basketball and football, and he went to Auburn with the goal of playing both sports.

Long before he won six SEC titles as coach of the Georgia Bulldogs, Vince Dooley was a quarterback at Auburn under Ralph "Shug" Jordan.

A knee injury ended his basketball career, but he continued to thrive at quarterback in the first years of Ralph "Shug" Jordan's tenure.

After his football career, Dooley spent two years in the Marine Corps. Following his military service, Dooley returned to the Plains, working as an assistant coach and a freshman coach. He picked up a master's degree in history to go with the undergraduate business degree he earned earlier.

Then he was hired at Georgia.

Dooley replaced Johnny Griffith, a former star player at Georgia, who had struggled through three consecutive losing seasons. It didn't take long for Dooley to win over fans. The Bulldogs won conference championships in 1966, 1968, 1976, 1980, 1981, and 1982.

After winning the national championship in 1980, Dooley received a strong pitch from his alma mater to take over as the Tigers' head coach. After considering the offer, Dooley decided to stay put. (Auburn, of course, eventually hired Georgia alumnus Pat Dye.) Dooley would go on to join Tom Osborne, Joe Paterno, and only a handful of others as the increasingly rare breed of coach associated with one school for his entire career.

Today, Dooley remains warm and engaging with fans and media alike.

There's more to the man than football. Gardening is among his favorite pastimes, and he's constructed an elaborate botanical garden in the backyard of his Athens, Georgia, home. A history buff, he's visited many Indian, Revolutionary, and Civil War battlefields.

He doesn't regret for a second the path his career took, even though it led him away from his alma mater.

"I had an incredible experience at Auburn," Dooley said. "I came very, very close to going back. If I hadn't been here for as long as I had, I would have jumped across the Chattahoochee."

46 Appreciate the Sacrifice of Two-a-Days

Two-a-days used to refer, quite literally, to practicing twice in one day. These days, there aren't many two-a-days left in two-a-days. But you won't find many players and coaches mourning the demise of those taxing practices.

Today "two-a-days" is a generic term for the month of August practices that take place prior to the season. There are only a handful of dates on which Auburn actually practices twice.

NCAA rules and common sense have reined in much of the excesses of the past. Rules prohibit teams from conducting two-a-days on consecutive days. Many coaches, including former Auburn coach Tommy Tuberville, find that more teaching can be done in a single practice session. "We call it two-a-days, but it's not really two-a-days anymore," Tuberville said.

Still, under Tuberville, coaches worked hard to cultivate a special atmosphere surrounding August camp that didn't exist in the spring or during regular-season practices. For one, two-a-days weren't conducted at Auburn's regular, well-groomed practice fields. For most of early August during the last decade, Auburn players got to practice by walking across lush green grass and expensive artificial turf. They crossed four lanes of traffic at Samford Drive (sometimes helped by a city police officer), crossed a bridge over a small creek, and finally arrived at the Auburn intramural fields.

For most of the year, these fields host fraternity softball and flag football games. Sometimes you'll catch international students using the acres of green space as a cricket pitch. But for a few weeks in August, this was the home of Auburn football…and not an especially glamorous home.

Auburn recreation facilities did some work on the turf before the summer of 2007, so it was in better shape in 2008 than it had been in the past. Gone were many of the uneven spots and rough patches. Ant hills were still around, but they're not nearly as prominent as they once were. The grass was baked in the long summer sun.

"It's a mental thing," said former Auburn defensive end Quentin Groves. "I think the coaches do this just to get in our heads."

Auburn has conducted practices this way for at least the last 10 years. Why hasn't Auburn used its beautiful practice fields in early

August? One reason is that the intramural fields provide convenient access for fans, who were usually allowed to watch the first several weeks of practice. Fans were able to park their cars and then walk a few steps to the field, something that would be impossible in the heavily fortified fields at the football complex.

Playing on the intramural fields also protects the regular practice fields from wear and tear, and it gives the team plenty of room to spread out. Kickers and punters can go off and do their own thing without having to trek down to the stadium to work out.

"If we ran two-and-a-half-hour practices every single day on [the complex] field, it would be gone. It would look like this field," joked former backup quarterback Blake Field in 2006.

The final advantage of the intramural fields is harder to quantify. Coaches are able to create a distinct atmosphere and attitude surrounding preseason camp, a mystique entirely separate from the rest of the year. "It's the idea that this is different from fall practice. This is camp," said tight end Cole Bennett.

New coach Gene Chizik will get to decide whether to continue the tradition when he opens up his first preseason camp.

Will Herring

Over four seasons, Will Herring never missed a game due to a bum ankle, a bad back, or a common cold. He was never suspended or benched. He's learned new positions without complaint. And in his senior season of 2006, Will Herring set a new Auburn record by starting in 49 consecutive games.

Herring's streak would have seemed unlikely five years earlier, when he was an unheralded recruit from nearby Opelika, Alabama. A quarterback in high school, Herring received interest from few major programs, and some doubted whether he could be a defensive contributor in the Southeastern Conference.

On Signing Day, Opelika head coach Spence McCracken said teams would regret overlooking Herring. In time, Herring proved him right.

After redshirting in 2002, Herring was a three-year starter at safety. In 2006 he switched to linebacker to help shore up Auburn's depth at the position.

In 2009 he's expected to start his third season with the Seattle Seahawks.

"Once you cross that bridge right there," said cornerback Jerraud Powers, "I'm like, 'Come on, let's get it rolling.' It's camp. It's supposed to be tough. It's nothing new. [The toughest part] is just knowing that you've got to do it. Just waking up and saying, 'Dang, we've got two practices today.' Once you're here, you're here."

Linebacker Chris Evans had a strategy for dealing with two-a-days: avoid naps. Waking up from a restful midday sleep is difficult, and it makes it seem as though two days have been crammed into one.

"If you go to sleep, it's a two-a-day; if you don't, it's just one day," he said. "That's the key thing for me. You just push through it. You're going to get tired, mentally and physically, but you just have to push through it."

Groves said the practice fields aren't as bad as some players imagine. "You can't have lavish conditions to play in or practice on," he said. "I think it's just the dread of walking all the way over here that gets in people's heads. [Coaches] mean for it to be hard, but it's only as hard as you make it."

Tucker Frederickson

By the 1960s the idea that great football players can—and should—play on both sides of the ball was nearing extinction. Auburn's Tucker Frederickson became one the last great two-way players, excelling on offense and defense for the Tigers in 1963 and 1964.

On offense, he was a bruising blocking back. On defense, he was a safety who could make plays all over the field. He led the team in interceptions in 1963 and rushed for 4.4 yards a carry in 1964. In both seasons, he was voted the top blocking back in the Southeastern Conference.

Tucker Frederickson (20) was one of the last great two-way players at Auburn and was the first overall pick in the 1965 NFL Draft.

Frederickson was from Broward County in south Florida, but came to Auburn because of its nationally known veterinary program (both his dad and his uncle were vets). Frederickson never became a vet, but he did become one of the great college football players of his era.

He was graceful and athletic on the football field. Frederickson, wrote longtime Auburn sportswriter Phillip Marshall, "was a man before his time. He combined size, speed, power, and finesse."

Fans respected Frederickson's career, making him the leading vote-getter on Auburn's Team of the Century, which was selected in 1992.

In 1963 he helped Jimmy Sidle become the first quarterback to amass more than 1,000 yards rushing. The Tigers finished 9–1 before losing to Nebraska in the Orange Bowl.

"We had a team that wasn't supposed to be as good as we were," Frederickson said. "We should have been undefeated. Jimmy Sidle was a great athlete. We had a bunch of kids that played together and liked each other."

Frederickson was an All-American at safety in 1964, although Sidle was injured and Auburn's offense struggled. His value became clear when the New York Giants made him the first overall pick of the 1965 NFL Draft.

"I signed a three-year contract with a $30,000 bonus and salaries each year of $27,500," Frederickson said. "I didn't have an agent. The most important thing to me was getting a three-year no-cut contract and going to New York. I had a chance to be the No. 1 draft choice in the AFL, too. Denver called and said, 'We want to pick you,' and I said, 'Don't waste your time, don't waste your pick, I'm going to New York.' Then Joe Namath had an agent and a couple of months later got a contract for $400,000. I thought, 'I guess I should have had an agent.'"

He spent six seasons with the Giants, having his best season as a rookie in 1965 when he rushed 195 times for 659 yards, caught 24 passes for 177 yards, and was selected to the postseason Pro Bowl. Over his career, he had 2,209 yards rushing and 1,011 yards receiving.

After his successful rookie year, he missed the entire 1966 season with a knee injury. Although he returned, he was never quite the same.

"I lost speed and explosion," he said. "I lost my weight. I had been 225, but I got down to 212. When you have that operation, you tape that knee up as tight as you can and slow yourself down. There were things I used to be able to do that I was not able to do because of the tape. Plus in your mind, you're vulnerable. I was never the same."

48 The 1942 Georgia Upset

Every Saturday in college football seems to produce a major upset somewhere on the national landscape, and sorting out the truly historic from the merely thrilling is a difficult task.

Judging the most meaningful or significant upset in Auburn history is equally impossible. So let's just say that Auburn's win in this game, for its time and moment in history, was a stunner.

On the surface, the meeting between Auburn and Georgia on November 21, 1942, seemed destined to have a lopsided outcome. The Bulldogs were the top-ranked team in the country and had demolished their three previous opponents—Alabama, Florida, and Chattanooga—with ease. Auburn was unranked and in the midst of a respectable but unspectacular season that included losses to Georgia Tech, Florida, and Mississippi State.

The nation was at war, and players and coaches could sense that college football's days were growing short. This would be the second-to-last game before Auburn suspended play. The games wouldn't resume until September 29, 1944.

But fans who saw one of the last War-era games were given a treat. Georgia was led by senior running back Frank Sinkwich, a Heisman Trophy winner and football legend. However, it was Auburn running back Ray "Monk" Gafford who stole the show, carrying 20 times for 119 yards and returning three punts for 92 yards to lead Auburn to a 27–13 win. Uncharacteristically,

Sinkwich struggled on the ground, rushing for only 31 yards on 21 carries, although he did pass for 177 yards.

"Monk Gafford showed what the coaches had been saying about him was true while the big boys up East were writing rave notices about Frankie Sinkwich," wrote *Birmingham News* sports editor Zipp Newman. "Gafford deserves All-America. He has played All-American football against the tough babies. With a more experienced Auburn team at the start he would have gotten the recognition due him."

The 1942 campaign was the ninth and final season for Auburn head coach Jack Meagher, who had to scramble to find new assistant coaches after losing much of his staff to military service. The *Glomerata* reported that "all that was left of our coaching staff after Uncle Sam had his way was soft-spoken Jack Meagher, whose job it was to find replacements enough to run his squad through another campaign. Congenial Jack did just that. He took his team through a long and arduous season with more than medium success."

The team improved as the season went on, peaking with the incredible win in Columbus, Georgia, on the 50th anniversary of the first Auburn-Georgia game in 1892. The series had already seen its share of memorable moments, and the Bulldogs led 21–20–5 entering the 1942 game.

Auburn was a "two-touchdown underdog with not many takers." Georgia newspapers "are certain of a Bulldog victory and that 'Auburn is just a warm-up before Georgia plays Tech,' but these scribes seem to know little of what's taking place in Auburn's camp," offered one reporter.

But the Tigers made 18 first downs and collected 355 total yards to Georgia's 227. Auburn operated exclusively from the T formation, attempting only five passes and failing to complete a single one. After Gafford, Jimmy Reynolds added 92 yards. Sophomore halfback Zach Jenkins was a "surprise performer" with 84 yards in seven carries.

Georgia coach Wally Butts was a "busy little round man, trying first this combination, then that, in a desperate effort to save the game."

While Butts' efforts were fruitless, Georgia's overall résumé was strong enough for the Bulldogs to be voted the national champions after a Rose Bowl victory over UCLA.

Auburn, meanwhile, could savor one of its sweetest upsets.

It was "the most startling upset of many years on a Southern gridiron," wrote Newman, and "probably the most outstanding victory for an Auburn team in all the 50 years of Auburn football."

49 The Auburn University Band

There is no moniker, nickname, or boastful title associated with one of the nation's top marching bands. And Auburn is perfectly content to keep it that way.

These words from former Auburn President Harry Philpott are used to introduce the band on Saturdays: "Some other institutions need to give descriptive names to their bands in order to praise them. The quality of the music, the precision of its drills, and the fine image that it portrays have made it unnecessary for us to say more than, 'This is the Auburn University Band.'"

For more than 100 years, the band has been an integral part of university life. Today it is an integral part of the gameday experience.

Auburn had a drum corps of 12 cadets in the early days of the school. In 1897 the university decided to add instrumental parts and make the corps into a true band. Students, faculty, and local businesses pitched in to raise money for instruments. Mechanical arts faculty member M. Thomas Fullan took the helm as the band's first director.

The Auburn Marching Band has become an essential part of every game day.

The band performed around the state at Mobile's Mardi Gras and other events. In 1915 it performed at a reunion of Confederate veterans in Selma and—owing to its military ties—was sent in 1916 to a border dispute with Mexico.

In 1917 director P.R. "Bedie" Bidez led the Auburn band into Europe during World War I. According to the band's official history, the unit played "Glory to Ole Auburn" as they crossed the Rhine from France into Germany and celebrated the Allied victory.

Bidez was one of the most influential directors in the band's history. Under his watch, the band tripled in size and the university established a Department of Music. It started traveling to several road games, and added female majorettes in 1946. In 1950, one year before Bidez's retirement, women began playing instruments in the band.

The band started looking more like the marching bands we know today when in 1957 it discarded its gray cadet uniforms for orange and blue. Deborah Whatley became Auburn's first female drum major in 1972. The uniforms were updated and a flag corps was added in 1985. An alumni band joined the students on the field for a home game in 1987, a tradition that continues today.

The band performed in its first ever St. Patrick's Day Parade in Dublin, Ireland, in 2008. It was the band's first international performance. The five-day itinerary included two days in Limerick and a performance at the Guinness Brewery. The band has now participated in three presidential inaugurations in Washington: Harry Truman in 1949, George H.W. Bush in 1989, and George W. Bush in 2005.

The marching band marked a major milestone in 2004 when it received the Sudler Intercollegiate Marching Band Trophy, the nation's highest honor for university marching bands.

What does that mean to students and fans? An introduction to the band's website put it this way: "Throughout its history, one of the primary goals of the Auburn University Marching Band has been to foster the Auburn Spirit. With more than 30 performances and exhibitions starting early in the fall and extending through the bowl season, the Auburn Band does exactly that."

50 The Bacardi Bowl

More than 40 years into its football history, Auburn made its first appearance in a bowl game. Appropriately, the first was also one of the most memorable and bizarre.

On January 1, 1937, Auburn played Villanova to a 7–7 tie in the Bacardi Bowl, or Rhumba Bowl, as it was also called. The game was not only played in the sweltering heat of Havana, Cuba, but it was held just days after a bloodless coup that unseated the president who helped organize the Sports Festival of which the bowl was a major part. The political climate was tense. President Miguel Mariano Gomez had been ousted in favor of Federico Laredo Bru, a handpicked puppet of strongman Fulgencio Batista. Batista would be overthrown by Fidel Castro in 1959.

But the festival went on as scheduled, and the Auburn football players who arrived via boat from Tampa and Key West were largely oblivious to the unfolding political drama.

"Music from a local band floated up from the platform as the boat docked," wrote Zipp Newman in a dispatch from Havana. "The natives were playing the Auburn alma mater, the victory song, and Touchdown Auburn. Their interpretation had a Spanish cadence, soft and dreamy."

Football wasn't the only event at the festival. There was amateur boxing, basketball, baseball, and an odd spectacle in which Jesse Owens raced—and defeated—a horse.

The 1937 game wasn't the first Cuban bowl, but it was the first that featured two schools from the United States. It almost didn't happen. Auburn was understandably concerned about the finances of the game and wanted to receive its payment up front.

In 1937 Auburn and Villanova played to a 7–7 tie in the Bacardi Bowl in Havana, Cuba.

The game itself at Tropical Stadium was somewhat anticlimactic. The crowd didn't live up to expectations, the heat was stifling, and the scoring was low. Auburn scored its lone touchdown in the first quarter on a 40-yard run by Billy Hitchcock. Villanova preserved the tie in the fourth quarter when Matthews Kuber blocked a quick kick and fell on the ball in the end zone. One writer opined that the heavily favored Tigers outplayed the Wildcats and should have won by two touchdowns.

"It was a savagely played game in a hot boiling sun," wrote Newman, "and it was remarkable how both the Auburn and Villanova players stood up under the intense heat."

Attendance was around 12,000 and "someone took a financial beating."

The local fans were reportedly most excited by fights that broke out in the second and fourth quarters. "It was the heat," players admitted after the game. The other big applause from the stands came when former president Gomez entered in the first quarter.

Auburn left immediately after the game for Miami, rested three hours, and then boarded a train for Opelika. The experience had been memorable, if not perfect.

"The Plainsmen should have won—but don't think this Villanova outfit wasn't the scrappingest team the Plainsmen faced all year," said Newman. "And they were happy, much happy with a tie."

Auburn and Villanova, now a Championship Subdivision or I-AA team, were scheduled to meet in 2006 to mark the 70th anniversary of the bowl, but the game was scrapped due to scheduling conflicts. The International Bowl is now played in Toronto—a location not as exotic or warm as Havana, but still outside the United States.

Meanwhile, in Cuba, Castro has entered semiretirement, and there are hopes that the chilly relationship between the United States and Cuba might begin to thaw, if only a little. Perhaps in 30 years, the Bacardi Bowl will be reborn and college football will return to the island of Cuba.

Aubie, the Lovable Mascot

Aubie turned 30 in 2009, although the exuberant mascot is still as fun-loving and young at heart as ever. The cartoonish, costumed Tiger has become a staple of Auburn athletic and community events over the last three decades, bringing a smile to young and old alike.

The concept of Aubie actually began 50 years ago as a drawing. *Birmingham Post-Herald* artist Phil Neel created the cartoon Tiger for an Auburn football program cover on October 3, 1959. The image was popular, and it remained a part of Auburn program covers for 18 years.

Aubie started out as a traditional, four-legged Tiger, but he evolved to stand upright in 1962. A year later, apparently feeling modest, he began to don human clothes—a blue tie and a straw hat.

Aubie came to life in 1979, when Auburn spirit director James Lloyd contacted Brooks–van Horn Costumes in New York to order a specially designed outfit. Using the old program covers as a model, the firm created the first Aubie costume for a cost of $1,350.

The new mascot's debut appearance was in the SEC men's basketball tournament at the Birmingham-Jefferson Civic Center. His presence helped first-year Auburn basketball coach Sonny Smith to a first-round upset over Vanderbilt and a four-overtime victory over Georgia the next day. Since then, Aubie has not only made fans smile, he's become an icon in the mascot community. Aubie has won six mascot national championships and was a member of the inaugural class of mascots in the Mascot Hall of Fame.

Who plays the role of Aubie? For the most part, it's spirit-oriented students who are in good shape and possess ample patience and good humor.

Former Aubie Justin Shugart, from Fairhope, Alabama, said he wanted to be Aubie in order to achieve a dream. "The dream was not being Aubie; it was having the opportunity to run out of the tunnel at Jordan-Hare with 87,000 people screaming their heads off," he said. "Because I wasn't built like a football player and figured it would be cooler to be Aubie than a water boy, I decided to go through with tryouts."

Tryouts are arduous and weed out any applicant who is just pursuing the position on a whim.

Aubie has become a fixture at Auburn football games and is one of the more recognizable mascots in college sports.

"The first round of tryouts gives each candidate the opportunity to perform a two-minute skit with props and music," Shugart said. "All participants are required to come up with their own original skit. The participants that made it past the first round of cuts participate in a five- to seven-minute impromptu session. Each individual will face several different scenarios depicting what Aubie can experience during regular experiences. It's basically about 20 appearances crammed into five minutes. After that, impromptu round cuts are made again, and those that survive advance to the interview portion of the process." The top three individuals coming out of the interview round are selected as Aubies—or "Friends of Aubie," as they say—for the upcoming year.

Much of Aubie's time is spent putting smiles on the faces of children. For Shugart, one interaction with a child was especially memorable. In the summer of 2007 Aubie and Shugart made an appearance at the UAB Children's Hospital to visit a girl who had just undergone successful triple-bypass heart surgery.

"Aubie walked into the recovery room where the little girl was lying in her bed," Shugart said. "She was covered in wires and tubes. It was by far one of the most moving things I have experienced to see such a small fragile body hooked up to so many machines. As soon as Aubie entered the room, the little girl's face beamed like the sun, she was so excited to see Aubie. Aubie walked over to the side of the bed and grabbed the girl's hand. The girl leaned back with all of her strength and said, 'I love you, Aubie.' She then asked Aubie to help her with a few Auburn cheers. Her favorite was 'Bodda Getta.' After spending close to 30 minutes with her, Aubie began to exit the room with the entire family, nurses, and doctors all taking in the moment. One of the doctors met Aubie at the door and stopped him from leaving. He grabbed his arm and gave him a hug and said, 'Aubie, you just performed a miracle. That little girl hasn't spoken a word to anyone for the past four days.' At that point I realized just how incredibly small I as an individual was, but how big of an impact Aubie has on the Auburn family."

Aubie stays busy. Shugart estimates that Aubie will make an average of 300 appearances a year, not including athletic events.

"You name an event, as long as it wasn't private or promotional, and Aubie more than likely attended," Shugart said.

52 Watch the Pregame Eagle Flight

If you believe in omens, the start of the 2004 season had to provide one of the best for Auburn football fans. In August of 2004 the university announced it had received clearance from the U.S. Fish and Wildlife Service to resume the popular eagle flights before football games. The eagles had always been present as a university symbol, but it wasn't until this decade that they began their breathtaking flights around Jordan-Hare Stadium prior to football games.

The show was an instant hit. Home fans loved it. Visiting fans couldn't wait to tell others about the experience. Reporters wrote about it.

But the flights were put on hiatus in 2003 as many birds at the university's Southeastern Raptor Center came down with illnesses. Golden eagles Tiger and Nova and bald eagle Spirit returned as the birds of prey on display in 2004. They were eased into the flying rotation cautiously.

Tiger was the experienced veteran, with several football flights and the 2002 Winter Olympics in Salt Lake City under her belt. Spirit and Nova were young and healthy, but less experienced in front of large crowds. Spirit wowed crowds before the LSU and Citadel games in 2004. Tiger made her comeback flight against Louisiana Tech, and has since taken a well-deserved retirement.

Make sure you've grabbed your seat about 15 minutes before game time to fully appreciate the flights. The raptor is toted in a cage to one of the upper ramps on the west side of the stadium. The public address announcer will direct your eyes to the flagpole. Find the bird or else you might miss the flight's first few seconds.

A handler opens the cage, and the bird takes off. Some flights are better than others. The best performances last the longest, as the bird literally circles the upper reaches of the stadium. Other times, the bird appears to linger just a few feet over the student section. At the end of the flight, the eagle identifies another handler who is racing toward the Auburn logo at the 50-yard line, dragging a leash with a hunk of meat attached. As the crowd's "War Eagle!" cheer reaches a crescendo, the eagle finishes with a dramatic landing at the center of the field. Or at least that's the idea. It works most of the time, although on days when the eagles don't bring their A-game, the flights can be considerably shorter.

In any event, the tradition is now an integral event at Auburn home football games and is eagerly anticipated by everyone in the stadium.

But there's a higher purpose to the flights, which are the work of Auburn's renowned raptor center. When Spirit took to the skies before the 2007 Ole Miss game, it was to commemorate the work of the nation's conservation groups that contributed to the resurgence of the bald eagle population and its removal from the Endangered Species List.

A pregame ceremony included government officials, the original founders of the raptor center, and elected representatives. Veterinary dean Timothy Boosinger accepted the honors on behalf of the "raptor center staff and volunteers who have contributed to the treatment of birds of prey for more than 30 years" and "the nation's raptor centers and thousands of others who have worked hard to protect these magnificent birds through conservation education."

The bald eagle was once nearly wiped from the American landscape. Today, the bird is flourishing. In the mid-1970s, when the bald eagle was placed on the list, Auburn veterinary faculty members Jimmy Milton and Gregg Boring founded the raptor center. The center has since sprouted a hospital, training facility, and educational amphitheater. Milton and Boring have moved on, but their legacy remains.

All birds used in Auburn's educational programs—like the pregame flights—are not able to be released into the wild. According to federal law, any bird capable of surviving in the wild must be released.

If you find an injured bird of prey, the raptor center should be your first call (334-844-6347). And if you're looking for a fascinating day at Auburn, one of the center's educational programs might be just the ticket.

Learn How to Tailgate on the Plains

Start on Magnolia and drift down Samford Avenue on a Saturday before a football game and you'll find a rich tapestry of sights and smells and good food. Tailgating on the Plains is a tradition that fans take seriously. This isn't Ole Miss, where tailgating turns into a high-end fashion show. At Auburn, it's about family and friends and good times. Some folks have a simple picnic-style spread. Other fans come prepared with tents and chairs. Satellites and televisions are increasingly popular. The food? It's as elaborate or as simple as you want it to be.

The vibe is festive but friendly. Interaction among tailgaters is encouraged and almost expected, even from fans of the enemy camp.

While rules limiting tailgaters have multiplied over the years, it's still an integral part of the game-day experience.

But while tailgating remains an integral part of Auburn Saturdays, it's hard to find a fan who doesn't reminisce about the way it used to be.

Some fans think the university is increasing its efforts to restrict tailgating.

"I truly hope that unlike other universities in the SEC, Auburn remains true to the fundamentals that made Auburn 'unique,'" one commenter wrote recently on a fan blog.

"I've been a season ticket holder since 1994, and the tailgates are one of the joys of my life," another poster chimed in. "While I fully appreciate the need to preserve the lawns by prohibiting parking on them, I think AU has gone as far as it needs to go. Parking at some shopping center in Opelika and riding a bus just don't cut it, especially for those of us who go the full nine yards with tents, TVs, and grills!"

Soon a topic that was unrelated to the subject was awash in tailgating feedback. Clearly, it's an issue that arouses a lot of passion in fans:

- "I really miss the days of tailgating right in front of Petrie Hall and watching the chimney sweeps fly in right at dusk. Some of my best memories in life happened right there. Tailgating and the whole game experience has suffered greatly in my opinion. Parking lots have so much less 'feel' of the campus and college football."
- "The lack of the tailgating environment is exactly why our family let our season tickets go. That made the difference. Please, please don't let that experience be diluted further."
- "Tailgating is truly one of the great pastimes of college football. It is almost as much fun as the games themselves when you're able to be with some of your oldest friends and family. It's a huge part of the environment around Jordan-Hare and the current administration needs to find plausible answers to the problems that new restrictions present."

So what's a viable solution? Clearly the old days of allowing cars to pull up onto lawns and park wherever they wish are long gone. Irrigation and landscaping aren't cheap, which is why many areas are fenced off, marked with "No parking" signs or partitioned with the hated "bollards." The campus is changing, too. Some areas now restrict cars. New buildings are sprouting where green space or lots used to be. There's no easy solution.

Ole Miss has a famous tailgating spot called The Grove. Mississippi State has tried to emulate that feel by designating a green space near the stadium for tailgaters—though this is not necessarily tailgating in the literal sense of eating and preparing food out of the back of a vehicle. There are plenty of open spaces on Auburn's campus fringes, but none within view of the stadium.

Tailgating is a part of the game-day heritage that Auburn people feel passionately about. That means it's a tradition worth preserving. But finding a way to accommodate thousands of fans on an increasingly crowded campus is an issue with which Auburn is still grappling.

54 Know What to Do When Auburn's on the Road

There's a nifty website that allows you to plot multiple locations on a map and find the geographic midpoint between all those locations. It makes a good timekiller at work if you want to find an equidistant point between, say, New York, Los Angeles, and San Antonio.

Try plugging all of the SEC schools into the geomidpoint.com map. After a few seconds of calculation, the site spits out an equidistant point: Blountsville, Alabama, just north of Birmingham, and not far from Auburn, Atlanta, Nashville, and other hubs of Auburn alumni.

Why is this relevant? It means Auburn fans are close to everything.

Perhaps that's why they travel so well. The only visit that requires a plane trip is when Auburn plays the Razorbacks, who are located way up in the hills of northwest Arkansas. Every other campus is easily drivable—even to locales like Baton Rouge, Louisiana, and Gainesville, Florida. For most road trips, however, Auburn keeps it close to home. Since the 2002 season opener at Southern California, the Tigers have traveled outside the region only once—a trip to West Virginia in 2008.

So let's concentrate on the SEC schools, starting with Auburn's five opponents in the SEC West.

Tuscaloosa, Alabama

Distance from Auburn: 159 miles

Auburn's record in Tuscaloosa: 6–1

In the stadium: Auburn fans cram into the corners of Bryant-Denny Stadium every other November, and if you look closely, you can even catch a few brave specks of orange in the Alabama student section. Tuscaloosa has been the site of some epic road celebrations in 2000, 2002, 2004, and 2006. The 2008 game didn't end as happily.

Final word: Allow plenty of time to get there, as interstate traffic is a nightmare. Tuscaloosa can be so hectic on a game-day weekend that many fans choose to stay elsewhere, even if they can find a hotel. If you're in town and can stomach the Paul Bryant Museum's obvious focus on the Crimson Tide, it might be worth a trip. It's perhaps the most impressive museum of Southern football on the SEC circuit.

Fayetteville, Arkansas

Distance from Auburn: 696 miles

Auburn's record in Fayetteville: 5–3

In the stadium: The Razorbacks have one of the most modern, NFL-like stadiums in the league. The high-definition replay board was an inspiration for Auburn's model.

Final word: This is the toughest road trip for fans, but northwest Arkansas doesn't deserve its "Fayette-nam" reputation. The area has a modern, albeit rural airport, and the cities north of Fayetteville are exploding with growth. Downtown Fayetteville has its own charm, and the region can be very pretty in autumn.

Baton Rouge, Louisiana

Distance from Auburn: 417 miles

Auburn's record in Baton Rouge: 5–13–1

In the stadium: This is one of the places where it's safer to stick with Auburn folks, especially when it's a night game and the locals have had time to get lubricated. The stadium is older, but has had some recent renovations. Bring your earplugs. It gets loud.

Final word: If you've got a thick skin, the pregame tailgate scene is said to be excellent. Baton Rouge is still recovering from a post-Katrina population surge, and the infrastructure often seems overwhelmed on game weekends.

Oxford, Mississippi
Distance from Auburn: 327 miles
Auburn's record in Oxford: 8–2
In the stadium: Vaught-Hemingway only seats about 60,000, and even Ole Miss players have sometimes criticized the fans for being too tepid.

Final word: Tailgating in the Grove is almost a cliché. For the uninitiated, it can be odd to see all the nice clothes and fancy spreads. Try to get a Rebel friend who knows the ropes to give you a tour of the Grove experience.

Starkville, Mississippi
Distance from Auburn: 269 miles
Auburn's record in Starkville: 11–4–1
In the stadium: Cover your ears. Seriously. The clanging of a single cowbell may be annoying alone, but thousands of the bells can make an ear-piercing metallic noise that impacts an opponent's offense as much as 100,000 screaming fans.

Final word: Starkville is another place that has an undeservedly poor reputation. If you haven't been lately, the campus has added some attractive new buildings, the downtown appears to be thriving, and there are ample opportunities for good eating and nightlife.

Athens, Georgia
Distance from Auburn: 187 miles
Auburn's record in Athens: 18–10

In the stadium: The field at Sanford Stadium is below ground level, affording a nice bridge view and ensuring the very attractive stadium doesn't dwarf the equally attractive campus. The stadium seats about 92,000 now, but an expansion plan under consideration could push the total above 100,000.

Final word: If you enjoy music and nightlife, there's no better city in the SEC—and possibly no better small city in the country.

Knoxville, Tennessee

Distance from Auburn: 322 miles

Auburn's record in Knoxville: 8–14–2

In the stadium: Neyland Stadium is huge. It seats 102,000, but seems even bigger. If you're on the chubby side, be ready for a tight squeeze. Neyland is known for offering very little room between you and your neighbor.

Final word: Tennessee isn't known for having the prettiest campus in the world, but the city is nestled in a scenic and hilly region. The drive up through the fall foliage is worth the trip alone.

Nashville, Tennessee

Distance from Auburn: 334 miles

Auburn's record in Nashville: 7–11

In the stadium: In a normal year, you might see more Auburn people than fans wearing black and gold. The fans are accustomed to losing, but when they win (like in 2008), the party is on.

Final word: If you can't find something to enjoy in Nashville, you won't be satisfied anywhere. It doesn't really count as an "SEC town" because of its size, but Nashville is a vibrant and fun Southern city. That may be why so many Auburn fans make the trip every five years.

Lexington, Kentucky

Distance from Auburn: 489 miles

Auburn's record in Lexington: 11–4

In the stadium: Yes, this is a basketball school, but the Wildcats have done well recently and fan interest has grown correspondingly. In the last 10 years the stadium has been expanded to about 67,000 seats.

Final word: Lexington has attractive neighborhoods and a nice downtown area, but the Bluegrass State is best known for its horse-racing. Check out the International Museum of the Horse, located in Kentucky Horse Park.

Gainesville, Florida

Distance from Auburn: 327 miles

Auburn's record in Gainesville: 9–23

In the stadium: Ben Hill Griffin Stadium at Florida Field is large, loud, and raucous. At the end of the third quarter, fans sway and sing, "We Are the Boys from Old Florida."

Final word: Yet another city that's almost too crowded to enjoy on game days. As long as you're in the neighborhood, why not take the kids to Disney World?

Columbia, South Carolina

Distance from Auburn: 321 miles

Auburn's record in Columbia: 2–0

In the stadium: South Carolina has great fans who have spent many years cheering for a bad team. Make sure to be in your seats for the pregame introductions when the theme from *2001: A Space Odyssey* is played. It's hard to describe, but it's cool.

Final word: Another miserable traffic situation, as the stadium is located near traffic-clogging railroad crossings. But Columbia's downtown "Congaree Vista" area is worth a stop. Stay close to downtown or campus if you can find a hotel room. The suburbs don't have nearly as much to offer.

A Greatly Exaggerated Demise: 1973 Showed New Life

How could the outlook be anything but bleak for the 1972 season?

Heisman Trophy–winning quarterback Pat Sullivan and receiver Terry Beasley were now in the NFL, and even with those two stars in the fold, the Tigers had been routed by Alabama and then Oklahoma in the two final games of the 1971 season.

Athletics director Jeff Beard retired after the season, and coach Ralph "Shug" Jordan reportedly mulled doing the same. But he stuck with it and instituted a demanding practice regimen that harkened back to his early days of coaching in the 1950s.

"These Tigers were scrappy if nothing else," wrote author and journalist Paul Hemphill. "Rarely did they go through a practice in the late-summer heat without fistfights and cries of 'Medic' breaking out all over the practice field. Jordan was in heaven…. It was No. 1 offense versus No. 1 defense, over and over again, the roughest preseason in two decades."

The team would eventually come to be known as the "Amazin's" for accomplishing what few thought that it could. There was, in fact, still a team and still hope without Sullivan or Beasley.

The wins didn't come easily. The Tigers survived four close games to open the season against Mississippi State, Chattanooga, Tennessee, and Ole Miss before dropping a blowout loss to then–No. 8 LSU. Auburn rebounded with wins against Georgia Tech, Florida State, and Florida to set up a climactic "Amen Corner" finish.

"Even a screenwriter would have his sanity checked if he dared propose what happened next," wrote Hemphill.

The Tigers downed Georgia in front of a frenzied Cliff Hare Stadium and then shocked Alabama 17–16 in the memorable "Punt, 'Bama, Punt!" game.

"Auburn, minus any stars or heroes, thought they could win…even though Pat Sullivan and Terry Beasley were gone," wrote David Housel. "They thought they could win on their own merit if they worked long enough and hard enough. Nobody else thought they could, but win they did."

The near-perfection of the season was capped by a 24–3 win against Colorado in the Gator Bowl. The Tigers finished the year ranked fifth by the AP and seventh by UPI.

There were still tough days on the horizon. Auburn would slip to 6–6 in 1973, but bounce back to 10–2 (and win another Gator Bowl) in 1974. Jordan's last season in 1975 was a disappointing 4–6–1, and the next five years under successor Doug Barfield produced only one winning season.

But the Amazin's carved out an important place in Auburn history, between the success of the Beasley-Sullivan era and the resurgence of the Pat Dye years. And they did it with players like Terry Henley, Bill Newton, Roger Mitchell, Gardner Jett, David Langner, and Dave Beck—players who probably weren't exactly household names before they became the Amazin's.

"It is a story in the finest tradition of the American Dream," wrote Housel, "a Horatio Alger story of the first degree."

56 The Powerbrokers: Behind-the-Scenes Influences

He's been called one of the most powerful boosters in America as recently as 2006, but is Auburn trustee and power broker Robert E. "Bobby" Lowder still worthy of the title?

That depends on whom you ask. Times, we are told, have changed. The old culture of Auburn athletics, in which decisions were micromanaged by boosters from above, no longer exists. Today things are supposed to be more transparent and progressive. There is supposed to be a clear chain of command, with the athletics director reporting directly to the president, not to any outside influences.

As documented elsewhere in this book, Auburn's recent coaching search appears to indicate that some things have, in fact, changed.

Athletics director Jay Jacobs promised a by-the-book, protocol-driven search. That didn't stop plenty of other names from being floated in the media. But Jacobs appeared to eschew candidates who would have required back-channel dealings—candidates like Ole Miss coach Houston Nutt or Florida State coach-in-waiting Jimbo Fisher. Instead, he interviewed primarily sitting head coaches after asking permission of their athletics directors.

Most agree that Jacobs' ultimate pick—Gene Chizik—was unlikely to have been stage-directed by Lowder or another prominent booster.

So why does Lowder have a reputation as a kingmaker and a meddler? Lowder has donated millions to Auburn, both the academic institution and its athletic department. His family name adorns more than one building on campus. Even so, he is a reviled figure to some.

Lowder's longevity (he's managed to remain on the Board of Trustees since 1983), his political influence (he is an important player in state campaigns), his wealth (he was CEO of Colonial Bank and is worth many millions), and his secrecy (he rarely talks to the media and shuns the limelight) have created the impression that he uses Auburn as his private fiefdom, exerting personal influence over the public university.

"Lowder's fingerprints have lingered for three decades in the hiring and firing of coaches and athletics directors alike—even university presidents. Thus, his brash micromanagement of his alma mater is as renowned as it is reviled," wrote Mike Fish in his profile of Lowder.

Lowder doesn't often get his hands dirty. When Auburn officials tried to oust Tommy Tuberville after a disappointing 2003 season, they used Lowder's private jet for their secret flight to Louisville to interview Bobby Petrino. Lowder wasn't present.

The incident came in the midst of an inquiry from Auburn's accrediting body, the Southern Association of Colleges and Schools, that ultimately led to a one-year probation and embarrassing headlines about the school and its board.

Whether the board's power has truly been reined in remains to be seen. In 2001 the board fired Auburn President William V. Muse, inspiring votes of no confidence in the Board of Trustees by both students and faculty. Today, new president Jay Gogue appears to have widespread support from all parts of campus, and he seems content to leave athletic department matters in the hands of Jacobs.

Lowder will serve on the board until 2011. That's according to an opinion from Attorney General Troy King, who was forced to decide, for reasons too complex to get into, whether Lowder was eligible to serve until 2007 or 2011. King returned a $10,000 campaign check from Lowder before making the decision.

When he retires—or if he retires—Lowder's tenure as a trustee will have spanned an astounding 28 years. His imprint on the university—for better or ill—is undeniable.

57 Walter Gilbert and the Award That Bears His Name

Walter Gilbert was one of the greatest college football players in the first half of the 20th century and one of the best ever to take the

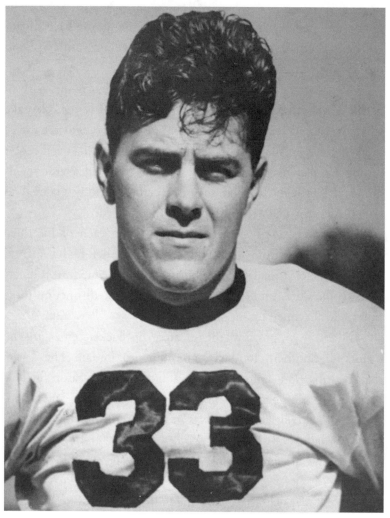

Each year, exceptional student-athletes at Auburn are given the Walter Gilbert Award, named after the Tigers' legendary center/linebacker.

field at Auburn. But the award that honors his memory has more to do with the accomplishments he achieved after his playing days were long over.

Gilbert was a Europe-based executive of international marketing at the end of a lengthy career at Texaco. He died in 1979. Two years later, Auburn began giving out the Walter Gilbert Award to honor his memory. The 28 recipients of the award have distinguished themselves both as Auburn student-athletes and professionals in their field.

Gilbert was a native of the Birmingham, Alabama, suburb of Fairfield who attended a prep boarding school in Rome, Georgia, where he played center on the football team. He caught the eye of then–Auburn assistant Ralph "Shug" Jordan, himself a great center during his playing days, and Auburn coaches paid a visit to his home in Fairfield. To their surprise, Gilbert already planned to attend Auburn. Their recruiting pitch wasn't needed.

Gilbert was an All-American at center in each of his three Auburn seasons, from 1934 through 1936. Before his arrival, Jimmy Hitchcock had been Auburn's only All-American. Gilbert remains the only Auburn player ever to earn the distinction three times. He also lined up on defense.

Gilbert was "possibly the greatest linebacker-center in the history of Southern football," according to Jordan. The Tigers struggled in 1934, Gilbert's first year and the first season for new coach Jack Meagher, but they rebounded in 1935 and 1936. Gilbert's final collegiate game was in the Bacardi Bowl in Havana, Cuba, on January 1, 1937.

Just days after graduating from college, he went to work at Texaco.

The 28 men who have won the Gilbert Award since his death include 20 former football athletes. Others competed in basketball, track, wrestling, baseball, and swimming. Three completed in more than one sport.

Among the group are executives, academics, coaches, and more.

Joe Stewart was the first recipient in 1981. Pat Sullivan was honored in 2008. The rest of the group includes: Thomas K. McGehee, Joel Eaves, David Middleton, William A. Fickling Jr., Ted Fereira, John Adcock, Bill Nichols, C.H. "Babe" McGehee, Billy Hitchcock, Vince Dooley, Jeff Beard, Morris Savage, Ed Dyas,

Lloyd Nix, Richard Guthrie, Jim Voss, Ernie Warren, James E. Martin, John Mengelt, Hal Herring, Jim Fibbe, Mac Crawford, Charles Carlan, David Marsh, R. Kenneth Johns, and D. Gaines Lanier.

Each summer, the university accepts nominations for the Gilbert Award from anyone who cares to offer one. If you know a former Auburn player doing great things in his life and career, send in a note.

The Championship Season of 1913

No modern team has ever come close to matching the defensive dominance of the Mike Donahue–coached clubs of the 1910s that produced Auburn's first Southern Intercollegiate Athletic Association championship in 1913.

These Tigers weren't just good. They almost never allowed opponents near the end zone.

Expectations were high for Auburn in 1913. The Tigers were coming off a 6–1–1 season that ended with a tie to Vanderbilt and a close loss to Georgia. In 1913 the Tigers barely broke a sweat until the final two weeks.

Auburn thrashed Mercer, Florida, Mississippi State, and Clemson to open the season by a combined score of 162–0. The Tigers then edged LSU in Mobile and whipped Georgia Tech 20–0 in Atlanta.

Auburn's toughest and most important game was November 15, 1913, against Vanderbilt, a school the Tigers had not beaten in 20 years. The game was played at Rickwood Field in Birmingham, and the *News* predicted the biggest crowd in the city's history: "The championship of the South is tottering on the fence today. Auburn arrived last night, confident, but not overconfident. Donahue is determined. He expects to win but would not say so. One could look upon his countenance and tell that he was determined that his hopefuls should walk from the field today victors.... All of the citizens are football wild. Old stars of the gridiron have flocked to the scene."

Roughly 10,000 fans attended the game, most in orange and blue. "Lots of money changed hands," reported the paper, although many fans lost big in predicting an Auburn rout. At halftime, 600 Auburn fans marched onto the field, formed the letter A, sang songs and cheers, and then "knelt as taps were played over the Vanderbilt goat, which meanwhile bucked and kicked and rared to go."

The game itself was classic, smashmouth football. Auburn used its pounding offense to control the ball. The Tigers completed no forward passes and used only a handful of sweeps. Mostly, they ran up the middle. Meanwhile, Vanderbilt coach Dan McGuigan's squad played "the new football," as the papers described it. The Commodores completed a forward pass to set up their lone touchdown. Auburn finished the game with a 62-yard touchdown drive in the fourth quarter to take a 13–6 win.

"It was a battle between a strong, powerful, experienced team, playing straight football and a bunch of less experienced men playing a desperate defensive game...and employing the new football on the offensive," said one description.

The headline the next day read: "Auburn Tigers Come from Their Lair and Viciously Claw and Tear the Flesh of Dan McGuigan's Commodores."

The newspaper description was written in the typically florid, overwrought style of the day: "The lean, lank Tiger of the Plains, held back from his prey for twenty tedious years, feasts at last upon the life-blood of the Commodore. Years of waiting had but added to his appetite until Saturday it was well-nigh insatiable. Even then, the Commodore fought the Beast of the Jungle back, until battered, clawed, scratched, beaten, he succumbed to the deadly attack."

Or something like that.

In any case, Auburn's victory set up a final game the following week against Georgia in Atlanta. The Tigers easily handled the Bulldogs to take their first of three SIAA championships.

Tech coach John Heisman was unamused, leading a call to arms to fans and players that the Yellow Jackets must improve or risk getting left behind by rivals like Auburn. "It is like the battle-ship building race between England and Germany. These two nations are never content with what ships they have; they both realize they must continue building and getting more, more if they wish to at all hold their own with rival nations," Heisman said.

Captain and senior running back Kirk Newell was the most important part of Auburn's offense in 1913. "The Dashing Darter from Dadeville" also played baseball and, occasionally, basketball, track, and soccer at Auburn. During his four years on the Plains, Auburn went 24–4–2 and outscored opponents 648–112. He gained 1,707 all-purpose yards in 1913 and had 5,800 rushing yards over his career.

The 1914 *Glomerata* yearbook gushed, "Captain Kirk Newell proved to be the sensation of the south. At all time heady and ready to take advantage of any slip by the opposing team, his directing of the attack was all that could be desired. Old football men declared him to be the greatest back who ever trod a southern gridiron."

Newell stuck around to help Donahue as an assistant for a few years and received a Distinguished Service Award for heroism in World War I. He died in 1967 and was posthumously inducted into the Alabama Sports Hall of Fame in 1994.

After 1913 Donahue and the Tigers picked up right where they left off. They were unbeaten in 1914 and—astonishingly—never allowed a point.

59 Tracy Rocker

Why were fans so thrilled when Tracy Rocker was hired as defensive line coach by Gene Chizik? For one thing, Tracy Rocker could hang an Auburn degree on the wall of his office when he moved back to the Plains in January. If there were room, he could have also displayed his Outland Trophy and Lombardi Award.

Rocker was not only one of the greatest defensive players in Auburn history, but many who watched him play say he could be one of the greatest defensive linemen to ever play the college game.

His NFL career was short and marred by injuries, but Rocker quickly found a niche in coaching. After six years working for Houston Nutt at Arkansas and Ole Miss, Rocker accepted Chizik's offer to return to his alma mater in January 2009.

Rocker's return to the Plains completed a journey that began more than 25 years earlier. As a senior at Atlanta's Fulton High School in 1983, Rocker was highly recruited by just about every major program in America. But he ultimately picked Auburn, which was coming off a Southeastern Conference championship under coach Pat Dye.

"Nebraska came to my house and pushed real hard, but I wasn't going that far away," Rocker said. "A lot of people were pushing me to go to Tech. I had a lot of friends there. I knew I wanted to be special in this game, and I didn't think I'd be special there because I'd have too many things to pull me away and I'd be too close to home. I wanted to get away from home, but not too far. When I met Coach Dye, I felt good about it. You have a gut feeling how you feel about someone."

Tracy Rocker won the Outland Trophy and Lombardi Award as a player, and returned to coach Auburn's defensive line in 2009.

Rocker ended up playing on two SEC championship teams, won those two prestigious trophies, and was inducted into the College Football Hall of Fame in 2004.

"People ask me, 'How did you do it?'" Rocker says. "I say, 'A lot of hard work.' I never felt anything was given to me. I worked my butt off to get there and had a lot of people behind me pushing me and motivating me."

Rocker said he thrived under Dye and defensive line coach Wayne Hall.

"I'd rather make the tackle than let somebody else do it," Rocker said. "Our mentality with Coach Hall was that the ball comes by us first."

After his NFL career, Rocker returned to Auburn to complete his degree and then signed on as an assistant coach at Auburn High School.

"All of a sudden, I am doing something I like doing and I have a big impact on people," he said. "I don't miss playing. I'm thinking this must be my calling."

His first college job was at West Alabama and he later made stops at Troy and Cincinnati. He landed in the SEC at Arkansas with Nutt, who's known as one of the better head coaches to work for.

"It was a great six years," Rocker said. "Houston provides a family environment, a very coachable environment. I enjoyed working with him. But there comes a time when we all have to part ways and move on in this business."

Rocker will supervise all four defensive linemen positions. Auburn has split those duties between tackles and ends for the last 10 years under former head coach Tommy Tuberville.

The philosophy Rocker plans to teach to his charges is built around toughness. "One thing I know about playing down there is that you don't really get an off down," he said. "You've got to lay it on the line on every snap. The most important thing is not so much talent, but doing your best and leaving it on the field and not getting back and saying, 'Well, coulda, shoulda, woulda.' I did my best and I left it all out there on the field."

The linemen on both sides of the ball have roles that can't be compared to the rest of the team.

"Playing defensive line, a lot of people don't quite understand that you run into people every day," Rocker said. "And you're expected to run into them even harder on the weekend. There's only a few guys who get to play flag football. And defensive linemen and offensive linemen don't get to play flag football. They run into people. So I'm expecting a challenge."

60 Crowd Control

The Georgia fans who decided to prance across the Jordan-Hare Stadium turf left Auburn very cold and very wet. And perhaps a bit more cautious in the future. But none of them seemed terribly angry after getting hosed down by water cannons in the aftermath of the Bulldogs' 20–16 win on November 15, 1986. They were too busy celebrating an improbable win in the Deep South's oldest rivalry.

It's a game now remembered more for what happened after the clock expired than before it. And thanks to the magic of YouTube, another generation of Auburn and Georgia fans are getting to watch the strange aftermath and either nod their heads in appreciation or mutter in disgust.

When the game was over, delirious Georgia fans stomped their way through the hedges and over the gates onto the turf, cheering the win as if the stadium were their own. Then someone flicked a switch and on came the heavy-duty sprinklers.

The television announcers calling the game for ESPN were dumbfounded, their tone alternately amused and admonishing.

"It's a little chilly to be getting drenched down there, but the Georgia fans probably aren't going to mind," one announcer said.

The sprinklers beamed their chilly spray from every corner of the field, but Georgia fans quickly discovered a safe spot near the midfield logo. That's when the next idea was hatched: fans could peel off pieces of the Auburn logo and take the turf home as a souvenir.

That indignity was too much for the ESPN broadcast crew. "You can't blame fans for celebrating, but you don't want them to tear up the field, either," one announcer said. "This is one of the prettiest fields in the country."

"Those souvenirs aren't going to last long," another added. "Dead grass doesn't make a great souvenir."

Predictably, the reaction to the incident divided along partisan lines. For Auburn fans, the impromptu shower was a perfectly sensible reaction to an outrageous breach of security and stadium protocol. For Georgia fans, it was the Auburn side that grossly overreacted to a harmless celebration.

An Atlanta columnist opined that the water "left its indelible stain on a once-civil rivalry" and cast Auburn as "the sorest loser imaginable." Another countered, "The big question is: why do idiots run on the field in the first place?"

Auburn coach Pat Dye was far from apologetic. While acknowledging that the water cannons "might not have been the thing to do," he said it was Georgia fans who acted recklessly. "If that [water] is the only way to get them off the field, that's fine," Dye said. "It doesn't hurt." Water was certainly better than billy clubs, he added.

There was one more interesting footnote to the story: more than 20 years later, a newspaper caught up with the man who gave the orders to drench the Georgia fans. Turns out, he was a Bulldog, too. Kermit Perry, Georgia class of 1955, was employed by Auburn at the time.

"I love Georgia, and the last thing I ever wanted to do was turn those cannons on," Perry told the *Atlanta Journal-Constitution*. "But that was our security plan. We had had that plan in place for five years, and we had never used it."

Perry retired to Newnan, Georgia, and still watches the rivalry closely. "I'm sorry it happened, but I'm not ashamed of it," he said. "It was just one of those crazy things."

Oh, by the way, there was a game, too. Auburn had started the 1986 season 7–0, winning each game by at least three touchdowns. The Tigers moved up to No. 5 in the national rankings, and many fans were thinking about a national title. But Auburn lost a heart-breaking 18–17 game at Florida in Week 8. The Tigers rebounded with a blowout win against Cincinnati a week later and approached their annual meeting with Georgia brimming with confidence. The Bulldogs were unranked, and their quarterback, James Jackson, missed the game to attend his grandmother's funeral. But backup Wayne Johnson threw one touchdown pass and rushed for another to lead the Bulldogs to a 20–16 win and ruin Auburn's hopes of a Sugar Bowl invitation.

Perhaps it was the utter surprise of the upset that prompted Georgia fans to dash onto the field. Perhaps it was the anger of the defeat that prompted Auburn to start dousing them. In either case, the day the Bulldogs got soaked has gone down as one of the more memorable chapters in the series' rich history.

61 How Auburn Made Nine Picks in One Game

On one incredibly strange day in 1969, Auburn's defense set a new record and made a future NFL quarterback look foolish. The Tigers intercepted nine passes thrown by Florida's John Reaves, a celebrated

Gators quarterback who would go on to be selected in the first round of the NFL draft and play professionally for 14 seasons. But on November 1, 1969, Reaves' nine air-mailed passes sent Florida to its first loss of the season and gave Auburn a season-changing victory.

Auburn coach Ralph "Shug" Jordan opined that the nine picks surely constituted an "all-world record." If not, it had to be close. "I've never been more proud of a bunch of men," Jordan said after the 38–12 victory at then–Cliff Hare Stadium.

How did Auburn come up with all the interceptions? It started on the defensive front.

"The key to the nine interceptions was the pressure we put on Reaves," Jordan said. "We were forcing him to do something with the ball."

Auburn broke the previous record of eight interceptions held by the Georgia Tech Yellow Jackets, who grabbed the picks against another top quarterback—Georgia's Zeke Bratkowski.

One of the reason Reaves (and Bratkowski) threw so many interceptions was because he had so many opportunities to throw them. Reaves threw 66 times, setting a new record. Three of those passes went to Auburn linebacker Sonny Ferguson. Linebacker Bobby Strickland and defensive backs Larry Willingham and Buddy McClinton had two each.

Auburn's offense was led more ably by quarterback Pat Sullivan, who completed 22 of 39 passes for two touchdowns and zero interceptions.

The game had been seen as the Gators' best chance in some time to break a 12-game winless streak at Auburn. Instead, it turned into a romp that turned around Auburn's season.

The Tigers went on to win their last three games, notching victories against Mississippi State, Georgia, and Alabama before losing to Houston in the Astro-Bluebonnet Bowl. Florida rebounded, too. The Gators didn't lose another game in 1969.

Head coach Ray Graves stepped down at the end of the season and became athletics director, clearing the way for Doug Dickey's arrival as the new coach.

The closest Auburn has come to a such an incredible mark of pass-thievery in recent history was October 2, 2004, during a rout of Tennessee at Neyland Stadium. The Tigers intercepted five passes from Tennessee quarterbacks Erik Ainge and Brent Schaeffer, and also took a fumble from Ainge.

Auburn defensive back Junior Rosegreen set a new team record when he caught his fourth interception late in the fourth quarter.

"When you're playing with young guys, there are going to be lessons learned along the way," then–Tennessee coach Phillip Fulmer said after the game. "I told Erik, 'This is an experience. Not a good experience, obviously.'"

Jimmy Sidle

Jimmy Sidle's career at Auburn was marked by tremendous accomplishments and enormous disappointments.

In 1963 he showed himself to be among the nation's best quarterbacks and led the Tigers to nine wins and an Orange Bowl trip. But the 1964 season, which was greeted with much promise, fizzled immediately when Sidle injured his shoulder. Not only did the Tigers not win the SEC title—as many believed they would—but it would be until 1970 before Auburn won nine games again.

Sidle went to Banks High School in Birmingham, where he was a talented quarterback with a sharp arm. But the arm was only a small part of his arsenal. At Auburn, Sidle was turned into one of the nation's most dangerous running quarterbacks. An All-American in 1963, Sidle became the first quarterback to lead the nation in rushing (1,006 yards). He also added 706 yards and five touchdowns through the air to lead the SEC in overall yardage.

Sidle ran alongside the impressive duo of halfback Tucker Frederickson and fullback Larry Rawson.

The most thrilling game may have come September 28 at Knoxville. "The score was 23–19, and how it came about on the gray and misty day is a story for Auburn men to marvel over many years from now," the *Birmingham News* wrote.

Auburn lost the ball five times on fumbles, and Sidle tossed an interception with the Tigers trailing late in the game. But when Auburn got the ball back, Sidle executed a flawless drive with runs of six, nine, and 16 yards, and a pass for 12. He reached the end zone on a one-yard run to give the Tigers the victory.

"Just like I've been saying all week, Sidle was the one we had to stop to win," said Tennessee coach Jim McDonald, who was in his first and only year at the Volunteers' helm.

Auburn coach Ralph "Shug" Jordan said it was the greatest game Sidle and Frederickson had ever played.

The Tigers finished 9–1 in 1963—a season marred only by a surprising upset to Mississippi State in Week 7—and went to the Orange Bowl, where they lost to Nebraska.

"Jimmy was one of the most talented athletes I've ever known," said Tom Bryan, who backed up Sidle in 1963. "He could have played college baseball, college basketball, or competed in track. He was good at pool, Ping-Pong, tennis, anything. Number one, he was talented enough to do it. Number two, he was extremely competitive."

Optimism was high heading into the 1964 season. Sidle was on the cover of a college football preview magazine, and many predicted great things for the Tigers. But disaster struck in the opening game. Sidle injured his throwing shoulder in a blowout win over Houston. He would never be quite the same quarterback for Auburn.

"I had a hole in my [rotator cuff] about the size of a silver dollar," Sidle said. "They tried everything." A specialist brought in by the team rubbed some concoction on the shoulder and Sidle thought briefly that he might be cured. "I went out to the parking lot to see if I could throw, and sure enough it felt like I could," he said. The good news was short-lived, and the shoulder problems were real. "I could [rest] for a few days and have four or five throws in me, but that was about all," he said.

Bryan and Joe Campbell took over most of the reps at quarterback, while Sidle moved to halfback. The disruption on offense was costly, as Auburn limped to a 6–4 record despite a very strong defense.

After his college career was done, Sidle played briefly in the NFL for Atlanta and then spent a couple of years in the Canadian Football League. He was estranged from Auburn for some time, but eventually came back into the fold later in life.

He passed away in 1999.

Visit the New Lovelace Museum

If you visit the location of the old Lovelace Athletic Museum and Hall of Honor today, you'll find a glassy entrance with a receptionist and two long corridors of offices for athletic department administrators. The museum is gone—or at least on hiatus. But it will return in the fall of 2010 when Auburn opens its new basketball arena across the street from Beard-Eaves-Memorial Coliseum.

The museum's new home will be wide-open and bright, with higher ceilings and more room to move about. "It will go in the lobby," said Randy Byars, Auburn's director of athletic facilities. "The north entrance will be the main area for fans. The [old]

Lovelace Museum was in a box. It had four walls, and you pretty much went left or right, but you couldn't go through. In this one, there are no walls. It will be an open format where you can just wander around. You can get up out of your seat and walk through any part of it. It will be much more open, more free-flow. We are trying to make it less an of an old-people's touring facility and get the young fans involved."

If you've ever been to Bud Walton Arena in Fayetteville, Arkansas, the museum there might provide the best glimpse of what Auburn is aiming for in its new arena. The downside is that the museum's hiatus means that many of the exhibits are inaccessible until the opening of the new arena.

The museum's mission statement is to honor "Auburn's athletic past, define its present, and inspire future generations. Documenting all of the intercollegiate sports played by Auburn men and women down through the years, the museum shows Auburn people, and those yet to experience the Auburn spirit, how Auburn's athletic programs have contributed to Auburn's historical traditions."

The museum featured multimedia displays for all 16 of Auburn's current intercollegiate sports, plus wrestling. A replica of Toomer's Corner and the Tiger Walk hall of mirrors are popular displays. Life-size dioramas of Bo Jackson going "over the top" and coach Ralph "Shug" Jordan discussing plays with quarterback Pat Sullivan are also a thrill for youngsters. It's still unclear how many of the traditional displays will be moved to the new arena.

The museum was named for Jonathan Bell Lovelace, who served as a graduate manager and assistant faculty manager on Mike Donahue's undefeated championship teams in 1913 and 1914. Lovelace founded the Capital Research and Management Company in 1931, now a 9,000-employee international firm known as the Capital Group of Companies. The privately held organization is one of the world's largest investment management companies.

The Lovelace Athletic Museum will reopen in 2010 in Auburn's new basketball arena.

While the museum is closed, there are other places to check out Auburn history. Wander in the front doors of the university's main athletic complex at Samford and Donahue and you'll find a hall of Auburn memorabilia to your immediate right. It's the Anthony J. Rane Family Reception Center, commonly known as the Rane Room. As long as the room is not being used for a function of some sort, fans are usually welcome to wander around. The Heisman Trophy is on display—twice—in the center of the room. There's also Tracy Rocker's Outland Trophy and Lombardi Award, murals, paintings, jerseys, and other memorabilia. You'll find SEC championship trophies, Carlos Rogers' Jim Thorpe Award, a display dedicated to

Terry Beasley and Pat Sullivan, and mementos from the 2004 Sugar Bowl. There's a bust of coach Ralph "Shug" Jordan and a sculpture of an eagle made entirely of shell casings from the Vietnam War.

It's not the full museum, but it will do until 2010.

64 The LSU-Auburn Hurricane Ivan Game in 2004

One of the most memorable games in recent Auburn history almost never occurred.

Set against the backdrop of a ferocious hurricane, Auburn's meeting with LSU in 2004 was in question until 36 hours before kickoff. Classes were canceled on both campuses as the unpredictable Hurricane Ivan danced through the Gulf of Mexico. But Auburn and Baton Rouge were both spared the brunt of the onslaught, and the game was played, adding another thrilling chapter in the SEC West's newest rivalry.

On September 13, the Monday of game week, officials at both schools first started taking Ivan seriously. ESPN canceled its *College GameDay* show and decided instead to go to East Lansing, Michigan, for a Notre Dame–Michigan State game. With an expensive outdoor set, the network didn't want to take any chances of getting caught in Ivan or its remnants. Auburn and LSU shared a common open date in November, so the SEC office was prepared if a cancellation had to be made.

"You have to have the discussion in place in case a call is made," said the SEC's Charles Bloom. "The current predicted path of the storm sends it right through south Alabama, so it's good just to have plans in place."

On Tuesday, as Ivan strengthened and approached the Gulf Coast, both schools called off classes for the rest of the week, told students to go home, and instructed nonessential personnel not to show up. Most of the bad stuff was predicted to be past Lee County by Saturday, but Auburn officials were concerned about the logistical hurdles of inviting 85,000 people to travel to Auburn in the wake of a major disaster. They wanted to make sure LSU could get to Auburn safely and fans could get to the stadium safely, while ensuring that the game didn't use police and emergency personnel needed elsewhere. Fans were told to be patient.

On Thursday, the remnants of Ivan hit the Auburn area, bringing some heavy wind and rain but no major damage. The eye of the storm made landfall near Gulf Shores, causing Alabama and Florida coastal areas to take the worst hit. Baton Rouge came out okay.

On Friday, the schools made it official: the game was on.

Both teams were forced to give up hours of practice time. Players couldn't live in their dorms. Nerves were frayed. To say that both teams faced heavy distractions before kickoff was an understatement. "You won't believe the distractions," said Auburn coach Tommy Tuberville. "That's what's tough about games like this, when you might not play it or you might play it. We haven't thrown a pass [in practice] since 11:00 [AM] on Wednesday."

The game itself was dominated by defense and field position. Auburn trailed 9–3 until the final minutes, when senior quarterback Jason Campbell led a 12-play touchdown drive culminating in Courtney Taylor's 16-yard catch in the end zone.

The extra point was an afterthought. After all, Auburn had made 190 consecutive extra points dating back to 1999. Fans and players were deliriously celebrating Taylor's catch. When John Vaughn's kick missed, the victory party ended abruptly.

"I just got sick to my stomach," Tuberville said.

The cruel twist came with a gift—an unusual penalty on LSU—and Vaughn connected on his second try. Auburn had won 10–9, beating Nick Saban and the defending national champions. They didn't know it at the time, but the Week 3 victory would be perhaps their most difficult test in the undefeated season to come. It was an especially sweet moment for Campbell and Tuberville, two embattled figures who would both reach new heights in the magical 2004 season.

But that historic significance was unclear in the immediate aftermath of the game. Instead, everyone wanted to talk about the strange extra point. "Ninety-nine percent of the time, it's probably the simplest play in football," Vaughn said. "But right there, it might have been the hardest." Snapper Pete Compton, a redshirt freshman, had struggled at times in 2004, and his snap came in low on the first attempt. Holder Sam Rives spotted the ball properly, but the kick sailed just outside the upright.

Then came the flag on LSU. "I guess the football gods were on our side," Rives said. Or, LSU coach Nick Saban might argue, the NCAA rules committee.

LSU's Ronnie Prude was called for a personal foul when he leaped into the air in an attempt to block the kick and landed on top of an Auburn lineman. "It's a new rule this year," Saban said. "That's a tough way to lose a game and a tough call to make to be a game-deciding call."

Saban, who actually serves on the rules committee, said the rule was designed to prevent injuries, but he found it vague and unfair.

"Who knows what happens when you're in the air?" Saban said. "But, obviously, I got outvoted on that. It's just kind of a cheap penalty to end up losing the game on."

The penalty gave Auburn a second chance to make the point.

"Settle down," Rives calmly told Vaughn. "It's not going to happen twice."

The snap was poor again, but this time Vaughn successfully booted it through the uprights.

"It's the pinnacle of my football career," said center Jeremy Ingle, one of several emotional players after the game. "When I saw Courtney come down with that pass, it's probably the first time in 10 years I've cried playing football. It was that emotional for me."

Campbell was unaffected by the week's distractions, leading the game-winning drive in the fourth quarter and showing impressive poise under fire on a crucial fourth-down conversion. "This kid is a lot better quarterback than people give him credit for, and I think he showed some of that," offensive coordinator Al Borges said. "He got knocked around and got up and picked himself off the ground to throw a touchdown pass."

The win made the Tigers 3–0 and gave fans the first inkling that the team might be better than anyone had imagined.

65 Watch Auburn Get the ODK Trophy at Halftime

When Auburn and Alabama meet in men's hoops, the basketball game itself is often secondary. The central attraction for many fans comes at halftime. That's when the victors in the Iron Bowl—of football—are presented with their trophy, and the losing school's student government president gets to belt out the winners' fight song. The ceremony is meant to be an exercise in good sportsmanship and good fun.

The trophy's unwieldy name is the James E. Foy/Omicron Delta Kappa Sportsmanship Trophy. For much of the last decade, Auburn got to revel in the win at Beard-Eaves-Memorial Coliseum. In 2009 the tradition—and the trophy—returned to Tuscaloosa and Coleman Coliseum.

It started in 1948, when the two chapters—or "circles"—of the Omicron Delta Kappa honor societies at Alabama and Auburn decided to sponsor a trophy devoted to sportsmanship and friendship between the two universities.

If you're lucky, you'll be in attendance at an Auburn basketball game during the presentation of the Foy-ODK Sportsmanship Trophy, given to the winner of that year's Iron Bowl.

The earliest tradition called for the trophy to be displayed at Loveman's department store in downtown Birmingham in the week prior to the Iron Bowl. In a parade before the game, a convertible carried the trophy and the ODK presidents from both schools. The parade came to an end in the 1960s, but the halftime basketball ceremony has stuck.

Thirty years after the trophy's creation, Foy's name was added to the honor. Foy, a beloved figure at Auburn, symbolizes the unity and friendship between the schools that the trophy is meant to convey. A University of Alabama graduate, Foy was the dean of students at Auburn from 1950 to 1978 after serving as an assistant dean at Alabama. He was also active as a faculty officer in ODK at both campuses.

When the trophy resided in Auburn, its home was the Lovelace Museum in the athletic complex. When the museum closed temporarily, the trophy was moved to the Rane Reception Room across the lobby. In Alabama, the trophy sits in the Ferguson Student Center.

The trophy itself has been dinged a bit during its 50 years of moving back and forth. Auburn master machinist Bill Holbrook is credited with saving the silver football player atop the trophy by inserting a steel rod through its inside. ODK officials believe the added strength will help the trophy survive many more ceremonies.

The ceremony itself has the feel of a pep rally. Coaches and players from the winning team file onto the floor. The head coach usually gives a pep talk of some sort, and officers from both ODK chapters say a few words. Then it's time for the singing of the fight song. The student government presidents are almost always good sports, singing with gusto and precision. Foy himself has made an appearance in recent years to lead the crowd in a "War Eagle" cheer.

In 2008 Alabama student president R.B. Walker had a warning: "I hope y'all enjoy this because this is the last time we're going to sing the Auburn fight song."

He was right...for at least one year.

If Auburn wins it back in 2009, get ready for a raucous ceremony in the new basketball arena in 2010. And, of course, stick around for the basketball game, too.

66 Roll Toomer's Corner on a Saturday Night

Toomer's Corner sits at College Street and Magnolia Avenue, where downtown Auburn meets the university campus. It's served as a central gathering place dating back to the earliest days of the college. Today it's best known as a place to celebrate Auburn victories.

"Rolling" Toomer's—or plastering the trees, wires, and anything else nearby with toilet paper—is one of Auburn's most cherished traditions for young and old alike. Gleeful celebrations after big wins can go on for hours and often end when the entire intersection is bathed in white.

The first rolling occurred in the early 1960s. The practice probably originated from the tradition of gathering at Toomer's Corner to celebrate and discuss Auburn road football games. It was a rallying place for fans who couldn't make the trip. Today it's not just football games that serve as an excuse to roll the corner. In fact, the constant rolling has taken its toll on the large oaks. Toomer's Corner is rolled for wins in other sports, championship celebrations, and miscellaneous causes—some avid supporters of Barack Obama even rolled Toomer's on the evening of his presidential victory.

The university has contracted with specialists to try to preserve the two live oaks. John Mouton, a building professor who earlier served as senior adviser to the president, said the arborists recommended that some of the trees' roots be cut to allow them to grow deeper. The arborist said the trees have "a lot of life left" if cared for properly.

But that's the rub.

"We can't continue to abuse them the way we have," Mouton told the Board of Trustees.

The rolling ritual itself doesn't damage trees, but the removal of the paper causes problems. City workers blast the branches with a high-powered spray of water after celebrations, the only practical way of removing the stuff from the trees. The water knocks leaves off branches and isn't good for the bark.

"It's not ideal, but there aren't a lot of good ways to get paper out of the trees," he said.

In the summer of 2008, traffic was shut down while specialists did more work on the trees. Dead limbs were removed, cables were attached to brace some of the weaker branches, and the compacted soil around the base of the trees was broken up. The crew also spread fertilizer and took care of bugs and pests. More root work was done in the summer of 2009.

Live oaks can live for a long time—sometimes hundreds of years—and the university said the Toomer's trees aren't ready for the wood chipper just yet.

The larger tree is even recovering from a gaping wound it suffered several years ago when it was hit by a car. Auburn foresters are growing younger trees from acorns harvested from the iconic Toomer's trees. So even if they were to die, they could be replaced

After an Auburn victory, head to Toomer's Corner with several rolls of toilet paper under your arm.

with "children" trees, so to speak. But even newer trees would have the same problems with the water-blasting, experts say.

So what should be done? One idea is to urge people to toss paper on nearby poles and wires.

Another solution?

"Doesn't Disney have artificial trees?" said trustee John Blackwell with a laugh.

67 How a "Hiring Committee" Landed Jordan and Dye

The closest thing Jay Jacobs came to a committee was the group that disembarked the Auburn jet one evening in mid-December in the midst of the search to hire Gene Chizik. Jacobs took a group of informal advisers to each of his roughly dozen interviews with candidates. Two members of the group were senior Auburn athletic department leaders—Tim Jackson and Mark Richard. A third adviser was Quentin Riggins, a former Auburn linebacker who now works as a Montgomery lobbyist and Auburn sideline reporter.

There was no committee and no vote. And despite rumors and speculation to the contrary, it appears that there was no outside influence from trustees or other boosters. Jay Jacobs made the call. Call it a one-man search committee.

That's increasingly the way it's done in college football these days. Many believe that traditional search committees are relics of the past. For a coaching search in which speed and confidentiality are vitally important, a committee can be unwieldy and prone to leaks.

Of course, Jacobs' search was hardly a cloak-and-dagger affair. He made a point of approaching each candidate through the "front door"—that is, he asked permission of the candidate's athletics director before going any further.

Most searches are much more stealthy.

Despite the sometimes soap opera–like quality of the Auburn athletic department in recent years, the school has actually had a remarkable degree of stability at the head-coaching position.

Tommy Tuberville was at Auburn for 10 years, an eternity in the coaching business. When he was hired from Ole Miss at the end of the 1998 season, the search was largely concluded while reporters and fans were still chasing names that were apparently never in the mix. Now *that* was a stealthy search.

People were equally caught off guard by the hiring of Terry Bowden in 1993. Bowden certainly had an impressive résumé and a fine pedigree, but most were surprised that a program of Auburn's stature hired a young coach from a lower-division program.

Chizik's hiring in December 2008 also defied conventional wisdom. Bowden's tenure produced several great seasons before crashing in 1998. Time will tell how Chizik fares.

Bowden's predecessor was Pat Dye, a respected figure in Southern coaching circles who had recently taken a self-imposed exile as head coach of Wyoming. After Auburn was turned down by alumnus Vince Dooley, who elected to remain at Georgia, Dye made a bold move to impress the search committee. He resigned at Wyoming and, fortunately for him, was ultimately hired by Auburn.

Of course, the search by which all searches are judged is the hiring of Ralph "Shug" Jordan. Sure, there was a committee, but there wasn't much of a "search." It was more of an anointment.

Auburn had passed on Jordan in 1948, and the result was a 3–22–4 record in three seasons. Athletics director Jeff Beard wasn't going to make the same mistake again, but Jordan also made it clear he had no interest in groveling for the job.

Four of the five men on the search committee were former Auburn players: Jimmy Hitchcock, Auburn's first All-American; Torrance "Bo" Russell; Bobby Blake; and Marion Talley. The fifth was Ken Lott, a former manager and alumnus.

The stage was set for Jordan's hiring. All the committee had to do was get him to formally apply. Beard convinced Jordan to send a one-sentence letter of interest. From there, the "search" was over.

Things usually aren't that easy these days. But Jacobs and Auburn fans hope it will be a while before they have to do it again.

68 Aundray Bruce

Aundray Bruce has been asked about the game more times than he can remember. And why not? His performance in 1987 against Georgia Tech might have been one of the most incredible feats ever accomplished by a defensive player at Auburn—or anywhere.

Bruce had three interceptions, the last returned 45 yards for a game-sealing touchdown. He forced a fumble that was recovered in the end zone for a touchdown. He had three quarterback sacks. He recovered another fumble. He had nine regular ol' tackles on top of that.

The victory continued what was then an undefeated season for the Tigers, although they later lost by a surprisingly one-sided margin to Florida State. The year would end in a Sugar Bowl tie against Syracuse detailed elsewhere in this book.

Bruce would finish the 1987 season as an All-America linebacker. Months later, he became the first overall player selected in the NFL Draft. For a player who grew up in public housing in Montgomery, the NFL millions were an incredible windfall. "For a kid coming out of Gibbs Village, it was all surprising," he said. "Having the opportunity to play pro football was like heaven for me.... The thing that always entered my mind was to take care of my mom, and I did that. That was one of my main reasons for playing sports, anyway."

Aundray Bruce was a dominating defensive force at Auburn before becoming the top overall pick in the 1988 NFL Draft.

Bruce was the 13th of 14 children and attended Carver High School in Montgomery, where he seemed to be a can't-miss athlete in basketball and football. Basketball was his first love, but he felt his 6'5" frame would be more advantageous on the football field. "I really wanted to play basketball, but I looked at my size and weight and determined that football was my best option," Bruce said.

He initially had a harsh adjustment to college football and was unprepared for the physical demands. Twice he quit the team only to be persuaded back by coaches Joe Whitt and James Daniel.

After winning All-SEC honors in 1986 and All-America honors in 1987, there were high hopes for Bruce's professional career. But he never became the star that the Falcons expected, and they cut ties with him after four seasons.

"What is important to me is establishing a reputation in this league, a reputation of being a dominant player," Bruce said in a critical *New York Times* story that ran after his release from the Falcons. "That is my childhood dream, that when it's all said and done to be in the Hall of Fame. There have been many obstacles that I have already overcome. I look at the way my career has started as just another obstacle to beat."

Bruce was picked up by the Los Angeles Raiders, where he played seven seasons as a steady but unspectacular reserve. His hopes of becoming a dominant player never materialized, but he did last 11 years in a cutthroat league, rarely missing a game due to injury.

69 Go to Fan Day and Get an Autograph...from a Backup

In August of 2005, with the euphoria of the previous year's perfect season still fresh, the annual Fan Day was more of a zoo than ever before. Fans packed Beard-Eaves-Memorial Coliseum, braving long lines for an autograph or a photo with the stars of the day—head coach Tommy Tuberville, offensive coordinator Al Borges, mascot Aubie, and several high-profile players placed strategically on the arena's floor. An Auburn employee had to rescue one of the heavily mobbed players at the end of the day. The player, who will remain unnamed, grasped the Auburn official and said, "Get me out of here."

So, yes, Fan Day can be a grind if you seek out the best-known attractions. The lines could last for an hour or more. Pictures with Aubie are in high demand. Popular players can be overwhelmed by the hordes. But there is a secret to getting the most out of the day.

Under Tuberville, fans could get to town early on Fan Day and take in a morning practice session. Gene Chizik still hasn't announced his practice policies, but it seems likely that he'll be more restrictive than Tuberville. If practice is open, Fan Day is a good day to watch. If not, head over to Beard-Eaves. If you want to get an autograph from a well-known coach or player, get to the basketball floor early. Better yet, stay in the outer concourse of the arena. Virtually every player on the team attends Fan Day, and most of them are seated at a table, alone and bored, for much of the two hours.

Running back Tristan Davis missed the 2007 fan day due to an injury, so the senior tried to savor the meet-and-greet in his senior season. "It's pretty rewarding," he said. "Fans are what make this sport so fun. The kids look at you like you're someone real special. It's pretty incredible. I'm just another guy out there on the field, but you're someone special with those kids."

The 2008 Fan Day was scheduled to last until 5:00 PM. That was after a three-hour, energy-sapping practice in the August heat. But with his line continuing to wrap around the coliseum floor at closing time, Tuberville continued signing autographs for another two hours until every last fan had been seen.

70 Paul "Bear" Bryant and Auburn

Paul "Bear" Bryant's relationship with his Auburn rivals across the state can be summed up in a two-word phrase that most fans are

Alabama coaching legend Paul Bryant and Auburn's Ralph "Shug" Jordan never let their rivalry on the field poison their professional friendship off the field.

not apt to forget. Bryant referred to Auburn as a "cow college" at some point prior to the 1972 Iron Bowl, although the exact context in which he said it is in some dispute.

In any case, Auburn people bristled at the elitism that under-pinned the remark. It was a battle that Auburn had been fighting for some time. During the 40-year break in the Auburn-Alabama rivalry, much of the resentment only simmered. The Tide excelled, while Auburn had less frequent success.

"Auburn people felt like second-class citizens. We were the butt of Alabama jokes. They went to Rose Bowls, and we couldn't even get Tennessee to come to our place," said early Tiger Babe McGehee.

But the rivalry went beyond the football field. Alabama produced lawyers and state legislators and such, and there was a smugness and arrogance directed at Auburn's land-grant roots that some say persists today.

Of course, that sort of manufactured elitism was as false in 1972 as it is now. Many Alabama fans had little or no connection to the campus in Tuscaloosa, while Auburn counts alumni as a large percentage of its supporters. And while Auburn continues to excel in land-grant staples like agriculture and forestry, it also can boast outstanding graduates in business, engineering, pharmacy, and the liberal arts. One positive aspect of the heated football rivalry is that many fans are now concerned about besting their rival in academic rankings, as well as sports rankings.

As for the "cow college" remark, some accounts quote Bryant as saying, "Sure, I'd love to beat Notre Dame, don't get me wrong. But nothing matters more than beating that cow college on the other side of the state." Another version goes, "I'd rather beat that cow college than beat Texas seven times."

You get the drift. Whatever the remark, Bryant was forced to eat crow rather quickly, as the 1972 game was of course the legendary "Punt, 'Bama, Punt!" game, which Auburn won 17–16.

Bryant admitted later that the comment was ill-advised, saying, "I ran off at the mouth and got those Auburn folks riled up."

He managed to have fun with it. When Auburn fans chanted, "Plow, Bear, Plow," he got his longtime sports information director, Charley Thornton, to extend his arms and act as a plow in front of him. The Auburn fans at Legion Field reportedly got a laugh out of it. When Alabama had a bad spring practice in 1973, Bryant said the Tide was playing like a cow college, before quickly changing the insult to "barber college."

Bryant's relationship to Auburn was more complex than just one remark, of course. Several assistant coaches worked on both sides of the rivalry. Auburn coach Pat Dye was a longtime Alabama assistant whom Bryant considered to be a protégé of sorts. Bill "Brother" Oliver played for Bryant and was a longtime assistant at both schools. Bryant and Ralph "Shug" Jordan maintained a respectful relationship and never let their longtime on-field rivalry spill over into public grievances.

Bryant's arrival at Alabama was much like Jordan's return to Auburn. It marked the end of a dark period for the football program. Jordan's return brought the Tigers out of an embarrassing slide and helped Auburn own the 1950s. During a four-year stretch, Auburn won the Iron Bowl by a combined 128–7. Then Bryant arrived and helped the Tide recover from the drought. He went 19–6 all-time against Auburn.

In the state of Alabama, it's still difficult to escape Bryant's shadow. And it's difficult to tell the story of Auburn football without Bryant getting a chapter.

71 Why Legion Field Never Really Felt Like Home

By the 1980s, Auburn wanted out of Birmingham and Legion Field, and it was going to do everything in its power to escape. Alabama, meanwhile, was trying to preserve what it considered the true home of the Iron Bowl for as long as it could.

The inevitable clash was won by Auburn when it moved the 1989 game to Jordan-Hare Stadium. (As a concession to Alabama and as an effort to avoid litigation, Auburn agreed to play one final home game in Birmingham in 1991.)

Why did the two fan bases have such drastically different views of Legion Field? Why did many Alabama fans treasure the traditional 50–50 split of fans while Auburn fans were intent on taking their games back to the Plains?

Much of the dispute has to do with the perceived neutrality—or lack thereof—at Legion Field.

"When you walk in that gate and there is a bronze monument of Bear Bryant, you sure don't feel like you are the home team," said Glen Gulledge, a longtime Auburn supporter and owner of Byron's Smokehouse.

Former Auburn athletics director David Housel said that was a common complaint. Like Alabama, Auburn often scheduled home games at Legion Field in the past to take advantage of the ample seating. But for Auburn, it was a venue. For Alabama, it seemed more like a second or even a primary home.

"Truth, like beauty, is in the eye of the beholder," Housel said. "For whatever reason, right or wrong, Auburn people always thought Alabama had a home-field advantage. Most Auburn people thought Legion Field was as neutral as the beaches of Normandy on D-Day."

Ticket distribution wasn't necessarily the main issue, although many Auburn fans thought the stadium never seemed to be a true 50–50 split. Each team had access to an equal amount of tickets, but other tickets set aside outside the purview of the two teams always seemed to fall in the hands of Alabama fans. Or so it was said.

Then-coach Pat Dye said he thought the ticket situation was fine, that Auburn usually had at least 50 percent representation in the stands. The real issue, he maintained, was that Auburn simply wanted to play its home games on its own campus in a perfectly suitable and newly expanded stadium—not two hours away in a big city.

He even suggested that Alabama might do the same and move its games to Tuscaloosa, a suggestion that didn't take hold until a few years later.

In any case, Auburn won the battle after some posturing by both sides. Actually, both sides eventually won, although they didn't necessarily see it that way at the time. A decade later, Alabama fans greeted the return of games to Tuscaloosa with almost as much enthusiasm as Auburn fans—well, perhaps not quite. Alabama has completed one stadium expansion and embarked on another that makes the crumbling Legion Field seem comically inadequate by comparison.

Auburn seems quite content with its own digs, too.

Somehow football in the state has survived without Legion Field. Some people understandably make the argument that the Iron Bowl name is due for retirement now that the game is no longer played in the "Pittsburgh of the South." But few make the argument that the game should return. And barring a major change in opinion on both sides, it's hard to imagine an Iron Bowl ever being played off campus again.

72 The Miserable 1950 Season

After almost a decade of SEC mediocrity, Auburn supporters were desperate for any shred of hope, any sign that might indicate brighter days were ahead.

That came in the final game of the 1949 season. Second-year coach Earl Brown had won twice, lost 12 times, and registered four ties during a forgettable stint on the Plains. But on December 3, 1949, Auburn stunned rival Alabama 14–13 in Birmingham. This was only the second year since the series had been revived and only one year removed from Alabama's 55–0 rout. Fans and alumni were thrilled. They were convinced that this was the evidence that Brown and the Tigers were turning a corner. They gave Brown a new car and a vote of confidence for 1950.

It was, of course, wishful thinking. The 1950 Auburn football team was atrocious. Vince Dooley was a freshman on the squad and called it "probably the worst football team I've ever seen."

The year started with a loss to Wofford, which was followed by a 41–0 blowout at the hands of Vanderbilt. Brown rested his team the following week, promising a rejuvenated squad in Week 3 against Southeast Louisiana. The result was an embarrassing 6–0 loss. "The boys will snap out of it," Brown promised. "Right now we're just got to lick that 'poor ol' Auburn' attitude."

The Tigers proceeded to lose every game of the 1950 season. They were outscored 255–31, including additional shutouts against Georgia Tech, Tulane, Mississippi State, Clemson, and Alabama.

Brown, an All-American at Notre Dame who was hired at the age of 32 from Canisius, was now 3–22–4 at Auburn, and his future seemed very much in doubt. He decided to be proactive. He signed 100 freshmen after the season, taking on anyone that had a recommendation—however dubious—from an Auburn alumnus.

Governor Gordon Persons, an Auburn graduate, was having none of that. He told Auburn President Ralph B. Draughon that it was time for Brown to go. Draughon blanched at the outside interference, and a faculty and alumni committee recommended that Brown be given another year to turn things around. But Persons never stopped his maneuvering, and Brown was never really safe. About a month later, the committee "reconsidered" its decision, and Brown was let go.

Furious, Brown complained that the administration and alumni at Auburn made for an impossible climate in which to succeed.

Ralph "Shug" Jordan was about to prove him wrong. Jordan's hiring brought immediate changes to Auburn's football culture.

The Tigers won five games in Jordan's first year—more than Brown's entire three-year tenure—and after a setback in 1952, rebounded with a winning season (7–3–1, 4–2–1 SEC) in 1953. Jordan's arrival also set the state for success against Alabama from 1955 to 1957, when the Tide was suffering through its own three-year stint under another less-than-successful coach, J.B. "Ears" Whitworth.

73 The Alma Mater and the Fight Song

War Eagle (Fight Song)

War...Eagle, fly down the field, Ever to conquer, never to yield.

War...Eagle fearless and true. Fight on, you orange and blue.

Go! Go! Go!

On to vic'try, strike up the band,

Give 'em hell, give 'em hell.

Stand up and yell, Hey! War...Eagle, win for Auburn, Power of Dixie Land!

The Alma Mater

On the rolling plains of Dixie

'Neath its sun-kissed sky,

Proudly stands, our Alma Mater

Banners high.

To thy name we'll sing thy praise,

From hearts that love so true,

And pledge to thee our

Loyalty the ages through.

We hail thee, Auburn, and we vow
To work for thy just fame,
And hold in memory as we do now
Thy cherished name.
Hear thy student voices swelling,
Echoes strong and clear,
Adding laurels to thy fame
Enshrined so dear.
From thy hallowed halls we'll part,
And bid thee sad adieu;
Thy sacred trust we'll bear with us
The ages through.
We hail thee, Auburn, and we vow
To work for thy just fame,
And hold in memory as we do now
Thy cherished name.
—Composed by Bill Wood, revised by Emmalu Foy

It took 40 years to unravel the mystery surrounding Auburn's alma mater, but it appears to have been solved.

Let's start this somewhat complex story at the beginning. In 1924 William Thorington "Bill" Wood, a glee club member and cheerleader, wrote Auburn's alma mater. In about 1960 several substantial revisions were made, but no one was sure who wrote the new lines, or why.

Dale Coleman, an Auburn professor of animal sciences, started researching the change. Eventually, the search led him to James Foy, the beloved dean of students at Auburn from 1950 to 1978. Foy had been linked to the alma mater from the beginning. When Wood's glee club traveled to Eufaula to perform, Wood stayed at the home of fraternity brother Simpson Foy, and taught the song he had written to a young James Foy. But when Coleman called the Foy household, he was in for a surprise.

"I thought you'd never ask," said Dean Foy's wife, Emmalu.

Mrs. Foy said she was the one who revised the alma mater in 1960, editing out references to API (Alabama Polytechnic Institute) and replacing them with Auburn, the school's new official name.

"Dr. [Ralph Brown] Draughon [then–university president] had recognized that there needed to be some changes in the song, and he first went to the alumni to see if they wanted to take on the project," Mrs. Foy said. "They declined. So he went to the SGA, and they agreed to do it."

The student government association placed an ad in the *Auburn Plainsman* seeking input and offering suggestions. One of the lines in the suggested verse contained the phrase "Auburn U.", which irked Emmalu Foy.

"I was talking with Jim about it, and he asked me how it could be changed since there's not much, if anything, that rhymes with Auburn. I told him that I would put Auburn in the middle of the line instead of at the end. When I told him that, he suggested that I submit a recommendation to the committee," she said.

Her recommendation was accepted, and the new words became part of the alma mater.

"I was delighted," she said. "Bill Wood's original words and music are so beautiful, I was just so excited that my work was going to be a small part of it."

Thanks to Coleman's fact-finding, Emmalu Foy received credit for her contribution in 2000.

"It's always been in the back of my mind," said James Foy. "I would go to football games and see the Alma Mater in the program and think, 'By golly, Emmalu revised that thing, and that should be known.' I'm gratified that she's finally getting some recognition, and I think it's the right thing to do."

Emmalu Foy passed away on January 21, 2004, at the age of 83. A few years earlier, Coleman had arranged a special honor for Mrs. Foy at an annual SGA banquet. The student government presented with her a resolution recognizing her work. Then four students approached to sing an a capella version of the alma mater in four-part harmony.

"It was truly an Auburn moment," Coleman said.

Auburn's fight song, "War Eagle," doesn't have such humble roots. In fact, an Auburn benefactor sought out an expensive and experienced composer and asked him to find a fitting tune for Auburn's new fight song.

In 1954 Auburn alumnus and supporter Roy B. Sewell offered to pony up the money for a new composition as a gift to Auburn. Robert Allen, who died in 2000, wrote hundreds of compositions, including classics like "Chances Are," and the ubiquitous Christmas song, "Home for the Holidays." He also composed "War Eagle," while music partner Al Stillman came up with the lyrics.

"I was on a committee of some nature examining the song, and I went to [Draughon's] office, and he called several people in and I played it on the piano for them," said Hubert Liverman, the head of Auburn's music department from 1951 to 1967. "They asked my opinion, and I told them that it was very, very good—extremely good—and that we ought to use it."

The song was played for the first time on September 24, 1955, in Auburn's win over Chattanooga.

"Auburn Victory March" was gradually phased out as the new song became more popular. But it wasn't an instant hit. Some didn't think it projected enough bravado.

"But imagine, if you can, in either supreme victory or utter defeat, Auburn's uncontainable spirit being vented in these driveling lines," an editorial in the *Montgomery Advertiser* complained. "This insipid, anemic attempt to versify one of the supreme bellows of our time is just plain tragic.... It's for the Ladies' Aid Society, not Auburn."

The song not only stuck but eventually became a fan favorite.

74 Kendall Simmons

In his rookie season, offensive lineman Kendall Simmons lived up to every expectation the Pittsburgh Steelers had when they selected him in the first round of the 2002 NFL Draft.

But when Simmons arrived at training camp in 2003, something felt different. He was dizzy, weak, and perpetually thirsty. He couldn't maintain his weight. Then he started losing it—rapidly. Finally, just before the season, he was diagnosed with type 1 diabetes. A new chapter in his life had begun.

"I wanted to just go ahead and keep doing things the way I'd done before," Simmons told a website focusing on the disease. "I didn't want to change my eating, I was embarrassed to take my shots in front of people. I just wanted the whole thing to go away.... The media didn't know what was going on with me medically, and I knew that I wasn't playing my best. I had to turn it around."

Eventually, Simmons got on track. His wife, Celesta, helped him with his diet and adjusted her cooking accordingly. Steelers owner Dan Rooney was especially understanding because he has a son with diabetes.

"I had worked too hard to make it to this point in my NFL career to let something like diabetes get in the way," Simmons said.

He overcame that obstacle and prospered in the NFL, starting every game in the Steelers' Super Bowl season of 2005. He was released after the 2008 season, and his NFL career may be done, but he can boast a solid seven-year career that might have been derailed even before it started if not for his perseverance.

Offensive lineman Kendall Simmons learned to manage his diabetes and won a Super Bowl with the Pittsburgh Steelers in 2005.

Simmons has never fit the stereotypical mold of a football player. On the field, he was an All-SEC player as a junior in 2000 after missing virtually all of the 1999 season with an injury. In 2001 he won the Jacobs Award as the SEC's best blocker.

Simmons was an art—or "visual communications"—major at Auburn and illustrated a portion of the team's media guide. He sketched drawings from photos of current and former Auburn players as well as coach Tommy Tuberville.

"I just didn't know what I was going to do in school," Simmons said. "Honestly, I'm like, 'You don't just want to be going to school to be going to school, so what are you going to do? Okay, you can draw, so how about you try this?'"

That's how he got the idea to major in art.

He stuck with it and skipped an early NFL opportunity in order to finish the degree.

"I had always told my mom, before I ever left college or did anything, I was going to graduate first," he said. "She's happy about all the football stuff and how everything's working, but she'd rather see me with a degree in my hand and working somewhere than being in the NFL and not able to come back and finish and get my degree."

The NFL thing worked out just fine. Plus, he was able to touch a few lives along the way.

During his Steelers career, Simmons frequently hosted local kids with juvenile diabetes.

"It's amazing to see these kids, the smiles on their faces," he said. "I know they're looking at me and thinking, *If he has diabetes and can do this, I can do anything, too.*"

75 Have a Sip of Toomer's Legendary Lemonade

Toomer's Corner a famous name.
How did it gain its fabulous fame?
A subject of many histories
And one hundred years of memories.
Toomer's is by definition

The soul of the War Eagle tradition
For its historic contribution
Made it an Auburn institution.
Auburn is a very special place
With a tradition of charm and grace
And its varied history ordains
The loveliest village on the plains.
I'm sure all of us will agree
Toomer's shares Auburn's history
And the Toomer's name still has merit
For it is the keeper of the spirit.
Serving Auburn for one hundred years
Toomer's helped students launch careers
It was a place where all could meet
Have lots of fun and shop and eat.
Now restoration is complete
Once again come meet, have fun, shop and eat
This is a firm affirmation
That Auburn will keep the Toomer's tradition.
—Everette E. Jones Sr., 1999, printed on the Toomer's
menu

Toomer's Drug Store occupies some of the most ideal real estate in downtown Auburn. Its windows offer a view of the bustling intersection of Magnolia and College. The famous, often toilet-paper-covered oak trees are just a few feet away. Every day, hundreds of students pass under the awning of the white building with blue trim.

But the interior of the building is decidedly simple. It's not a pharmacy—it doesn't offer prescription medication—but there's plenty of over-the-counter stuff and other convenience supplies. Auburn memorabilia and mementos line the walls. Plenty of T-shirts and other apparel are for sale. Black-and-white photos from the old days of Auburn and portraits of former owners of Toomer's Drugs give the place an even more nostalgic feel.

If you're hungry, an old-fashioned soda fountain offers about a dozen seats, and small tables in the back of the cafe provide more seating for groups. Toomer's is a great place for a quick lunch. Virtually every menu item is less than $5. Grilled sandwiches, ham sandwiches, turkey sandwiches, clubs, melts, hot dogs, baked potatoes, soups, and chili are all available.

Of course, the most famous item at Toomer's Drugs—and, honestly, the one thing on the menu that isn't cheap—is the fresh, hand-squeezed lemonade. The staff members at the cafe put real elbow grease into the lemonade-making process every day. The result is a cold, tasty, tart drink with a souvenir cup to take home. The soda jerk can also make you any sort of ice cream concoction, shakes, malts, floats, sodas, or sundaes. And if you get a stomachache, they'll be able to help you with that, too.

Toomer's is the oldest building in downtown Auburn, but its existence has been tenuous in recent years. The Haisten family purchased the store after it had sat empty for several years. Don Haisten passed away in 2006.

"Even in Don's last weeks at Auburn, he was developing another way to enhance the game-day experience for the fans," his wife Betty remembered. "He was creative, never happy with the status quo, loved Auburn, both the university and the community, and never cared for any recognition for himself. He was all about Toomer's and preserving the tradition for the fans."

Sheldon Toomer was the original owner, and the drugstore stayed in his hands from its founding in 1893 until 1952. After his graduation from Auburn, Toomer joined his stepfather, Benjamin Lazarus, in running the store and later opened a hardware store down the street.

In its early days, Toomer's was a community gathering place and gave politicians a forum for stump speeches. According to legend, Auburn football coach John Heisman used to drop in for a glass of lemonade. Previous owners and managers of Toomer's include Mac Lipscomb, Mark Morgan, and James Echols.

"I really just think it's always been a gathering point," said Toomer's manager Michael Overstreet. "It's so close to campus and just naturally a spot for people to gather."

The humble storefront made *Esquire* magazine in 2001 as one of "162 Reasons It's Good to Be an American."

"When God was a little boy and He needed extra money, He put up a card table outside His folk's house," the magazine said. "This [Toomer's Lemonade] is what He sold."

Bring the Kids to the Game

Most folks have a few indelible childhood memories from sporting events they saw as a kid—whether it was their first big-league baseball game or a Saturday of college football in the afternoon or an intense basketball matchup in a big arena. What will your kids remember about their trips to Jordan-Hare Stadium?

As any parent, uncle, big brother, grandparent, etc., can tell you, a football game can be an exciting but also overwhelming experience for a youngster. The long day of travel, anticipation, and traffic can also be taxing on even older kids.

After the game, most fans are eager to visit Toomer's Corner or hit the road quickly.

But the time before the game can be a great time to traipse around campus and get some of the kids' pent-up energy from the car ride out of their systems.

Aubie is an obvious attraction for little ones, but Saturdays are a busy day for Auburn's mascot. There are thousands of kids and only one of him. Still, if you're patient and persistent, he's usually good for a photo-op.

If you can, an up-close visit with the eagle before or after his pregame flight is often a neat idea. The birds are enormous and mesmerizing when you're within a few feet.

Kids love parades, and what is Tiger Walk but a scaled-down parade with all their favorite stars? But for the height-challenged, Tiger Walk usually requires early planning to get a good spot near the procession or find an elevated vantage point from which to view the players.

What about face painting? That's always a good timekiller. There are usually other kid-friendly stations set up in the vicinity of the stadium.

But there's nothing wrong with keeping things simple. It's hard to walk a few feet on Saturdays without walking by a group of kids throwing the football. Find a grassy spot, bring the Nerf, and you'll probably have a pickup game going on before you know it.

If you get restless, take a walk downtown. Stroll down College Street and keep your eyes on the ground, where you'll see dozens of Auburn greats immortalized in the cement.

Early games can be hot and late-season games chilly, so plan accordingly for young ones. And, of course, take plenty of pictures. That way even if the game doesn't reach the level of unforgettable memory, at least you'll have something to jog their memory.

77 Terry Bowden

On January 2, 2009, Terry Bowden stood before a crowd of roughly 100 people at the University of North Alabama and celebrated his return to college football after a more than decade-long hiatus.

Terry Bowden amassed a 47–17–1 record as the head coach at Auburn before resigning midway through the 1998 season.

When Bowden resigned from Auburn in the middle of the 1998 season, no one thought it would be this long before he reentered the game. And few would have imagined that the scion of one of college football's most prominent families would have to restart his career at such a low rung on the coaching ladder.

But the departure from Auburn soured Bowden's enthusiasm on the game. And when he wanted back in many years later, he found few takers. That's why he found himself in Florence, Alabama, on that day, grateful and eager to coach a successful Division II program in a state where he had both great successes and great failures.

"Thank you for making me feel like this is going to be my home," Bowden said. "I apologize for getting emotional, because I've been wanting this for a long time. I've known in my heart that it was meant that I come back into coaching.

"It had to be the right time and it had to be the right place. A couple of years ago, I knew I had to get back in. The passion came back to coach football. They say don't go into football because you love it but because you can't live without it. I knew a couple of years ago I couldn't live without it."

On paper, Bowden's record as a head coach was difficult to match. He was 111–53–2 in 15 years at Salem (West Virginia) College, Samford University, and Auburn. He took Samford to the brink of a national championship and was voted Coach of the Year in 1993 after leading Auburn to an undefeated record.

Coach of the Year

Tommy Tuberville won five Coach of the Year awards after Auburn's undefeated 2004 season. He was honored by the SEC, the American Football Coaches Association, Schutt Sports, and the Associated Press. He also became the second Auburn coach to win the Paul "Bear" Bryant Award. Terry Bowden was honored in 1993.

Bowden won 20 straight to start his Auburn career, but left when the program began to unravel in 1998. He said he quit after a 1–5 start because he would have been fired after the season, anyway. Many Auburn fans found the departure distasteful, no matter what the circumstance.

Bowden took time off, then started dabbling in television and radio. He became a frequent guest on the speaker circuit, started writing a weekly Yahoo Sports column, and became an avid blogger, even sharing recipes and weight-loss tips with anyone who cared to read.

For two seasons he tried hard to get back into coaching and nearly got the West Virginia job when Rich Rodriguez departed for Michigan after the 2007 season. But other attempts were less successful. He got barely a sniff from schools like Iowa State and San Diego State, despite open lobbying and campaigning for the jobs.

He knew he couldn't go another off-season without a job, so he jumped when the North Alabama Lions, a perennial Division II power, showed interest.

"The purpose I was longing for was to make an impact on young people's lives," Bowden said. "[In] television and broadcasting and writing…you reach millions but you touch nobody. In coaching, you touch individuals and you have an ability to make an impact.

"Maybe I just hit my middle-age crisis and I knew I had to look in the mirror and say, 'Is this what I want to do the rest of my life?' I knew I had to get back to what I thought was my purpose."

Although it was expected that Bowden would go into the family business, he took an unusual path to get to that point. His father, Bobby, is a longtime head coach at Florida State and one of the game's most celebrated figures. Brothers Tommy (a former head coach at Tulane and Clemson) and Jeff (a former coordinator at FSU) are both in the business.

Bowden attended West Virginia, graduating magna cum laude with an accounting degree. He did postgraduate work at Oxford

University in England and then earned a law degree at Florida State. The coaching world beckoned, but Bowden continued to pursue an unconventional direction. He became the nation's youngest head coach when he was hired by Salem College in 1983 at age 26. After a year as an assistant at Akron, Bowden moved to Samford, his dad's alma mater, in 1987, where he directed a successful transition to Division I-AA scholarship football.

His final coaching leap was the biggest, and in many ways, the most unexpected. Auburn officials interviewed seven candidates, but settled on the young coach just up Highway 280. Still only 36, Terry joined his father as the sixth father-son coaching pair in the NCAA but the first at major universities.

Beneath the surface, the story may have been far less happy. Bowden retained five coaches from Pat Dye's staff, but he also later claimed in a series of recordings that he inherited a corrupt system of paying players. Despite his coaching lineage, Bowden's youth and lack of major-college experience may have made him a bit naïve about what he would encounter when he got to Auburn.

Bowden's first two years were brilliant and the plaudits rolled in. But Auburn was ineligible for bowls in 1993 and 1994 because of NCAA sanctions, and the program seemed to decline when many of the Dye-recruited players were gone. The Tigers went 16–8 overall and 9–7 in the SEC in 1995 and 1996, but seemed to bounce back in 1997.

The Tigers beat Alabama 18–17 in the Iron Bowl to close a nine-win regular season, and then lost a heartbreaking SEC championship game to Tennessee, 30–29. The year ended with a Peach Bowl victory against Clemson, and things seemed to be looking up.

Although many claimed to see the 1998 disaster coming in retrospect, few predicted it at the time. Indeed, it was incredible how rapidly a seemingly strong program had deteriorated. After a blowout loss to Florida in the sixth game, Bowden was gone.

78 Doug Barfield: Following a Legend

Ron Zook's tenure at Florida was short-lived, while Urban Meyer is prospering. Ray Perkins led a succession of brief-tenured coaches at Alabama. Ray Goff never approached Vince Dooley's success at Georgia.

It's accepted as gospel in the coaching business: following a legend is never easy and sometimes almost impossible.

That's the situation Doug Barfield was thrust into when he was tapped to succeed Ralph "Shug" Jordan when the legendary coach retired after the 1975 season. Barfield lasted five seasons and went 29–25–1, including two games later forfeited by Mississippi State due to NCAA sanctions.

There were two distinctive years in his tenure. In 1977, his second year, Auburn was 5–0 in the SEC and competing for a conference title until the last game of the season, a 48–21 loss to then–No. 2 Alabama. Amazingly, Auburn lost all four of its non-conference games that year—to Southern Mississippi, North Carolina State, Georgia Tech, and Florida State—finished 6–5, and was left out of a bowl game.

Two years later, Barfield had his best season. The Tigers went 8–3, losing to Tennessee, Alabama, and a very good Wake Forest team. But the Tigers regressed in 1980, losing every conference game, and Barfield was let go.

"It's fairly traumatic when you get canned," Barfield said recently. "But you get in the profession realizing that it could happen."

After his Auburn tenure ended, Barfield was a successful high school coach in Alabama, coaching at Hillcrest-Evergreen,

Andalusia, and Opelika. He was athletics director at UMS-Wright in Mobile until 2001.

Even after retirement, Barfield didn't really retire. He went to work for the Alabama High School Athletic Association and later became director of sports medicine for Encore Rehabilitation.

Though the Tigers made no bowl games and went 0–5 against Alabama during his five years on the Plains, Barfield's tenure will be remembered as a bridge between the Jordan and the Dye eras.

"I made a lot of friends there," Barfield said. "I still have some good memories, along with those that aren't so good."

Unlike most modern coaches who exit with a fat severance check, Barfield made only $48,000 in his final year at Auburn.

"I might change a few things along the way, but I would do it all over again," he said.

How Auburn Snagged Carnell Williams

In the winter of 2000 Carnell Williams was the state of Alabama's top recruit. But to Tommy Tuberville and the Auburn coaching staff, he was more than that. He was a once-in-a-career player, the type of athlete who fit Auburn's rushing attack so perfectly that it would be a crime to see him play anywhere else.

So when news leaked that Williams had verbally committed to Tennessee, Tuberville didn't panic. Instead, he directed an elaborate recruiting effort centered on Williams' living room in Attalla, Alabama. The prep running back wasn't going to get away without a fight.

"I wanted to show him how important he was to our program," Tuberville said.

Tuberville grabbed six assistant coaches—everyone available—and hit the road for Attalla, an old railroad town of about 7,000 people not far from Gadsden. The impressive show of strength spilled from Williams' living room into the kitchen, where Williams found extra chairs to accommodate the larger-than-expected group.

The unorthodox recruiting strategy paid off. Williams had been impressed. By the time the coaches stood up to depart, Williams had agreed to take an official visit to Auburn. He would eventually change his mind about becoming a Volunteer and sign instead with the Auburn Tigers.

"It just makes you feel that much more special as a player," Williams said later. "He just did something different. Most coaches just bring two or three coaches, but he brought his whole staff."

Tuberville said the plan succeeded because he set modest expectations. He didn't want Williams to immediately renounce the Vols or commit to the Tigers. He just wanted Williams to visit campus.

"I came real close [to going to Tennessee]," Williams said. "After my visit with them, I really felt like that's where I was going. Coach Tub came to my home and changed my mind. I came on a visit and liked it much better than Tennessee."

Williams wasn't the only Tiger who nearly went to Knoxville. Ronnie Brown, Williams' longtime partner in the backfield, also committed to Tennessee before choosing Auburn. He was spooked by an academic tutoring scandal going on at Tennessee at the time.

"I felt pretty comfortable [in Auburn], so it was pretty much a toss-up," Brown said. "When that started going on, I just thought about them being on probation and stuff like that and just decided I'd come to Auburn."

The loss of the two backs had to be particularly vexing for Tennessee coach Phillip Fulmer. In 2004, the senior season for both

Williams and Brown, the Tigers routed the Volunteers 34–10 at Neyland Stadium on their way to the Sugar Bowl and a perfect season.

After his change of heart, Williams continued to get calls from Fulmer—always friendly, he stressed—but stuck with the Tigers.

"If I could do it all over again," Williams said, "I would choose Auburn again."

80 The Coldest Game Ever in Alabama? The 2000 Iron Bowl

Auburn fans are unlikely to experience the Ice Bowl on the Plains or even on any SEC road trip. Sure, it can occasionally get chilly in Fayetteville, Arkansas, or Lexington, Kentucky, but most of the SEC's games are played in temperate Southern autumn temperatures.

The exceptions are always interesting, and not always pleasant.

When Auburn traveled to Morgantown, West Virginia, in 2008 to play the West Virginia Mountaineers, gallons of ink were spilled debating the impact the weather would have on the game. After all, Morgantown represented the northernmost city in which Auburn had played outdoors since opening the 1984 season in East Rutherford, New Jersey, against Miami (Florida). And it was the northernmost city in which Auburn has played later than Columbus Day (October 13) since a trip to Villanova in Philadelphia on November 22, 1941.

As it turned out, all the fret was largely for nothing. The game was brisk but hardly cold, although television viewers who saw the parka-clad Tommy Tuberville could be excused for thinking otherwise.

Typically, the biggest weather threat comes late in the season—and that means the Iron Bowl. Alabama-Auburn games are played in the back end of November, which means chilly temperatures can be a factor, especially during night games.

The 2000 Iron Bowl in Tuscaloosa was the coldest Auburn game of the decade, according to Auburn's sports information staff. Temperatures prior to 2000 are either unavailable or too tedious to dig up.

In any case, while it probably wasn't the coldest Auburn game ever played, it probably felt a lot like it to the fans and participants. It's a good bet that Auburn fans felt just a little warmer. The game-time temperature was 41 degrees on the gray and dark November day, but it seemed to plummet as the game went on. Fans were pelted with a chilly rain that turned slushy and then icy in the second half.

It didn't help that the game was incredibly boring. Auburn managed three field goals. Alabama didn't score at all.

At the start of the year, the Tide had hoped to celebrate a successful season and win its first Iron Bowl at Bryant-Denny Stadium. Instead, the atmosphere was like that of a funeral. Mike DuBose had resigned and was finishing out a miserable 3–8 year.

Alabama fans quickly cleared out. When word filtered around the stadium that Mississippi State had lost its game, the hardy Auburn fans remaining could celebrate an SEC West title in only Tommy Tuberville's second year.

The Tide finished with three wins, matching its preseason No. 3 ranking. Mike DuBose choked back tears in his final press conference.

"No one thought that Auburn's fans would chant 'SEC! SEC!' in Bryant-Denny Stadium this season," wrote Joe Medley of the *Anniston Star*. Auburn's players could be heard chanting those three letters from their locker room as coach Tommy Tuberville spoke from across the tunnel to media.

"At the beginning of the year, I put up on my wall, in my office, in my locker downstairs, we were picked bottom 50 in the country," Tuberville said. "We talked about it with our players. I think we've overcome that a little bit."

In 1999, Tuberville's first year, Alabama spoiled the 10-year anniversary of the first Iron Bowl played at Jordan-Hare Stadium. Tuberville was glad for revenge at the first Iron Bowl at Bryant-Denny.

"This is a game for all of Auburn University," he said. "When you play Alabama, you're playing for the right to brag about it, and to beat them on the road, I mean it took them 10 years to beat Auburn in Auburn.

"It took us one year."

81 Fob James

The life story of Fob James encompasses that unique American intersection of sports and politics.

Of course, being a sports hero is no guarantee of success in politics. There's a long line of beloved sports figures who could never make the cut in elections. But James is one of those rare individuals who gets to declare on his résumé that not only was he a college football All-American, he was also elected governor. Twice. As a Democrat and a Republican. That's quite an accomplishment, but then James is quite a character.

Forrest Hood "Fob" James Jr. was born September 15, 1934, in Lanett, Alabama. He and his father were named after Confederate generals Nathan Bedford Forrest and John Bell Hood. He went to Baylor Military Academy in Chattanooga, Tennessee, but returned to his home state for college.

As a running back at Auburn, he rushed for 879 yards on 123 carries in 1955, including 178 against Chattanooga. When he left the Plains, he was Auburn's all-time leading rusher with 1,913 yards. The record stood for 21 years.

Fob James left Auburn as the school's all-time leading rusher in 1955, then won two terms as governor of Alabama.

James was named a Movietone News and International News All-American in 1955 and was selected as the SEC's Back of the Year by the Atlanta Touchdown Club. He received his degree in civil engineering in 1956 and didn't leave Auburn before eloping with homecoming queen Bobbie May Mooney of Decatur. James played pro football in Canada for the Montreal Alouettes for a year, then served two years in the U.S. Army Corps of Engineers.

His professional life was equally successful. In 1962 he helped found Diversified Products, a company that eventually had sales of more than $1 billion annually.

James started his career as a Republican. The South was moving in that direction, but Democrats still controlled statewide offices, and after an unsuccessful run for the Republican state executive committee, James switched parties in 1977. In 1978 Governor George Wallace was finishing his third term—and his second consecutively—and could not seek another. James was a long-shot candidate running against former Governor Albert Brewer, Lt. Gov. Jere Beasley, and Attorney General Bill Baxley. But James used extensive television advertising to finish as the largest vote-getter, beat Baxley in the Democratic runoff, and then routed Republican Guy Hunt in the general election.

James distanced himself from Wallace by appointing several African Americans to key cabinet positions, but his tenure was doomed by the bad national economy and struggles dealing with the legislature. He chose not to run for reelection in 1982, paving the way for Wallace to return, yet again, for a fourth and final term.

But James' taste for politics wasn't done. He ran and lost in the Democratic primary in 1986 and 1990. In 1994 James switched back to his original party, qualifying as a Republican at the last moment. He stressed ethics and defeated incumbent Jim Folsom Jr.

By winning the election, James become only the second Republican governor in Alabama in modern times. But in his second term, James was never to reclaim the moderate label he had in first term. He became embroiled in the Ten Commandments controversy and was often lampooned in the media for his whimsical public statements, like wishing the state government ran as well as a Waffle House. Once again, he exited office after one term, this time defeated by Don Siegelman, who campaigned largely on a state lottery that never came to be.

That was it for James' political career, although his son Tim is active in politics and could run for governor in 2010.

Even if his two terms weren't entirely politically successful, James will go down in history as one of Auburn's most notable sons: a star on the football field, a successful businessman, and a savvy politician.

82 Auburn: The "Loveliest Village of the Plains"

Sweet Auburn, loveliest village of the plain,
Where health and plenty cheered the labouring swain,
Where smiling spring its earliest visit paid,
And parting summer's lingering blooms delayed:
Dear lovely bowers of innocence and ease,
Seats of my youth, when every sport could please,
How often have I loitered o'er thy green,
Where humble happiness endeared each scene;
How often have I paused on every charm,
The sheltered cot, the cultivated farm,
The never-failing brook, the busy mill,
The decent church that topped the neighbouring hill,
The hawthorn bush, with seats beneath the shade,
For talking age and whispering lovers made.

So begins "The Deserted Village," a poem by Anglo-Irish poet Oliver Goldsmith. According to legend, it was this pastoral poem about the little village of Auburn written in 1770 that inspired the founders of Auburn, Alabama, about 60 years later.

The legend holds that Judge John J. Harper was leading some of the original settlers of Auburn in the 1830s. His son Thomas stayed the night in Jones County, Georgia. It was there he met 15-year-old Lizzie, who had just read the poem and suggested that the new village be named Auburn. Thomas later married Lizzie, they moved to Auburn, and presumably lived happily ever after.

While the first line or two of the poem is often quoted, few people realize that the entire work is some 3,400 words and not easily digestible in a single sitting. There are a few other quirks. While the Alabama village is fondly referred to as "the plains," the poem never uses that term, although the phrase "plain" is used five times. And while the poem does in fact celebrate the beauty of "Auburn," its tone is wistful, mourning the demise of the countryside to the rapacious growth of the cities.

The poem took Goldsmith about two years to write and was published on May 26, 1770. It was an immediate hit, running through six different editions in its first year. Goldsmith's aim was to illustrate the evils of accumulation of wealth and the decay of the villages and countryside.

Where was Goldsmith's Auburn? Many point to the Irish village of Lissoy, where Goldsmith grew up and where his brother was a curate. But other critics say the Auburn of the poem is "distinctly an English village," and "doubtless Goldsmith mingled his recollections of both countries."

Goldsmith was born about 1730, the second son of Rev. Charles Goldsmith. He was admitted to Trinity College in Dublin as a sizar, essentially a scholarship student. He managed to graduate after the death of his father and his participation in a school riot, but failed to be ordained by the Church.

After several short attempts to pursue a career in medicine, Goldsmith began traveling—and writing. He joined a literary circle with other writers of the age like Samuel Johnson and published works like *The Vicar of Wakefield* (1766), *The Deserted Village*, and a handful of plays. He also gained a reputation as a hack for the prolific output needed to pay his tremendous debts. The story of Goldsmith's life is often written in tragic terms. He died at about the age of 44.

While the literary quality of Goldsmith's poem is respected, some of his critiques of modernization have been disputed. Goldsmith's grand-nephew, also named Oliver, emigrated to Canada, where he wrote "The Rising Village," a much more optimistic view of pastoral life in the New World.

83 Auburn's Athletic Facilities

Auburn fans worried about their standing in the facilities arms race are usually focused on the size, infrastructure, and amenities of Jordan-Hare Stadium. But the most important enhancements happening on campus right now might be a few blocks to the west. That's where Auburn is building new student residential housing that will help bolster the university's on-campus housing inventory and give athletic teams an attractive option to pitch to recruits.

Athletic dorms or sport-specific dorms have long been banned by the NCAA under the idea that student-athletes shouldn't be segregated from the rest of the campus community, nor should they get special perks in housing. But coaches have complained that it was a lot easier to keep tabs on athletes (and keep them out of trouble) when they were living in a nearby dorm. Eventually, clever schools figured out a compromise. They build gleaming new on-campus residential centers, offer 51 percent of the rooms to regular students, and have 49 percent available for athletes.

Many—or perhaps most—Auburn football players live off campus. But for the youngsters who live on campus, their housing options are dreary. Many players reside in Sewell Hall, which may have been a nice place to live in the 1960s (although probably not) but is far from state-of-the-art today. Sewell Hall's biggest asset is its location. It's a short walk across the street from Auburn's athletic complex and football practice fields, and it's also next to the dining hall that players use for their daily training table meal.

The new dorms will still be a short walk from Jordan-Hare Stadium and the athletics complex, and they'll offer a view of Auburn's new basketball arena, which is being built next door.

They'll also let Auburn football coach Gene Chizik offer potential freshmen a nice future residence, rather than forcing him to gloss over the details of Sewell Hall on the campus tour.

The roughly $90 million basketball arena is expected to rejuvenate Auburn's struggling men's basketball program, but it could also have an impact on football. Why? A good basketball team gives the football team an opportunity to spice up recruiting trips. Auburn's basketball coaches love taking recruits to football games to let them soak in the atmosphere. But there's not much atmosphere for football recruits to soak in at Beard-Eaves-Memorial Coliseum, a place that is often bleak, depressing, or both.

What else is in the works or on the agenda for the football program? The coaches' offices at the athletic complex were recently spruced up, and the locker rooms were revamped and expanded. Hot tubs, cold tubs, and swimming rehab pools were updated. Architects carved a lounge area out of increased locker room space.

Former coach Tommy Tuberville would amusingly press for a 100-yard indoor football facility whenever a few drops of rain hit.

Auburn's athletic facilities are in the process of being upgraded, including new office space and player dorms.

Auburn's current 40-yard indoor facility is largely useless for anything other than simple drills. The Tigers do have a 100-yard outdoor turf field that is helpful during drizzles. A 100-yard indoor facility is in the department's master plan, according to athletics director Jay Jacobs, but it's not on the front burner. The new building will eventually go on the site of the old track, which is behind Auburn's grass practice fields and across Biggio Drive.

Down the street at Jordan-Hare Stadium, other work has been completed in the last several years. Spiffier luxury boxes and new scoreboards have been added. The fuzzy public-address system has been reconditioned. Improvements have been made in restrooms and concessions.

Outside the stadium, the entranceways have been adorned in an attractive brick facade. A plaza was built outside the ticket windows near Donahue Drive, but that "quick fix" will eventually be improved and expanded and tie into the new arena and residence halls near the stadium.

Now the big question: just how big will Jordan-Hare Stadium get? Right now it seats 87,451 fans. Expansion plans are out there, but they aren't a pressing short-term priority. For now, at least, bigger isn't better.

84 Dameyune Craig

His promising coaching career followed a rewarding playing career. Now Dameyune Craig is back home. The only question is how long he will be there before a major program snatches him up again.

A former Auburn and NFL quarterback with an impeccable reputation in the football business, Craig was hired in January 2008 to be part of the first coaching staff at the University of South

Alabama. South Alabama is starting a Bowl Subdivision (Division I-A) football program from scratch with plans to start limited competition in 2009. Craig was the first assistant hired by USA head coach Joey Jones and might be one of the most important. A native of Prichard, just outside Mobile, Craig knows the region and its high school coaches well.

"[Craig] is a man of great character," Jones said. "I was very impressed with the passion he has for coaching and recruiting, but more importantly, I am impressed with the desire he has to be a positive influence on the young men who will play here at South Alabama."

Craig went to Blount High School, a football powerhouse that has sent many players into college football over the years. Even though he grew up as the "baby of the family" and struggled with asthma, it soon became clear that he was an incredible athlete. He won two state titles at Blount and arrived at Auburn with high expectations. He was a backup for longer than expected, playing behind Patrick Nix in 1994 and 1995, but was declared the starter entering the 1996 season.

"Craig had been causing murmurs of amazement at practices for three years," wrote Phillip Marshall in his book *The Auburn Experience*. "He could outrun most of the running backs. He had a knack for escaping seemingly impossible situations. He had a powerful and accurate right arm. Now, at last, he was going to get his chance."

Talk to people who followed Auburn's program closely around that time, and they'll tell you it's no secret why the Tigers crumbled after Craig graduated. He was the glue that held the team together in 1996 and 1997 and might have been one of the most underrated players in the country. The Tigers went 8–4 in 1996, including a four-overtime loss against Georgia, a one-point loss to Alabama, and an Independence Bowl victory against Army. In 1997 Craig passed for 3,277 yards, leading the Tigers to the SEC West title.

Quarterback Dameyune Craig led Auburn to an SEC West title in 1997. In 2008 he joined the coaching staff at the University of South Alabama.

The Tigers reached as high as No. 6 in the national rankings, beat Georgia and Alabama, lost a heartbreaker to Tennessee in the SEC championship game, and then beat Clemson in the Peach Bowl.

The season was all the more remarkable because just one year later Terry Bowden would resign amid a disastrous 1–5 start. Despite playing only two full seasons, Craig is near the top of most Auburn passing categories. He's fifth in career passing yards (6,026) and threw 39 career touchdown passes.

Surprisingly, Craig wasn't drafted by any NFL team. He might not have fit a prototypical NFL mold, or perhaps he just came 10 years too early and would find more teams willing to take a chance on him today. He did, however, catch on with the Carolina Panthers and served as a backup there for four seasons. He also has the distinction of passing for 611 yards and five touchdowns in one game for the Scottish Claymores in NFL Europe.

After a brief stint in arena ball, Craig got started on his coaching career. He served as an assistant at Blount before getting the call to join Nick Saban as a graduate assistant at LSU. He followed Saban to the NFL's Miami Dolphins, then coached quarterbacks at Division II Tuskegee for two seasons.

Now he's back home at South Alabama, helping start a program from the ground up.

"This," said Craig, "is a great opportunity."

85 Topping Florida in 2001

Florida entered Jordan-Hare Stadium on October 13, 2001, as the No. 1 team in the nation. When the game was over, Auburn fans were raiding the goalposts, and Florida coach Steve Spurrier was forced to acknowledge, "They were definitely the best team out there."

Florida's hopes for a national title and an SEC crown were dashed, although the Gators still finished No. 5 in the nation. But the victory would be the highlight for what would otherwise be a strange 2001 season for the Tigers.

Auburn went 7–4 in the regular season, losing to Syracuse (in the first game played in New York after the September 11 attacks) and LSU (in a game rescheduled at the end of the season due to the attacks). In between, Auburn lost to Arkansas and Alabama by wide margins and narrowly survived an overtime upset bid by Louisiana Tech only seven days after the Florida win. But for one day, in the wind and rain at Jordan-Hare Stadium, Auburn managed to put everything together and pull off a stunning upset.

Quarterback Daniel Cobb was at the heart of the victory. Returning from a shoulder injury, Cobb replaced starter Jason Campbell and completed 11 passes for 152 yards. Kicker Damon Duval hit a 44-yard field goal—his third game-winning kick in as many weeks—to give the Tigers a 23–20 win.

"It doesn't get any bigger than this," said Auburn coach Tommy Tuberville.

While the late fireworks were on offense, it was the defense that carried much of the load, holding Florida's top-ranked scoring offense 29 points below its average. Middle linebacker Phillip Pate, just back from knee surgery, caught his first career interception in the third quarter. Reserve Mayo Sowell intercepted a pass in the fourth. Karlos Dansby picked off yet another to set up Auburn's game-winning drive.

"It's not Houdini. It's not magic," said linebacker James Callier. "No one thought we could do it.… It is a surprise to the world, but we kept saying we believe, and we're going to shock the world."

The same Florida receivers who caught eight touchdowns passes in two games against the Tigers in 2000 had only two on this day.

"We wanted to make them have to work for it and not let them score easily," said then–defensive coordinator John Lovett. "We wanted to keep the game close, because they're not used to that, and we thought they might get a little impatient.... It was an 11-man effort on defense. It was an entire defense playing well together."

"What transpired at blustery Jordan-Hare Stadium," wrote the *Anniston Star*'s Phillip Tutor, "proved to be the quintessential story—maybe the textbook case, even—about how an unranked and underdog team should go about playing college football's high and mighty. No, Auburn didn't do everything right. Daniel Cobb fumbled into the end zone. Casinious Moore fumbled, too. The Tigers' defense let one of those road-runner Florida receivers get behind it for an 80-yard touchdown. Perfection it was not. But style didn't matter. Who cares about style? What mattered was that Tommy Tuberville's team laughed at the doubters...dug in and did its job."

86 Alabama-Auburn Freshman Game of 1968

Freshmen weren't eligible to participate when Pat Sullivan and Terry Beasley played, so that means fans eager to see the two sensations on the field had to be content with the annual junior varsity game against Alabama.

Normally the games attracted only minimal attention. After all, this was before the era of round-the-calendar recruiting coverage and celebrity high schoolers. But Sullivan and Beasley were different. Everyone knew about them, and every Auburn fan knew what their arrival could mean for the Tigers.

The duo whetted fans' appetites during a high school all-star game in the summer, as Sullivan connected with Beasley three times on long passes. The j.v. game promised more fireworks.

It didn't start out that way. In fact, it started like most of the games of the 1960s. Alabama jumped out to a 27–0 lead and seemed poised to continue its streak of j.v. wins. But the Tigers, led by Sullivan and Beasley, thrilled the crowd with 36 unanswered points and a comeback victory. Beasley caught a 72-yard over-the-shoulder touchdown and had a 38-yard reception to set up another touchdown. He finished his freshman season with 19 catches, 418 yards, and five touchdowns.

The freshmen heroics in what was essentially a meaningless exhibition provided Sullivan and Beasley with confidence when the games were more important.

Two years later, Auburn was in the midst of an impressive 1970 season, marred only by losses to LSU and Georgia. The Tigers were actually favored to win the Iron Bowl against an Alabama team that was struggling uncharacteristically. But the Tide jumped out to a quick 17–0 lead.

"Get ready, Beez," Sullivan supposedly said to his receiver. "We're going to win it just like when we were freshmen."

The Tigers tied the game with two Sullivan touchdown runs and a 26-yard field goal by Gardner Jett. When 'Bama retook the lead with a field goal, Jett answered with a 37-yarder to tie. Sullivan hit Robby Robinett on a 17-yard touchdown pass to give Auburn its first lead. But Alabama quarterback Scott Hunter responded with a 54-yard touchdown pass to George Ranager. The Tide's two-point conversion gave Alabama the lead until Auburn's Wallace Clark dashed in for a winning touchdown with less than four minutes to play.

In a repeat of two years ago, Auburn had come back from a large deficit. Did the freshman game really matter that much?

"Anytime you've been down to somebody like Alabama and you came back and beat them, it has to build your confidence," Sullivan said. "Subconsciously, you think, *We've done it once, we'll be able to do it again.*"

87 Al Del Greco and Other Great Kickers

A consistent kicker is usually taken for granted until he's gone. Then the lack of one becomes a crisis that rears its head every time the team nears the red zone. Auburn has had a string of great kickers in the modern era, many of whom went on to successful careers in the NFL. But none can match the longevity of Al Del Greco.

Del Greco grew up in the Miami area and played both soccer and football at Coral Gables High School. At Auburn, he kicked 110 of 111 extra points and set the SEC record for field goals made and attempted (six out of seven) in a game against Kentucky in 1982. He finished his four-year career with 236 total points, fifth-most in Auburn history, behind only two kickers—John Vaughn and Damon Duval—and two running backs—Carnell Williams and Bo Jackson.

His NFL career lasted an astounding 17 years and included stints with three franchises, Green Bay, St. Louis/Phoenix, and Houston/Tennessee. He was part of three games so memorable they have their own NFL Films–style nicknames: the Comeback (Buffalo-Houston in 1993), the Music City Miracle (Buffalo-Tennessee in the post-1999 playoffs), and the Tackle (Tennessee–St. Louis in Super Bowl XXXIV). Del Greco kicked 347 field goals and 543 extra points and entered 2009 ranked 14th on the NFL's all-time scoring list. He now hosts a popular morning sports talk show in Birmingham, Alabama.

While Miami was a decent distance for an Auburn recruit to travel, Neil O'Donoghue had to make it across the ocean. The native of Dublin, Ireland, started his career as a soccer player at tiny St. Bernard College in Cullman, Alabama, but transferred to Auburn in 1975. He had only seen college football played twice before, and

Kicker Al Del Greco left Auburn fifth on the school's all-time scoring list, then played 17 years in the NFL.

now he was participating in it. He's best remembered for hitting a 57-yard field goal against Tennessee in 1976 that stood as an Auburn record until Philip Yost tied the mark in 2003.

In his first season, O'Donoghue made 9-of-10 field goals from inside the 43. But he was even more impressive in long-range opportunities. In 1975 he kicked a 54-yarder against Mississippi

Notable Auburn Special-Teams Records

Yards-per-kickoff-return average in a game (min. 3): Tim Carter, 46.3 (September 16, 2000, against LSU)

Yards-per-kickoff-return average in a season (min. 10 returns): Rick Neel, 28.1 (1975)

Yards-per-kickoff-return average in a career (min. 20): James Brooks, 27.5 (1979)

Yards-per-punt-return average in a game (min. 3): Mike Fuller, 57.7 (September 21, 1974 against UT-Chattanooga)

Yards-per-punt-return average in a season (min. 10): Mike Fuller, 19.1 (1974)

Yards-per-punt-return average in a career (min. 25): Mike Fuller, 17.6 (1972–1974)

Yards-per-punt average in a game (min. 5): Skip Johnston, 53.3 (November 4, 1978 against Florida)

Yards-per-punt average in a season (min. 30): Terry Daniel, 46.9 (1993)

Yards-per-punt average in a career (min. 100): Terry Daniel, 44.5 (1992–1994)

State and a 53-yarder against Virginia Tech. A year later he had three field goals longer than 50 yards and was named an All-American by *Football News*. O'Donoghue spent nine years in the NFL with three different franchises.

Damon Duval had a curious Auburn career marked by run-ins with Tommy Tuberville and occasionally tuba players in the opposing team's band, but he also managed to put up eye-popping numbers as both a kicker and a punter.

He was named an All-American in 2001 after making 16-of-26 field goals, including three game-winning kicks. His most memorable was a 44-yarder in the wind and rain to help Auburn beat No. 1 Florida at Jordan-Hare Stadium. He was a finalist for the Lou Groza Award and was an All-SEC selection as both a kicker and punter, the first player ever to be recognized at two different positions.

After failing to stick with an NFL team, Duval found a niche in the Canadian Football League, settling in Montreal and playing for the Alouettes. Duval may have even outkicked his coverage, so to speak, when he married the daughter of the team's president and CEO, Larry Smith.

88 The Legend of War Eagle

The best legends shouldn't be scrutinized too closely, and that is certainly the case with "War Eagle." The story is almost certainly a myth, but it's a good myth, and absent any other reliable explanation for the origin of Auburn's cheer, it serves just as well as any.

Legends are by definition unverifiable. They're handed down by tradition and folklore and popularly accepted as historical—or at least as close to historical as we're going to get. Such is the case of the War Eagle legend, which may have been invented by an enterprising *Plainsman* editor in the 1950s.

Auburn's media guide reprints the story annually, although it offers several caveats. It's labeled a "fable" and said that the facts "cannot be authenticated." In any case, here is the story:

It begins in 1864 at the Battle of the Wilderness in Virginia. An Auburn student was fighting with Confederate troops under the command of Gen. Robert E. Lee. He suffered wounds during a long battle and was left for dead on the battlefield. When he regained consciousness, there sat a baby eagle by his side.

The soldier adopted the wounded bird, nursed him to health, and took him to Auburn as a pet of sorts. That student—by now a faculty member—was in attendance on February 20, 1892, the day Auburn and Georgia met in the first installment of what is now the oldest rivalry in the Deep South. The "war eagle," of course, was still at his side.

When Auburn scored the first touchdown, the eagle broke free and soared above the field, prompting Auburn fans to shout "War Eagle!" At the end of the game, the old eagle collapsed and died "having given his all in pursuit of victory for Auburn."

That's the version penned by Jim Phillips in the late 1950s. He probably never expected it to be taken seriously or adopted as a sort of quasi-official history. But his penchant for storytelling earned him that distinction.

There are other versions, of course, although they're not nearly as interesting. Noted Alabama folklorist Kathryn Tucker Windham recounted the following story in her recent book: at a 1913 pep rally at Langdon Hall before a big Auburn-Georgia game, cheerleader Gus Graydon riled up the crowd by shouting, "This is war!" At about that time, cheerleader E.T. Ensen saw something fall from his hat. Ensen, who was in military uniform, soon discovered that a metal eagle had dropped to the ground from his hat. Another student asked what it was, and soon a chant of "War Eagle!" ensued.

Dale Coleman, an Auburn associate professor of animal sciences, endorses that version of the story, which coincides with the introduction of the eagle as a mascot about the same time.

Why "War Eagle?" Windham suggests the phrase does, in fact, have some origins in the Civil War. A fast sailboat, or schooner, was used to slip by the blockade of Mobile Bay and deliver supplies from Bon Secour to the city. Near the end of the war, the *War Eagle* was purposely sunk to prevent the Union from taking it. Later it was raised and rebuilt, and perhaps provided an impetus—conscious or unconscious—for the battle cry that Auburn now uses.

Carlos Rogers

Carlos Rogers was so thrilled when Gene Chizik was hired to be Auburn's new head coach that he caught a flight south, donned a very dapper suit vest, and showed up to greet the new coach in person.

Carlos Rogers won the Jim Thorpe Award as a member of Auburn's 2004 undefeated team.

Rogers was a cornerback on Auburn's undefeated 2004 team for which Chizik was the defensive coordinator, and it was in that season that Rogers won the prestigious Jim Thorpe Award.

"What we did our senior year comes from him coming in my sophomore year and saying, 'Once y'all get my program down, you'll see a difference,'" Rogers said. "In two years, we had it down and y'all know the results.... I have a real tight relationship with him. It was real important to come down here and just see him again. He's like a father to me."

Rogers' endorsement was an important one for Chizik, who was still trying to soothe fans surprised or upset by his hiring.

"We had a coach that loved players and loved football," Rogers said. "You have to take that same enthusiasm and passion he has for the game and tie it into your game."

Rogers was a standout at George D. Butler High in Augusta, Georgia. He made a detour to Hargrave Military Academy before landing at Auburn. His performance didn't always show up in the box scores, largely because opposing quarterbacks usually shied away from testing him, but he grew into a valuable member of Auburn's secondary.

After a solid 2003 season, he announced he would return for his senior season in 2004. That decision was overshadowed by similar choices made by running backs Carnell Williams and Ronnie Brown. But Rogers' choice proved to be just as, if not more, important. His decision to return solidified Auburn's defense and gave him a chance to be part of a special season.

"The things I wanted to do are happening," Rogers said before the season-ending Sugar Bowl. "I'm very proud of the way I handled that situation by coming back and the way the season has been going for me individually and as a team."

Auburn's sports information staff had to crunch some unusual numbers to promote Rogers for postseason awards in 2004 because he didn't have any flashy statistics that would immediately catch voters' eyes. Opposing quarterbacks didn't test him often. Only 17 passes were completed against him in the regular season out of 62 balls thrown his way. Quarterbacks threw to his side only 20 percent of the time (62 out of 309 attempts).

Coaches and scouts picked up those things even if others didn't.

"I think they see a lot of aggressiveness. I think they see a lot of confidence," Chizik said at the time. "They see a guy who will challenge receivers and is not afraid to get up on them and challenge them in both the running game and the passing game. He's got great sudden quickness and he's just been very aggressive whether it be the pass or the run."

Rogers became the highest Auburn defensive back ever drafted when he was selected with the ninth overall pick in the 2005 NFL Draft by the Washington Redskins. Rogers has been a regular starter since the end of his rookie season, although he was sidelined with a knee injury in 2007. He has six career interceptions, including one returned for a touchdown.

90 Jay Jacobs

Jay Jacobs was an Auburn student-athlete and has spent his entire professional life—the last 23 years—working for the Auburn athletic department. But things changed when he moved upstairs to the athletics director's suite in January of 2005. After laboring in relative obscurity for many years, he was now at the forefront of the department, charged with making difficult and sometimes controversial decisions and justifying them to an often skeptical fan base.

In the last year alone, Jacobs has been heckled at the airport, denounced during a pro–Tommy Tuberville march on campus, and been subject to a barrage of message-board vitriol. But Jacobs has stood firm, confident that his decisions have been best for Auburn.

He has always worn his emotions on his sleeve. After his introductory press conference in 2005, Jacobs choked up when talking about having to make tough decisions—like firing coaches—for the greater good of the department and the university. In 2008, when Tuberville resigned, Jacobs got emotional when describing their final conversations.

When Jacobs made his first change, letting a tennis coach go in 2005, few even noticed. But that didn't make the decision any less difficult.

"The thing that people who have had to do that before realize—and maybe the thing that people who have never had to do before don't realize—is that it doesn't really matter whether they are the best-known coach or the least-known coach," Jacobs said. "When you sit in front of a person and tell them that they're no longer going to be employed here, it impacts their wife and their children. No great leader lacks compassion, and it's a tough thing to do. However, my responsibility is as the steward of this department, and those decisions have to be made. It's a tough thing to do personally. Professionally, it's the right thing to do. I just have to stay focused on the fact that this isn't my department. This is not about one particular person. It's about what's best for Auburn. I'm not going to make a decision that creates longevity for me. I'm going to make decisions that move Auburn forward."

Jacobs grew up in nearby LaFayette, Alabama, but finished high school in Jacksonville, Florida. He played at Auburn for Pat Dye and stayed on to earn an MBA while serving as an assistant strength coach and graduate assistant. After a few more years on the coaching side, he moved into athletic administration in 1991. He was promoted in 1994 and again in 2001 to head up Tigers Unlimited, the department's fund-raising arm.

When former AD David Housel retired after the 2003 season, former baseball coach Hal Baird assumed departmental responsibilities on a temporary basis while then–interim president Ed Richardson searched for a new director.

Jacobs was one of four finalists, and the only internal candidate. In the post-Jetgate climate, that made many fans suspicious of his candidacy. But Jacobs won over Richardson and got the job. He started just after the undefeated championship season of 2004 and not long after the hirings of baseball coach Tom Slater, men's basketball coach Jeff Lebo, and women's basketball coach Nell Fortner.

At the time, it seemed like a period of calm might be settling over the department after a couple of tumultuous years. "I hope so," Jacobs said in 2005 when asked about that possibility. "But in order to be stable, you can't be static. You've got to keep moving. If you're green, you're growing; if you're ripe, you're rotten. We're going to be green and growing for a long time, I hope.

"Having these folks on board is a great thing, but we've got to produce every day.... This isn't a maintenance program, and we're not going to be status quo."

Sure enough, Slater was let go after the 2008 season and Lebo survived only after a strong finish in 2009.

But the biggest move came after Tuberville's surprise postseason resignation. While many were focused on big names like Florida State's Jimbo Fisher, Georgia Tech's Paul Johnson, or Houston Nutt at Ole Miss, Jacobs conducted a by-the-book search that eschewed some of the coaches who might have been splashy hires.

Tulsa coach Todd Graham and Buffalo coach Turner Gill had good interviews. So did Georgia assistant Rodney Garner, a former Auburn player and coach. But ultimately Jacobs went in a direction that stunned nearly everyone. He hired former Auburn defensive coordinator Gene Chizik from Iowa State.

"The thing that I walk through the door thinking about every day—and I've said it since four years ago when I took the job—my number-one concern is those student-athletes," Jacobs said. "So my number-one concern is what gives them the best chance to compete on the field and in the classroom and in the community. And I know that with the support of the student-athletes and what the football players are going to say about Gene, the Auburn people will latch on to that. The great thing about it is we've got a lot of passionate fans, but when our student-athletes start responding like they have the last few days, the Auburn people will adjust to that. Here's a guy who went undefeated here as a defensive coordinator, went to Texas, won a national championship as a coordinator, and he's had two years as being experienced as a head coach making some tough choices at a tough place. It's not an easy business. I like all that."

And what about Jacobs' critics? The devout Christian responds, as he frequently does, with passages from the Bible.

"I'm not disappointed at all," he said. "I've just stood on Exodus 14:14 and am going to keep walking by faith and not by sight. And I know that at the end of the day, I'm going to put on my coat of armor from Ephesians 6:10, and I know that we got the right guy here to do the right thing for Auburn. Our student-athletes are going to have an unbelievable experience playing for a guy that loves them and is going to work them as hard as he can possibly work them, push them to a new limit. And all the people will be proud and get on board."

91 Auburn Players in the Hall of Fame

The path to the National Football Foundation's Hall of Fame is rigorous, which means the 12 players and coaches in the Hall with links to Auburn are among the greatest of the great.

Founded in 1951, the National Football Foundation Hall of Fame occupies a handsome building in South Bend, Indiana, where it moved 15 years ago. A replica football field is painted on the building's front concourse.

The process by which candidates are nominated, elected, and enshrined is demanding. For players, the first hurdle is having received major first-team All-America recognition. A player becomes eligible 10 years after his last year of college football. The foundation also takes off-the-field conduct into consideration.

"While each nominee's football achievements are of prime consideration, his post-football record as a citizen is also weighed," the NFF guidelines state. "He must have proven himself worthy as a citizen, carrying the ideals of football forward into his relations with his community and his fellow man with love of his country. Consideration may also be given for academic honors and whether or not the candidate earned a college degree."

A coach becomes eligible three years after retirement, or immediately following retirement if he is at least 70 years old. Active coaches become eligible at 75—that's why Florida State's Bobby Bowden and Penn State's Joe Paterno are already in. Coaches are required to have coached at least 100 games in 10 years with a .600 winning percentage.

Any NFF member can nominate candidates, who are screened by NFF staff. The NFF membership votes on the approved candidates, and results are forwarded to the group's 13-member "honors court," which ultimately picks the candidates to be enshrined.

Understandably, the 12 players and coaches who came through Auburn have found their own chapters in this book.

But if you ever swing through South Bend, this crowd is worth checking out:

- Coach Mike Donahue. Head coach from 1904 to 1906 and 1908 to 1922. Inducted 1951.
- Coach John Heisman. Head coach from 1895 to 1899. Inducted 1954.
- Halfback Jimmy Hitchcock. Played at Auburn from 1930 to 1932. Inducted 1954.
- Center Walter Gilbert. Played at Auburn from 1934 to 1936. Inducted 1956.
- Coach Ralph "Shug" Jordan. Head coach from 1951 to 1975. Inducted 1982.
- Quarterback Pat Sullivan. Played at Auburn from 1969 to 1971. Inducted 1991.

- Fullback Tucker Frederickson. Played at Auburn from 1962 to 1964. Inducted 1994.
- Running back Bo Jackson. Played at Auburn from 1982 to 1985. Inducted 1998.
- Receiver Terry Beasley. Played at Auburn from 1969 to 1971. Inducted 2002.
- Defensive tackle Tracy Rocker. Played at Auburn from 1985 to 1988. Inducted 2004.
- Coach Pat Dye. Head coach from 1981 to 1992. Inducted 2005.
- Running back/linebacker/kicker Ed Dyas. Played at Auburn from 1958 to 1960. Inducted 2009.

92 Auburn in the NFL

The list starts at Tommie Agee, a bruising fullback who spent seven years in the NFL and won back-to-back Super Bowls with the Dallas Cowboys. It ends with running back Mickey Zofko, a late-round pick by the Detroit Lions who lasted four years as a return specialist in the early 1970s.

In between are dozens of former Auburn players who made it to the National Football League. Some were there for just a cup of coffee. Others made lasting careers.

Offensive tackle Willie Anderson, a Vigor High graduate from Prichard, Alabama, was part of Auburn teams that went 20–1–1 in 1993 and 1994. He left Auburn after his junior season for what has turned out to be a lengthy and lucrative professional career. After 12 seasons as an every-game starter with the Cincinnati Bengals, he signed a free-agent contract with the Baltimore Ravens in 2008.

Anderson has made four Pro Bowls and is among active NFL leaders in number of games started.

Another offensive lineman, Tom Banks, parlayed a late-round draft selection into a 10-year NFL career, making four Pro Bowls as a member of the St. Louis Cardinals from 1971 to 1980.

Forrest Blue was also a four-time Pro Bowl selection during an 11-year career with San Francisco and Baltimore from 1968 to 1978.

Running back James Brooks was a first-round draft selection of the San Diego Chargers in 1981 and survived 12 years in the league. (Unfortunately, he squandered much of his pro riches and was arrested in an embarrassing and highly publicized child-support case in 1999. When he claimed to be "barely literate" as a defense, Auburn mounted an aggressive campaign to cast doubt on that assertion.) Brooks remains 41st on the NFL's all-time rushing list, between Garrison Hearst and Thomas Jones.

Another running back had even more success despite considerably less hype coming out of college. Stephen Davis was only a fourth-round selection of the Washington Redskins in 1996, but went on to a record-setting career for more than a decade. He was the league's top rusher in carries in 2001, and leader in yards per game and touchdowns in 1999. He's in the top 40 all-time in NFL rushes, yards, and rushing touchdowns. Davis won an NFC championship with Carolina in 2003, but narrowly lost in the Super Bowl to New England.

Chris Gray is another offensive-line success story. Picked in the fifth round of the 1993 draft, he's started 170 career games, largely for Miami and Seattle.

The muscle-bound former linebacker/defensive end Kevin Greene still comes by to watch Auburn practice from time to time. In a 15-year career, he made 160 sacks, third in history behind only Bruce Smith and Reggie White.

Linebacker Chris Martin spent 12 years in the league with four teams and has the rare distinction of returning three fumbles for touchdowns. Only seven players have done better.

Fullback Tony Richardson will open his 15th NFL season in 2009. The Daleville (Alabama) High graduate is a three-time Pro Bowl player who has played in 192 career games.

Longevity in the cutthroat league is impressive, but some players manage to pack a lot into shorter careers. William Andrews was a four-time Pro Bowl selection and among the league's leading rushers in his career with the Atlanta Falcons from 1979 to 1983. He blew out his knee and attempted a short-lived comeback in 1986 before retiring. The Falcons retired his jersey out of respect for what he did and what he could have done.

93 Al Borges

Tommy Tuberville may have made the most important hire of his career over lunch at a local barbecue joint. In February 2004, Tuberville called his coaching staff and asked them to meet Auburn's final candidate for its vacant offensive coordinator position. He wanted to see how his coaches would react to their potential colleague in an informal setting. After a few minutes of talking football and eating barbecue, the feedback was unanimously positive.

"The coaches said, 'No question about it. We can learn something from this guy. He can help us,'" Tuberville said. "They were very impressed."

The candidate was Al Borges, a 30-year coaching veteran who forged his reputation out west but had spent two chilly seasons in the coaching purgatory of Indiana. The Auburn job was a chance to revive his career, and Borges would eventually revive Auburn's offense.

Rod Smith

Smith didn't have an invitation to walk on at a Division I school, let alone a scholarship offer.

A speedy high school football player in suburban Atlanta, he had no serious interest from major schools, so he decided to follow his friend, scholarship receiver James Swinton, to Auburn and walk on to the team. Most successful walk-ons are "invited"—that is, they were either recruited out of high school or their arrival on campus is anticipated in some way. Smith just showed up.

But he played on the scout team and quickly turned heads. One catch in particular caught the attention of then-coordinator Al Borges, who was looking for receivers.

Before long, Smith was in the regular rotation. Prior to his junior year in 2007, coach Tommy Tuberville awarded him a scholarship in a team meeting.

Smith became Auburn's most consistent receiver, finishing his career with 114 career catches for 1,598 yards and 10 touchdowns. He's ninth all-time at Auburn in receiving yards and is sixth all-time in receptions.

Borges' four-year tenure on the Plains ended unhappily after the 2007 season, when Tuberville fired him and made the ultimately disastrous move to a spread offense in 2008. But Borges' impact in Auburn's undefeated 2004 season can't be overstated. He inherited an offense with plenty of weapons but no identity, and he helped transform quarterback Jason Campbell into an elite college player.

It's also easy to forget just how incredibly popular Borges was in 2004. To say he was a fan favorite doesn't do him justice. A gregarious talker and football junkie, Borges won over fans with both his offense and his personality. Even after he was let go, Borges could still be seen frequently at Auburn baseball games wearing his trademark Hawaiian shirt and usually lugging at least one of his kids.

But even at the apex of his popularity, he understood the fickle nature of the football business. "Believe me, I appreciate the appreciation," Borges said in 2004. "But you can never take yourself too seriously. In this profession, you're only as good as your last game."

Borges should know. He left a successful gig at UCLA for a new job at California before the 2001 season, jumping at a sizable pay

Al Borges masterminded the Tigers' offense from 2004 to 2007. The team went 42–9 during his four-year tenure.

increase and a chance to turn around the Bears. The move turned out to be a disaster, and when Tom Holmoe was fired a year later, Borges was out of a job. After two years of struggles at Indiana, he jumped at the chance to come to Auburn.

A native of Salinas, California, Borges graduated from Cal State–Chico and had spent virtually his entire coaching career in California or on the West Coast until arriving at Indiana.

His first love was baseball, but he found coaching football more challenging and fun.

"I was about 19 when I had what I call a case of the terrible toos—too small, too slow, too unskilled," Borges said. "I found that the most enjoyable sport to coach was football because you could probably have the most impact on winning and losing."

Borges caught on to the emerging West Coast offense of Bill Walsh's San Francisco 49ers and has used the system throughout his career. His high mark was during UCLA's 20-game winning streak in 1997 through 1998 under quarterback Cade McNown.

Borges freely admitted that for most of his career he tried to keep relationships with players professional, rather than personal. But he made an exception for Campbell, an immensely talented quarterback who had struggled through multiple systems and coordinators at Auburn and had sometimes been made an unfair scapegoat for the team's problems.

In 2004 they teased each other about their roots. "I always mess with him about beaches in California," Campbell said. "He always talks about picturing himself lying on the beach."

Told of this, Borges broke into a laugh. "He doesn't know anything about California," Borges said. "He's so far from California in both distance and thinking that he has no clue. I try to keep him up on what's going on in the world outside of Taylorsville, Mississippi, and Auburn, Alabama, but it's a full-time proposition."

When Campbell was drafted by the NFL's Washington Redskins, Borges and Campbell continued their friendship.

"I don't really get too close to players I coach. But with Jason, I probably let my guard down a little more because I felt like he needed it," Borges said. "He was a guy that needed someone to tell him he was pretty good and get on him when he did it wrong. I probably got closer to him than I did most kids. It's still reflective of our relationship.

"He knows I don't have any life. He can call me and talk about football."

94 Know Where to Eat in Town

Why does this topic deserve its own chapter? Auburn fans should already know where to find a bite to eat on the Plains, right? Perhaps. But the overflowing lines at the chain restaurants on football weekends provide ample evidence that many folks still need a primer on dining options in Auburn and Opelika.

Here are the ground rules for the list: first, these are restaurants with staying power. The restaurant business is a fickle one, and the list is intended to stay accurate for years to come. Second, most of the major national chains are excluded. Nothing against them, but this list is seeking a unique Auburn perspective. Finally, the list is not exhaustive and some are bound to be left off. That doesn't mean they aren't good places to grab a meal.

Classy
- Amsterdam Cafe, 410 S. Gay St. Upscale-casual dining with good food and friendly service. Attractive indoor and terrace seating. Great fresh seafood and regular American fare.
- Arricia, 241 S. College St. This restaurant/bar is tucked away inside the Auburn Hotel and Conference Center. Most fans

recognize it as the home of the weekly *Tiger Talk* radio show. Sunday brunch is a popular treat. Reservations are helpful.

- Provino's, 2575 Hilton Garden Drive. This upscale Italian restaurant is a good place to bring a date.

Affordable Fun

- Loco's, 1120 S. College St. This deli and pub is a popular gathering spot near campus. The service is always friendly and the food is very good. Beers are on tap and affordable. Limited outdoor seating is available in nice weather. Try the black-and-blue burger.
- Momma Goldberg's, 500 W. Magnolia Ave. This Auburn institution is now franchising, believe it or not. A second location is now open at 217 E. Thach Ave. There's even a Momma G's in Tuscaloosa! The sandwiches are still cheap and made fresh, and the nachos remain a simple but satisfying treat.
- Niffer's Place, 1151 Opelika Rd. This quirky Auburn landmark has great specials, including cheap beer, every night, so getting a quick seat can be difficult. The American food is simple but good, and Niffer's is frequented by families and college students alike.
- Veggies to Go, 1650 S. College St. This down-home, meat-and-three joint serves up an entree plus side options every day. The food is ready to go (or eat) in a hurry. In fact, it's usually much faster than a fast-food drive-thru.

Good Lunch Spots

- Block and Barrel Deli, 323 Airport Rd. Offering freshly made deli sandwiches, this is a popular spot for lunch. Located in the shadow of the Auburn-Opelika airport.
- Byron's, 450 Opelika Rd. This barbecue smokehouse is a popular football weekend treat. The restaurant has close

links to Auburn University—Tommy Tuberville was a regular customer—and its catering business is worth trying.

- Chappy's, 754 E. Glenn Ave. This deli bills itself as "New York flavor with Southern hospitality." It's a great place for a quick and affordable lunch, and it also has a very loyal breakfast crowd.

Specialty

- Brick Oven Pizza, 217 N. Gay St. Casual outdoor dining with nice outdoor patio during the summer. Just a few steps from the railroad, so you can wave at the conductors as they come by. Most get pizza, but their calzones and salads are just as good.
- Creole and Seafood Shack, 1288 Shug Jordan Pkwy. This place was a well-kept secret until it was featured on an ESPN broadcast of an Auburn game. Now it's frequently crowded. You can't miss it—it's the "shack" on Shug Jordan near campus.
- Laredo, 1710 Opelika Rd. Probably the most popular Mexican restaurant in town, Laredo is often packed on weekends. Get there early for margarita specials. If there's a wait, Tino's down the street is worth a try.
- Mellow Mushroom, 128 N. College St. The Auburn branch of this popular small chain boasts great pizza and beers. The downtown location is convenient to campus.

95 The Story of Team Chaplain Chette Williams

In the summer of 1999 team chaplain Chette Williams was serving as pastor in Spartanburg, South Carolina, when Tommy Tuberville called him up to offer a new opportunity. Tuberville was Auburn's new head football coach and he was looking for a team chaplain. He could think of no better candidate than Williams.

"I knew when we first talked to Chette he'd be the right guy," Tuberville said in a 2000 interview. "He played here, went through tough times, had a change of attitude, and turned out to be a minister. He enjoys working with young people. He felt like this was his calling. He accepted the challenge and has been a tremendous help."

Williams writes in his memoir, *Hard Fighting Soldier: Finding God in Trials, Tragedies, and Triumphs*, that he was a "mean, bitter, angry young man." He was nearly kicked off the team by coach Pat Dye and then vowed to turn his life around.

Today Williams tries to mentor young people in a similar predicament. As the campus director of the Fellowship of Christian Athletes, Williams is paid by private funds but maintains an office in the athletic complex.

"Nobody is beyond redemption," Williams said. "You want them to turn that switch as soon as you talk to them. It doesn't always happen. You see them going through the same things you went through, and they don't have to. What really breaks your heart is when one has to leave. Some people dismiss that side of it. I can't. Those guys are who I'm here for."

Williams joined Auburn's football program as a walk-on in 1981. But he was unhappy. Plagued by worries over his parents' divorce, he turned to alcohol and marijuana.

"For almost a year and a half, I never smiled," Williams said. "I was just a mad, upset, mean person."

Kyle Collins had the locker next to Williams. "Chette was probably the single most bitter person I've ever been around," Collins said. "I never saw his teeth for a year because he never smiled. In the Bible study group I was in, they asked me who I was going to pray for. When I said Chette Williams, they said, 'Hey, pray for somebody that has a chance.'"

The impetus for Williams' change was Dye's threat to boot him from the team. Dye thought Williams' attitude was beginning to infect younger players. Despondent, Williams sought out Collins.

"I'm not saying God opened up the clouds and spoke to me or anything like that, but I could feel something I'd never felt before," Williams says. "I had all this stuff on me—school, being kicked off the team, my dad's problems, everything. I could just feel it leave me that night."

Collins and Williams went on to become best friends, and Williams decided to make a career of the ministry. That career path landed him back in Auburn in 1999.

In 2004 his impact on the team started garnering national attention, as players on the undefeated team embraced his "Hard Fighting Soldiers" mantra and began walking into the stadium locked arm in arm.

"I hate for people to think it's gimmicky," said nose guard Tommy Jackson. "That's not what it is at all. That's just what happens when guys get close."

96 Fear the Thumb

One of the reasons Auburn coach Tommy Tuberville was so popular with fans—and reporters—is that he didn't take himself too seriously. He wasn't afraid to be provocative, tweaking opponents with a Steve Spurrier–like glee that delighted Auburn fans and flustered opponents. Auburn's winning streak against Alabama provided plenty of fodder for that mischievous side of Tuberville.

Let's start the story in 2005. Auburn was about to vanquish then–No. 8 Alabama for the fourth consecutive game, recording a school-record 11 sacks on the way to a 28–18 win. As the seconds

Tommy Tuberville (and Aubie) warned rival Alabama to "Fear the Thumb" after Auburn's Iron Bowl victory in 2005, then backed up the boast by winning again in 2006, the Tigers' fifth straight victory over the Crimson Tide.

ticked off the clock, the Jordan-Hare Stadium scoreboard zeroed in on Tuberville. Perhaps spontaneously, perhaps not, Tuberville raised four fingers. The crowd immediately roared its approval. But some Alabama fans simmered.

Meanwhile, Auburn fans started thinking about No. 5. A month after that fourth-consecutive win, as Auburn arrived for bowl practice in Orlando, Florida, Tuberville was photographed outside the team hotel wearing a "Fear the Thumb" T-shirt—the thumb being the fifth digit to be raised if Auburn were to win a fifth-consecutive time. The photo was circulated through email in-boxes and message boards, and an unlikely catchphrase was born.

Soon fans could order "Fear the Thumb" T-shirts, hats, and sunglasses, most featuring an Aubie-like character menacingly holding up a paw with four raised digits.

It seemed like tailor-made bulletin board material for the 2006 game. In the week leading up the Iron Bowl, Auburn players were unanimous in their hesitance to talk about the Thumb. Even Tuberville, while never expressing regret for his fashion choice, downplayed the incident.

"You really don't need any motivation to play this game," he said. "It's going to be good talk in the newspapers, I'm sure."

He was right about that. In the days leading up the Iron Bowl, when media interest in the state sometimes approaches an absurd level, talk of the Thumb dominated talk radio and Internet conversation. "That's a fan deal," said Auburn receiver Courtney Taylor, summing up the views of most of his teammates. "We know every year we're in for a war with these guys." Still, Taylor admitted, if he were an Alabama player, the endless Thumb talk would get on his nerves. "Those guys are going to be fired up anyway," he said. "The Fear the Thumb deal, that's just adding to the fire."

Needless to say, when Auburn won number five —a 22–15 victory in Tuscaloosa—the celebration was especially sweet.

For the Auburn seniors who left college with an unblemished record, the bragging rights would never end. "I can live the rest of my life here and never have to answer any questions about this rivalry," said offensive guard Ben Grubbs, a native of Eclectic, Alabama. "I'll be the only one talking. I can tell my kids that I never lost to Alabama."

Win No. 6 came with a 17–10 win at Jordan-Hare Stadium on November 24, 2007. Perhaps feeling win No. 7, Tuberville held up seven digits while celebrating a flag football win with troops during his tour of the Middle East. (The image was, of course, widely circulated back home.)

Auburn wasn't so fortunate in 2008, as the streak ended with Alabama's emphatic 36–0 victory. Rather than hold up an index finger—or even a less polite digit—to signal No. 1, many Tide fans responded with seven fingers of their own to represent Auburn's seven losses.

"All streaks must come to an end," Tuberville said. "And ours came to a screeching halt."

97 Bowden's First and Last Seasons

The final days of Terry Bowden remain shrouded in controversy more than a decade after his departure from Auburn University. For a tenure that started with almost unprecedented promise and enthusiasm, Bowden's demise was incredibly sudden.

Let's start at the beginning. The undefeated season in 1993. The 20 consecutive victories to start his tenure. The excitement that seemed to suggest that Auburn had latched onto a coach that would one day be mentioned alongside legends of the sport.

After the lofty start, the Tigers hummed along smoothly, having solid if unspectacular eight-win seasons in 1995 and 1996. While many claimed to see signs of imminent downfall leading up to the 1998 season, few had the courage to voice those opinions. Only with the benefit of hindsight have many said that they saw it coming.

It's worth remembering that entering the 1998 season, Bowden had posted a sterling record of 46–12–1 and was coming off a 10-win season that ended with a narrow loss to Tennessee in the SEC Championship Game and a victory over Clemson in the Peach Bowl.

But the 1998 season started on a sour note almost immediately. The Tigers were shut out 19–0 by Virginia at Jordan-Hare Stadium. After recovering with a solid victory a week later at Ole Miss, Auburn lost four consecutive games to start the season 1–5. Auburn didn't play particularly well in any of those four straight losses, but three of the opponents (LSU, Tennessee, and Florida) were ranked in the top 10. In other words, the Tigers weren't losing to weak teams.

While the 1–5 record was certainly alarming, it wasn't cause for program-altering panic. Was it?

After the 24–3 loss at Florida, athletics director David Housel said he met with Bowden and told him he needed to put together a plan to share with the president and others that would describe how to restore the program to its formerly healthy shape. "No mention was made of staff changes, only that a plan must be prepared to assure Auburn people, especially alumni leaders, that the 1–5 start was an aberration in an otherwise strong program," Housel wrote in his recent book.

Bowden evidently didn't interpret his discussion with Housel, or the planned postseason evaluation, in such an innocuous light. He asked specifically whether he would be fired. Housel said he replied that while staff changes were never discussed, "the 1–5 start made it clear that concerns needed to be addressed."

"Well if that's the case, I'll just quit right now," Bowden said, according to Housel. Bowden returned later to say that he had changed his mind and would "fight for his job," starting with his radio show that evening. But those listening to the show would hear no such impassioned plea.

The next day, Housel wrote, Bowden's attorney showed up at the athletic complex and said Bowden wanted to resign immediately. That day. One day before Auburn's game against Louisiana Tech.

Bowden would say that he resigned because he was convinced he would be fired. That explanation didn't satisfy the fans who believed the coach quit on his team.

No matter the quality of Louisiana Tech, it's remarkable that Auburn's players managed to put aside the distractions enough to win the game 32–17. Interim coach Bill Oliver finished the season 2–3, picking up another nonconference win against Central Florida but losing by respectable margins to Arkansas, Georgia, and Alabama.

Oliver would throw his hat into the ring for the head-coaching job that would eventually go to Tommy Tuberville.

Because of the unusual, soap-operatic quality of Bowden's departure, Auburn faced an intense national media glare and earned a reputation for administrative meddling and impatience that persists to this day. That view isn't entirely fair, of course, but few dispute that the wounds from Bowden's last season took time to heal.

98 Know Where to Grab a Cold One

Whether your college days ended decades ago or they're still in progress, it never hurts to have a place to celebrate a win or drown your sorrows after a loss. Auburn has a wide variety of pubs, clubs, and taverns—some glamorous, others dives.

Like the restaurant list, this list will focus on bars that are local, distinctive, and hopefully will keep their doors open (although the precariousness of the bar business makes that difficult to predict).

On a per-capita basis, Auburn probably has fewer bars than most SEC towns. City residents probably don't consider that a bad thing, but the lack of competition means lack of variety and few of the outrageous specials for which college towns are known. This list is far from exhaustive—in particular, it doesn't include many of the places down Wire Road—but it's a good starting point for the novice.

Classy

- Eight and Rail, 807 S. Railroad Ave., Opelika. Nestled in a historic portion of downtown Opelika, this upscale spot is best known for its extensive martini list. Comfortable seats and candlelighting give the place an attractive ambiance.

College Crowd

- 17–16, 154 E. Magnolia Ave. Yes, this bar is named for the final score in the iconic "Punt, 'Bama, Punt!" game. But don't expect a sports bar–style atmosphere with memorabilia on every bit of wall space. The owners spent oodles of money renovating the place, and the brick interior gives it a classier touch. The crowd can range from undergrad to grad to older, depending on the night.
- Bodega, 101 N. College St. The bar stands on an iconic corner of College Street and Magnolia Drive in the old Auburn Bank building. The big windows provide a nice view of Toomer's Corner. On crowded nights, patrons can use an upstairs bar with pool tables and a Nintendo Wii. The large back deck is also popular on warm evenings.
- In Italy, 145 E. Magnolia Ave. This is an upscale bar with a large college clientele. It has a sleek, modern design with plenty of comfortable couch seating.
- Olde Auburn Ale House, 124 Tichenor Ave. Attractive tavern-style arrangement with plenty of seating. The ale house brews its own beers and can recommend the right one for your taste.
- Quixote's, 129 N. College St. This building has been through many different incarnations, but the current name has stuck for several years now. The establishment has front

and back patios, a stage for bands, and a large wraparound bar. Check out the specials. There's usually something good before 9:00 PM.

- War Eagle Supper Club, 2061 S. College St. This quintessential dive bar is an Auburn institution. Membership is required—it is a "club," after all—but the fee is only nominal.
- Sky Bar, 136 W. Magnolia Ave. A club to see and be seen. Frequently a line and a steep cover on busy nights. You might draw stares if you're over 30.

99 Tony Franklin and Gus Malzahn

When Gus Malzahn was introduced as Auburn's new offensive coordinator just after Christmas Day in 2008, he spoke cautiously. He knew Auburn had an uneasy relationship and an ugly breakup with the spread offense, so he chose his terms with care.

He didn't talk much about the "spread." Instead he used phrases like "smashmouth," "physical," and "run-first" to describe what his offensive philosophy would be like under first-year Auburn coach Gene Chizik.

And what about his predecessor, Tony Franklin, who was fired by Tommy Tuberville in the middle of the 2008 season? "I'm not very familiar with him," Malzahn said. "I've never met him. I'm not very familiar with his system and can't tell you much about it."

Malzahn produced one of the nation's top offenses at Tulsa in 2006 and 2007. But he said the spread stereotypes go out the window after that.

"We're going to be a run, play-action team," Malzahn said. "I know a lot of people categorize me as a spread team, [but] if you really look back at my history, we're going to play smashmouth football. We're going to set up the pass with the run. I really think the difference [between] us and most run/play-action teams is we're going to throw the ball vertically down the field and we're going to do that quite often."

Although he had no prior relationship with Malzahn, Chizik said he knew the coach by reputation and targeted him from the beginning of his search. He gave Malzahn full autonomy to run the offense without interference.

"I don't want to micromanage," Chizik said. "I think that's why you hire great people. I know with Gus what I'm getting. I've seen it. I've done my homework on this one. I feel very comfortable with Gus running the offense. Period."

Former Auburn head coach Tommy Tuberville hired spread guru Tony Franklin to much fanfare just after the 2007 season. But Franklin was fired at midseason after the offense struggled and he failed to mesh with Tuberville's existing assistant coaches.

Malzahn, on the other hand, is getting in on the ground floor with a first-year head coach. He didn't even have to reference Franklin's struggles because he went through a similar experience himself. His one-year stint at Arkansas in 2006 produced 10 wins but also was marred by a soap opera atmosphere involving head coach Houston Nutt, parents of some of the players, and assistant coaches.

Malzahn was quickly hired by first-year head coach Todd Graham at Tulsa, where Malzhan cemented his reputation as an offensive innovator, leading the Golden Hurricane to the nation's top-ranked offensive production in 2007 and number two in 2008.

"Any time you can get in on the front end and you actually can establish your plan and build it like you need to build it, I think that's very important," Malzahn said.

That was a luxury that Franklin didn't have in the 10th and ultimately final season of Tuberville's Auburn tenure. Franklin came to

Auburn from Troy after a phone call that he never expected about a job that he didn't even bother striving for. The idea that a spread offense guru would find a home at Auburn, a team built around a running attack and a strong defense, was too fanciful for Franklin to even entertain.

"I was basically a little taken aback when [Auburn] called me," Franklin said. "It was not something I ever thought would happen."

Franklin spent two seasons building a nationally recognized offense at Troy. Before that, he helped dozens of high schools install his system—a fast-paced, spread offense with multiple receivers and almost no huddles.

But although his professional accomplishments were similar to Malzahn's, he later acknowledged that the experiment at Auburn was probably doomed to fail from the start. After his stunning ouster, Franklin said he was foolish not to realize that head coach Tommy Tuberville's loyalty to his core of long-term assistants would trump his commitment to Franklin's new spread offense.

"I'm a history teacher and a history student," Franklin said. "When you look at the history of [Auburn under Tuberville], coordinators come in, coordinators leave, and those guys [assistants] stay."

Franklin's demise started with Auburn's embarrassing loss to Vanderbilt on October 4. Fearing he had lost the team, Franklin decided to coach with renewed and almost maniacal enthusiasm the following week. On October 7, he barked out a "George Patton speech" in a team meeting. Later, during practice, he coached every position on the offense.

"I was 25 years old again," Franklin said. "I ran routes. I ran and grabbed people. I got in people's faces."

When practice was over, he felt satisfied. Players seemed encouraged. Tuberville even told the team to support Franklin. "I thought maybe the gamble had paid off," Franklin said. "Maybe I needed to be more aggressive on the field and not so concerned about feelings."

The next morning, he said, nothing seemed amiss. By the afternoon, he had been fired.

"I took a chance. I knew that we had to do something desperate," Franklin said. "I had a talk with Coach Tuberville about making some changes and really letting me go with it. I thought it might happen until he walked in the door. I looked at him and knew I was going to be fired. He said, 'This thing isn't working. I feel like I've got to do something.' I said, 'Coach, are you trying to fire me?' He said, 'Yeah, I am.'"

In a now-infamous scene, Franklin packed up his office and tossed his belongings into the back of his car while being filmed and photographed by media.

Auburn fans hope Malzahn's tenure has a happier ending.

100 The Story of the 1988 Sugar Bowl

Pat Dye will never be wanting for garish or ugly ties. Frustrated Syracuse fans ensured more than 20 years ago that Dye's wardrobe would always be full.

With the tie game now extinct in the NCAA football—and replaced at times by an unwieldy series of overtimes—it's easy to forget how frequent and vexing ties could be in the old days.

One tie was especially rankling for the Syracuse Orangemen and their fans.

Syracuse entered the Sugar Bowl following the 1987 season with an undefeated 11–0 record and a No. 4 national ranking. With a victory, the Orange could claim an undefeated season and at least a share of the national championship.

With seconds remaining and Auburn on the Syracuse 13, Dye opted for a game-tying field goal rather than an attempt at the end zone. The Tigers finished the season 9–1–2. Syracuse finished 11–0–1 and very, very bitter.

"I have no idea what he was thinking," said Syracuse coach Dick MacPherson said. "What did they come here for in the first place? I told my players after we kicked the field goal to go ahead that it was as good as a touchdown. I was shocked when he went for the field goal. For someone to allow that little guy to come out and kick, I just don't understand."

MacPherson said he thought Dye's sole intention was to prevent Syracuse from reaching a perfect season.

"I gotta believe his menu was to stop us from being 12–0," he said.

Kicker Win Lyle said that some of his teammates were shouting for him not to go. Quarterback Jeff Burger admitted he wanted to go for the win, but Dye said Auburn had played too hard to lose on a high-risk final play.

Dye got stuck with the derisive nickname "Pat Tie," but won't apologize for his decision. He said Syracuse players were hanging all over Auburn's top receiver, Lawyer Tillman, and the Tigers couldn't draw a flag.

"They were holding, tackling, doing anything they could to keep him from getting downfield, and the officials wouldn't call it," Dye said. "They about tore his uniform off him, and the officials would not call a penalty on Syracuse.

"I was so mad when it came down to fourth down, I said, 'Well, our kids played too hard and too good to get beat. If they ain't going to call a penalty, we're going to kick a field goal.'

"That upset Syracuse fans, but I wasn't concerned about that. I was concerned about our football team. I thought they played well enough to win. If I thought Lawyer Tillman could get off the ball and have a fair chance to make it to the end zone, I probably would have gone for it. He was a 6'4", 225-pound wide receiver, so if you throw it up to him, you've got a 50–50 chance to get a touchdown.

They knew that, and that's the reason they weren't going to let him get off the line of scrimmage."

There's another twist to the story that lets it end on a bit of a lighthearted note. After the bowl game, a Syracuse radio station collected 2,000 ties and mailed them to Dye in Auburn. Happy to take the joke, Dye autographed each of the ties and sold them at an auction, raising about $30,000 for Auburn's general scholarship fund.

Sources

1. Ralph "Shug" Jordan

"Alabama Academy of Honor: Ralph 'Shug' Jordan." Alabama Department of Archives and History. 16 Mar. 2009 <http://www.archives.state.al.us/famous/Academy/r_jordan.html>.

Donnell, Rich. *Shug: The Life and Times of Auburn's Ralph 'Shug' Jordan*. New York: Owl Bay, 1993.

Flynt, Wayne. *Alabama in the Twentieth Century*. Tuscaloosa: University of Alabama, 2004.

Hester, Wayne. *Where Tradition Began: The Centennial History of Auburn Football*. Birmingham, Ala: Seacoast Pub., *Birmingham News*, 1991. p. 36–37, 40.

Marshall, Phillip. *Stadium Stories Auburn Tigers (Stadium Stories Series)*. Guilford: Globe Pequot, 2005. p. 49.

2. The 1957 National Championship Team

Boyles, Bob. *Fifty Years of College Football a History of America's Most Colorful Sport*. New York, NY: Skyhorse Pub., 2007. p. 86.

Housel, David. *Auburn University Football Vault*. Grand Rapids: Whitman, 2007. p. 71.

Marshall, Phillip. *Stadium Stories Auburn Tigers (Stadium Stories Series)*. Guilford: Globe Pequot, 2005.

3. When Alabama Came to Auburn: The 1989 Iron Bowl

Housel, David. *Auburn University Football Vault*. Grand Rapids: Whitman, 2007. p. 108–9.

Maisel, Ivan. "Home is where Auburn's heart is." *Dallas Morning News* 2 Dec. 1989.

Medley, Joe. "Special feelings come with memories of the Iron Bowl." *Anniston Star* 19 Nov. 1999.

4. George Petrie: Coach and University Leader

Bolton, Clyde. *War Eagle A Story of Auburn Football*. Strode Pub, 1979. p. 4.

Browning, Al. *Kick 'Em Big Blue: Memorable Games and Memorable Names in Auburn University Football History.* Mason: Five Points South Pubns, 2001. p. 15–20.

Hester, p. 3.

Jernigan, Mike. *Auburn Man: The Life & Times of George Petrie.* New York: The Donnell Group, 2007.

5. The 2004 Undefeated Team

Woodbery, Evan. "BCS controversy motivates Tigers; AU uses anger." *Mobile Register* 17 Dec. 2004.

Woodbery, Evan. "Tigers wanted shot at Orange." *Mobile Register* 6 Dec. 2004.

6. Punt, Bama, Punt! The Story of the 1972 Iron Bowl

Fiutak, Pete. "Scout.com: 100 Greatest Finishes—No. 81 to 90." College Football News. 9 July 2007. 16 Mar. 2009 <http://cfn.scout.com/2/654773.html>.

Forde, Pat. "Iron Bowl turns mortals into heroes." ESPN. 19 Nov. 2004. 16 Mar. 2009 <http://proxy.espn.go.com/ncf/columns/story?columnist=forde_pat&id=1926783>.

"Punt Bama Punt." YouTube. 16 Mar. 2009 <http://www.youtube.com/watch?v=VIsbeUefKNM&feature=related>.

7. Jordan-Hare Stadium

Dodd, Dennis. "Top 25 college football stadiums." CBSSports.com. 16 Mar. 2009 <http://www.sportsline.com/collegefootball/story/6437023>.

Hayes, Matt. "No venue more intimidating than Autzen Stadium." *Sporting News.* 7 Aug. 2006. 16 Mar. 2009 <http://www.sportingnews.com/yourturn/viewtopic.php?t=115554>.

Woodbery, Evan. "AU running rotation limited." *Press-Register [Mobile]* 2 Sept. 2007.

Woodbery, Evan. "Road, Sweet Road." *Press-Register [Mobile]* 27 Sept. 2007.

Woodbery, Evan. "Stadium gets a new look." *Press-Register [Mobile]* 13 July 2007.

8. Bo Jackson

Flatter, Ron. "Bo knows stardom and disappointment." ESPN. 16 Mar. 2009 <http://espn.go.com/sportscentury/fe tures/00016045.html>.

Schaap, Dick, and Bo Jackson. *Bo Knows Bo*. New York: Doubleday Books, 1990.

Wulf, Steve. "It Hurts Just To Watch Him." *Sports Illustrated* 16 Mar. 1992.

http://vault.sportsillustrated.cnn.com/vault/article/magazine/MAG10 03543/index.htm

http://espn.go.com/sportscentury/features/00016045.html

9. Pat Dye

Auburn University Athletics. "Jordan-Hare Stadium Field To Be Named After Pat Dye." Press release. 16 Sept. 2005. Auburn University.

Bolton, p. 289, 291–94.

Dunnavant, Keith. *Coach: The Life of Paul "Bear" Bryant*. Boston: St. Martin's Griffin, 2005.

Dunnavant, Keith. *The Missing Ring: How Bear Bryant and the 1966 Alabama Crimson Tide Were Denied College Football's Most Elusive Prize*. New York: Thomas Dunne Books, 2006.

10. Pat Sullivan

Auburn University Athletics. "Former Auburn Football Player Pat Sullivan Named Walter Gilbert Award Recipient." Press release. Auburn Tigers. 7 Nov. 2008.

Bolton, Clyde. "Superman Sullivan, Boy Wonder Beasley: Together, they win huge game over Georgia." *Birmingham News* 13 Nov. 1971.

Bolton, Clyde. *War Eagle: A Story of Auburn Football*. Strode Pub, 1979.

Hester, p. 87–91.

"1971–37th Award." Heisman.com.

"Player Bio: Pat Sullivan." Samford University, Official Athletic Site. 16 Mar. 2009 <http://samfordsports.cstv.com/sports/m-footbl/mtt/sullivan_pat00.html>.

11. The Iron Bowl

"Jason Bosley." Personal interview. 18 Nov. 2008.

"Jerraud Powers." Personal interview. 24 Nov. 2008.

Walsh, Christopher J. *100 Things Every Crimson Fan Should Know & Do Before They Die*. Chicago, Il: Triumph Books, 2008.

12. Jimmy Hitchcock: Auburn's First All-American

Akin, William. "Jim Hitchcock." The Baseball Biography Project. Society for American Baseball Research. 16 Mar. 2009 <http://bioproj.sabr.org/bioproj.cfm?a=v&v=l&bid=286&pid=6373>.

Hester, p. 24.

13. Mike Donahue

Browning, p. 68.

Hester, p. 15–20.

Marshall, Phillip. *Stadium Stories Auburn Tigers (Stadium Stories Series)*. Guilford: Globe Pequot, 2005. p. 11-12.

"Mickey Logue and Jack Simms, Auburn: The Loveliest Village Photograph Collection, RG 798." Auburn University Libraries. 17 Mar. 2009 <http://www.lib.auburn.edu/archive/find-aid/798/0000001d.htm>.

Umphlett, Wiley Lee. *Creating the Big Game: John W. Heisman and the Invention of American Football*. Westport, Conn: Greenwood Press, 1992.

14. Auburn-UGA in 1971

"Auburn wins thriller, 35–20: Passing of Sullivan good for four TDs." *Birmingham News* 13 Nov. 1971.

Dooley, Vince, and Blake Giles. *Vince Dooley's Tales from the 1980 Georgia Bulldogs*. Grand Rapids: Sports Publishing, 2007.

Housel, David, comp. *Auburn: 100 Years of Football Glory*. 1992. p. 96.

15. The Auburn Creed

Jernigan."Sesquicentennial Celebration." Auburn University. 17 Mar. 2009 <http://www.auburn.edu/communications_markeking/150/creed.html>.

16. Backfield Built for Two: Ronnie Brown and Carnell Williams

Glier, Ray. "Stars of Auburn's Backfield Are Aligned in an Unselfish Quest to Win." *New York Times* 2 Jan. 2005.

Klein, Gary. "Auburn's Complete Fleet." Latimes.com. 16 Mar. 2009 <http://articles.latimes.com/2003/aug/28/sports/sp-auburn28>.

Mandel, Stewart. "Four Score." *Sports Illustrated* 18 Aug. 2003. SI.com. 16 Mar. 2009 <http://vault.sportsillustrated.cnn.com/vault/article/web/COM1033381/index.htm>.

Medley, Joe. "Split decision: Expect Williams, Brown to share more carries in '04." *Anniston Star* 18 Jan. 2004.

Silver, Michael. "From Auburn to the NFL." *Sports Illustrated* 2 May 2005. SI.com. 16 Mar. 2009 <http://vault.sportsillustrated.cnn.com/vault/article/magazine/MAG1111017/index.htm>.

17. An Era of Great Defense: Bill Oliver, Gene Chizik, Will Muschamp

Hicks, Tommy. "Four Downs with Bill Oliver." *Press-Register [Mobile]* 4 Oct. 2006.

Woodbery, Evan. "Muschamp's intensity a hit with players." *Press-Register [Mobile]* 17 Oct. 2007.

Woodbery, Evan. "WILL POWER: Muschamp's players on edge." *Mobile Register* 5 Mar. 2006.

18. The 1983 Season: Shunned by the Poll

"Auburn Fullback Dies After Sprint in Practice." *New York Times* 21 Aug. 1983.

Bolton, Clyde. "Poll says Miami can become No. 1 with Orange win." *Birmingham News* 2 Jan. 1984, sec. B: 5.

"College Football Belt Top 25: 1983 Auburn Tigers." The College Football Belt. 17 Mar. 2009.

Hollis, Charles. "Being shunned by poll just part of AU's growing pains." *Birmingham News* 4 Jan. 1984, sec. B: 1.

Hollis, Charles. "'We deserve a better fate,' Dye says of No. 3 ranking." *Birmingham News* 4 Jan. 1984, sec. A: 1.

Suggs, Rob. *Top Dawg: Mark Richt and the Revival of Georgia Football.* Thomas Nelson, 2008.

Winslett, Deric. "Auburn Football: Will The Tigers Defeat The Ghosts of Championships Past?" Bleacher Report. 23 June 2008. 17 Mar. 2009 <http://bleacherreport.com/articles/32015-auburn-football-will-the-tigers-defeat-the-ghosts-of-championships-past>.

19. The Best 10 Games of the 2000s: What the Fans Say

"Tuberville's Top Ten." Auburn Athletics. 17 Mar. 2009 <http://auburntigers.cstv.com/sports/m-footbl/spec-rel/top-ten/tuberville-top-ten-results.html>.

Woodbery, Evan. "Reversal of fortune." *Press-Register [Mobile]* 17 Sept. 2006.

20. First Auburn-Alabama game in 1893.

Dunnavant, Keith. 2007. *The Missing Ring.* New York: St. Martin's Griffin. p. 23.

Marshall, Phillip. 2005. *Stadium Stories: Auburn Tigers.* Guilford, Conn: Insiders' Guide

21. Experience Tiger Walk

"Al Borges." Personal interview. 15 Oct. 2006.

Maisel, Ivan. "The best Walk in America." ESPN. 17 Mar. 2009 <http://espn.go.com/page2/s/maisel/031120auburn.html>.

"Walter McFadden." Personal interview. 8 Nov. 2008.

23. The History of Auburn's Uniforms

"The Helmet Project." NationalChamps.net. 17 Mar. 2009 <http://www.nationalchamps.net/Helmet_Project/>.

Woodbery, Evan. "Hood gets professional opinion." *Press-Register [Mobile]* 6 Nov. 2008.

24. Terry Beasley

Beasley, Terry, and Rich Donnell. *God's Receiver: The Terry Beasley Story.* New York: Donnell Group, 1999.

Fitzgerald, Francis J. *Sullivan to Beasley: Memories of a Special Time.* Birmingham: Epic Sports, 1999.

25. The SEC: How the League as We Know It Came to Be

"About the Southeastern Conference." SECSports.com. 17 Mar. 2009 <http://www.secsports.com/index.php?change_well_id=9993&s>.

"New College Body Planned in South: Twelve Universities Take Steps to Break Away From Intercollegiate A.A." *New York Times* 12 Dec. 1920.

Roza, Greg. *Football in the SEC.* New York: Rosen, 2008.

"Stories of Character: Celebrating 75 Years." SECSports.com. 17 Mar. 2009<http://www.secsports.com/index.php?s=&url_channel_id=22&url_article_id=9234&change_well_id=2>.

26. The "Wreck Tech" Tradition and Auburn's 1955 Win

Auburn University. Communications and Marketing. "Wreck Tech Pajama Parade, Pep Rally Set for Friday Evening." Press release. Auburn University. 30 Aug. 2005. 17 Mar. 2009 <http://www.ocm.auburn.edu/news_releases/wrecktech05.html>.

Browning, p. 31–32.

Danforth, Ed. "Hungry War Eagle Claws Tech, 14-12: Tigers End Long Famine, Win First Here Since 1940." *Atlanta Journal* 16 Oct. 1955, sec. D: 1.

27. David Housel

Auburn University. Athletics. "Jordan-Hare Stadium Press Box Named After David Housel." Press release. Auburn Tigers. 29 Oct. 2005. 17 Mar. 2009 <http://auburntigers.cstv.com/sports/m-footbl/spec-rel/102905aaa.html>.

Coulter, Jay. "It's Weird Not Having David Housel Around." Football Saturday In The South. 21 Oct. 2005. 17 Mar. 2009 <http://footballsaturday.blogspot.com/2005/10/its-weird-not-having-david-housel.html>.

Hancock, Bill. *Riding with the Blue Moth.* Grand Rapids: Sports, 2006.

28. Recruiting Players to the Plains

"Walter McFadden." Personal interview. 14 Dec. 2008.

29. Pumping Iron: Auburn's Strength Program

Marshall, Phillip. "Far from the cheering crowds, Yoxall molds Auburn players." Auburn Undercover. 1 July 2008. 17 Mar. 2009<http://auburnundercover.com/news/articles/2008/7/1/far-from-the-cheering-crowds-yoxall-molds-auburn-players>.

"Player Bio: Kevin Yoxall." Auburn Athletics. 17 Mar. 2009 <http://auburntigers.cstv.com/sports/mfootbl/mtt/yoxall_kevin00.html>.

Wilner, Jon. "Yoxall Helps Bolster Bruins' Brawn." *Los Angeles Daily News* 30 Aug. 1996.

Yoxall, Kevin. "The Strength Report: Developing the Explosive Athlete: Auburn's Off Season Training." *American Football Monthly* Nov. 2007.

30. On the Air: Auburn Radio Broadcasters

Auburn University. "Auburn Play-by-Play Announcer Jim Fyffe Dead at 57." Press release. 17 Mar. 2009 <http://www.ocm.auburn.edu/news_releases/fyffe.html>.

Fyffe, Jim. *Touchdown Auburn: Memories and Calls from the Announcer's Booth.* New York: Donnel Group, 1996.

Murphy, Mark. "Why Bramblett Is The New Voice Of Auburn Sports." Inside the Auburn Tigers. 24 June 2003. 17 Mar. 2009 <http://auburn.scout.com/2/117629.html>.

31. A Modern Rivalry: Auburn-LSU

Woodbery, Evan. "Showdown of Tigers holds key to future." *Mobile Register* 18 Sept. 2004.

Woodbery, Evan. "Top-10 Tigers tangle today." *Press-Register [Mobile]* 16 Sept. 2006.

32. Family Traditions

Bean, Josh. "Family Ties: Williamson's Terrance Coleman one of five from Mobile to sign with Tigers." *Press-Register [Mobile]* 5 Feb. 2009.

Caldwell, Jason. "Brother of AU Player a LB Prospect, Too." Inside the Auburn Tigers. 22 Jan. 2008. 17 Mar. 2009 <http://auburn.scout.com/2/722131.html>.

Marshall, Phillip. The Auburn Experience. 2004. p. 215-216.

33. John Heisman

Browning, p. 31

Hester, p. 13.

Pennington, Bill. *The Heisman: Great American Stories of the Men Who Won*. New York: Harper Entertainment, 2005. p. 6.

Umphlett, p. 48–56, 68

34. Jeff Beard

Housel, David. *Jeff Beard: Auburn Man*. Auburn, 1994.

35. Zeke Smith

Marshall, Phillip. *The Auburn Experience*. 2004. p. 139

36. Gene Chizik

"Antarrious Williams." Personal interview. 13 Dec. 2008.

"Carlos Rogers." Personal interview. 15 Dec. 2008.

Herndon, Mike. "'The right guy:' Former coaches, players say Chizik is up to the challenge at Auburn." *Press-Register [Mobile]* 16 Dec. 2008.

37. The Sacrifices of James Owen and the First Black Players

Gossom, Thom. *Walk-On*. Ann Arbor: State Street Press, 2008.

38. Jason Campbell

Heckert, Justin. "REVERSING FIELD: To understand just how Jason Campbell makes it work for the Redskins, we had to reveal his life …in reverse." *ESPN The Magazine*. 17 Mar. 2009 <http://sports.espn.go.com/espnmag/story?section=magazine&id=3660356>.

Judge, Clark. "Camp tour: 'Skins QB has ability and, finally, stability." CBSSports.com. 23 Aug. 2007. 17 Mar. 2009 <http://www.cbssports.com/nfl/story/10303350>.

Woodbery, Evan. "Campbell enjoying payback." *Mobile Register* 7 Oct. 2004.

Woodbery, Evan. "Four Tigers go in first round." *Mobile Register* 24 Apr. 2005.

39. Tommy Tuberville

Birmingham Christian Family Magazine. 8 Jan. 2009 <http://www.birminghamchristian.com/pdfs/BCF0903center.pdf>.

Crise, Doug. "Arkansas Sports Hall of Fame: Tommy the technician." *Arkansas Democrat Gazette [Little Rock]* 28 Jan. 2008.

Marshall, Phillip. "Small-town values serve Tuberville well as he heads toward his 10th Auburn season." Auburn Undercover. 16 July 2008. 17 Mar. 2009 <http://auburnundercover.com/news/articles/2008/7/16/small-town-values-serve-tuberville-well-as-he-heads-toward-his-10th-auburn-season>.

40. Go to an Auburn Club Meeting and Meet the Coach

Woodbery, Evan. "Multi-taskers: Coaches are public relations directors, recruiters, fundraisers, disciplinarians, but still must produce wins." *Press-Register [Mobile]* 23 July 2008.

41. Jimmy "Red" Phillips

Marshall, Phillip. *The Auburn Experience.* 2004. p. 130.

Lee, Spencer. "Twenty-one questions with Jimmy "Red" Phillips." Buzzle Web Portal. 9 July 2002. 17 Mar. 2009 <http://www.buzzle.com/editorials/7-9-2002-22043.asp>.

43. In the Classroom: Great Student-Athletes, Past and Present

"Dontarrious Thomas." 49ers.com. 17 Mar. 2009 <http://sf49ers.com/team/roster_detail.php?PRKey=172&section=TE%20Roster>.

"Dr. Win Lyle." Kenny Howard Athletic Training Fellowship. 17 Mar. 2009 <http://www.khowardfellow.org/wynlyle.php>.

Marshall, Phillip. *The Auburn Experience.* 2004. p. 78, 142.

44. The Eric Ramsey Case and Auburn's Run-Ins with the NCAA

"Legislative Services Database." 17 Mar. 2009 <https://web1.ncaa.org/LSDBi/exec/homepage>.

Rhoden, William C. "I May Have Been Lax, Says Beleaguered Dye." *New York Times* 4 Nov. 1991.

Telander, Rick. "No Hero In Sight: What of an ex-Auburn football player who chose to take the money and run his tape recorder?" *Sports Illustrated* 4 Nov. 1991.

45. Vince Dooley

"About Vince." Vince Dooley: The Documentary. 17 Mar. 2009 <http://www.vincedooleydvd.com/vince/index.htm>.

Marshall, Phillip. *The Auburn Experience.* 2004. p. 91.

Starrs, Chris. "Vince Dooley (b. 1932)." New Georgia Encyclopedia. 17 Mar. 2009 <http://www.georgiaencyclopedia.org/nge/Article.jsp?id=h-1999>.

"Vince Dooley." Telephone interview. 2006.

46. Appreciate the Sacrifice of Two-a-Days

Woodbery, Evan. "Auburn football team sweats through two-a-days." *Press-Register [Mobile]* 6 Aug. 2007.

47. Tucker Frederickson

Eisen, Michael. "Where are They Now? Tucker Frederickson." Giants.com. 18 Jan. 2005. 17 Mar. 2009 <http://www.giants.com/news/eisen/story.asp?story_id=5086>.

FHSAA. "FHSAA announces 33-member All-Century football team." Press release. 12 Dec. 2007. 17 Mar. 2009 <http://www.fhsaa.org/news/2007/1212.htm>.

Marshall, Phillip. *The Auburn Experience.* 2004. p. 96-98.

"Tucker Frederickson." College Football Hall of Fame. 17 Mar. 2009 <http://www.collegefootball.org/famersearch.php?id=60063>.

48. The 1942 Upset of Georgia

Browning, p. 59–60.

Newman, Zipp. "Dusting 'Em Off." *Birmingham News* 21 Nov. 1942.

Phillips, Bob. "Monk Gafford Outshines Bulldog Star Sinkwich In Surprise of the Year." *Birmingham News* 21 Nov. 1942.

"Plainsmen Set to Face Georgia." *Birmingham News* 20 Nov. 1942.

49. The Auburn University Band

"History." Auburn University Bands. 17 Mar. 2009 <http://www.auburn.edu/auband/history/>.

50. The Bacardi Bowl

"The Bacardi Bowl 1937." MMBolding.com. 17 Mar. 2009 <http://www.mmbolding.com/bowls/Bacardi_1937.htm>.

Newman, Zipp. "Dusting 'Em Off column." *Birmingham News* 1 Jan. 1937.

Newman, Zipp. "Wildcats Get late tally to gain 7-7 draw." *Birmingham News* 2 Jan. 1937.

Nissenson, Herschel. Tales from College Football's Sidelines. Grand Rapids: Sports, 2001.

51. Aubie: The Lovable Mascot

"History of Aubie." The Official Website of Aubie the Tiger. 17 Mar. 2009<http://www.auburn.edu/student_info/student_life/aubie/history.html>.

"Justin Shugart." Email interview. 9 Jan. 2009.

52. Watch the Pregame Eagle Flight

Auburn University. "AU's Spirit to fly in recognition of bald eagle's removal from Endangered Species List." Press release. Wire Eagle. 24 Oct. 2007. 17 Mar. 2009 <http://wireeagle.auburn.edu/news/223>.

"Eagles to return to sidelines at football games this fall." Auburn E-Commons. Aug. 2004. 17 Mar. 2009 <http://www.ocm.auburn.edu/ecommons/august04/story4.html>.

55. A Greatly Exaggerated Demise: 1972 Showed New Life

Hemphill, Paul. *A Tiger Walk Through History.* Tuscaloosa: University of Alabama P, 2008. p. 134–38.

Housel, David. *Saturdays to Remember.* The Village P, 1973. p. 201–2.

56. The Powerbrokers: Behind-the-Scenes Influence

"Board of Trustees Biographies." Auburn University. 17 Mar. 2009 <http://www.auburn.edu/administration/trustees/members.html>.

Fish, Mike. "A Tiger of a trustee." ESPN. 13 Jan. 2006. 17 Mar. 2009 <http://sports.espn.go.com/ncf/news/story?id=2285976>.

57. Walter Gilbert and the Award that Bears His Name

Auburn University Athletics. "Auburn University Seeking Nominations for the Walter Gilbert Award." Press release. Auburn University. 17 Mar. 2009 <http://grfx.cstv.com/photos/schools/aub/sports/tigers-unlimited/auto_pdf/gilbert-award-release.pdf.>.

Auburn University Athletics. "Former Auburn Gootball Player D. Gaines Lanier Namer Walter Gilbert Award Recipient." Press release. Auburn Athletics. 26 Oct. 2007. 17 Mar. 2009 <http://auburntigers.cstv.com/genrel/102607aaa.html>.

Marshall, Phillip. *The Auburn Experience.* 2004. p. 102.

58. The Championship Season of 1913

Browning, p. 35–48

Chappell, James E. "Mike Donahue's Men Overcome Stubborn Defense in Smashing Style." *Birmingham News* 16 Nov. 1913.

"Kirk Newell." Alabama Sports Hall of Fame. 17 Mar. 2009 <http://www.ashof.org/index.php?category=Football&refno=252 &search=distinguished&src=directory&srctype=display&view=co mpany>.

"Stage is Set for South's Best Game." *Birmingham News* 15 Nov. 1913.

59. Tracy Rocker

Marshall, Phillip. *The Auburn Experience.* 2004. p. 134.

"Tracy Rocker." Telephone interview. 12 Jan. 2009.

60. Crowd Control

Barnhart, Tony. "Some strange but true UGA-Auburn finishes." *Atlanta Journal-Constitution* 10 Nov. 2007.

Bradley, Mark. "Between the Hoses." *Atlanta Journal-Constitution* 18 Nov. 1986.

"Dye: Water better than using billy clubs." *Atlanta Journal-Constitution* 19 Nov. 1986.

Hudspeth, Ron. "Fans on field spoil the fun for everyone." *Atlanta Journal-Constitution* 20 Nov. 1986.

Westerdawg, Paul. "Game Between the Hoses: UGA vs. Auburn." Georgia Sports Blog. 11 July 208. 17 Mar. 2009 <http://georgias-ports.blogspot.com/2008/07/game-between-hoses-uga-vs-auburn .html>.

61. How Auburn Made Nine Picks in One Game

Johnston, Joey, and Josh Poltilove. "Ex-Football Star Reaves Says Police Planted Cocaine." *The Tampa Tribune.* TBO.com. 4 Aug.

2008. 17 Mar. 2009 <http://www2.tbo.com/content/2008/aug/04/041709/ex-football-star-reaves-arrested-drug-charges/news-metro/>.

Woodbery, Evan. "AU peels Orange." *Mobile Register* 3 Oct. 2004.

62. Jimmy Sidle

Marshall, Phillip. *The Auburn Experience*. 2004. p. 138.

"Ol' devil Sidle does Vols in." *Birmingham News* 28 Sept. 1963.

63. Visit the New Lovelace Museum

Marshall, Phillip. "Construction days away on basketball arena; football locker rooms, training rooms are like new." Auburn Undercover. 9 July 2008. 17 Mar. 2009 <http://www.auburnundercover.com/news/articles/2008/7/9/construction-days-away-on-basketball-arena-football-locker-rooms-training-rooms-are-like-new>.

"Welcome to the Lovelace Museum & Hall of Honor." Lovelace Athletic Museum & Hall of Honor. 17 Mar. 2009 <http://www.lovelacemuseum.com/>.

64. The LSU-Auburn Hurricane Ivan Game in 2004

Woodbery, Evan, and Thomas Murphy. "Game calls to come today." *Mobile Register* 17 Sept. 2004.

Woodbery, Evan. "AU decision will ignite criticism." *Mobile Register* 16 Sept. 2004.

Woodbery, Evan. "AU, LSU working to play on Saturday." *Mobile Register* 15 Sept. 2004.

Woodbery, Evan. "AU wins by toenail." *Mobile Register* 19 Sept. 2004.

Woodbery, Evan. "Showdown of Tigers holds key to future." *Mobile Register* 18 Sept. 2004.

65. Watch Auburn Get the ODK Trophy at Halftime

"The James E. Foy, ODK Sportsmanship Trophy." Auburn University. 17 Mar. 2009 <http://www.auburn.edu/odk/Trophy.htm>.

66. Roll Toomer's Corner on a Saturday Night

""Rolling" Toomer's Corner." Rocky Mountain Auburn Club. 17 Mar. 2009 <http://www.coloradotigers.com/concourse/traditions_toomers.htm>.

"Tree experts giving makeover to Auburn's historic Toomer's oaks." Wire Eagle. 17 June 2008. Auburn University. 17 Mar. 2009 <http://wireeagle.auburn.edu/news/372>.

Woodbery, Evan. "AU president to meet with coaches." *Press-Register [Mobile]* 2 Nov. 2007.

67. How a "Hiring Committee" Landed Jordan and Dye

Housel, David. *Auburn University Football Vault.* Grand Rapids: Whitman, 2007. p. 61–64.

68. Aundray Bruce

George, Thomas. "After His Fall From Grace, Aundray Bruce Starts Over." *New York Times* 22 Mar. 1992.

Marshall, Phillip. *The Auburn Experience.* 2004. p. 75.

69. Go to Fan Day and Get an Autograph...from a Backup

"Tristan Davis." Personal interview. 2 Aug. 2008.

70. Paul "Bear" Bryant and Auburn

Browning, Al. I *Remember Paul "Bear" Bryant.* New York: Cumberland House, 2001. p. 117.

Dunnavant, Keith. *Coach: the Life of Paul "Bear" Bryant.* New York: Thomas Dunne Books, 2005. p. 141–42.

Mandell, Ted. *Heart Stoppers and Hail Marys.* New York: Hardwood Press, 2006.

Shepard, David. *Bama, Bear Bryant and the Bible.* New York: Writers Club P, 2002. p. 35.

71. Why Legion Field Never Really Felt Like Home

Marshall, Phillip. *Stadium Stories Auburn Tigers (Stadium Stories Series).* Guilford: Globe Pequot, 2005. p. 128–30.

72. The Miserable 1950 Season of 1950

Housel, David. *Saturdays to Remember.* The Village Press, 1973. p. 19–20.

73. The Alma Mater and the Fight Song

"Auburn Fight Song, Alma Mater and Creed." Auburn Athletics. 17 Mar. 2009 <http://auburntigers.cstv.com/trads/aub-trads-fight-song.html>.

Auburn University. University Relations. "AU Prof Discovers Long-Anonymous Author of Alma Mater." Press release. Auburn University News. 7 June 2000. 17 Mar. 2009 <http://www.auburn.edu/administration/univrel/news/archive/6_00news/6_00almamater.html>.

Auburn University. University Relations. "Robert Allen, "War Eagle' Composer, Dies of Cancer at 73." Press release. Auburn University News. 5 Oct. 2000. 17 Mar. 2009 <http://www.auburn.edu/administration/univrel/news/archive/10_00news/10_00wareagle.html>.

74. Kendall Simmons

Kaplan-Meyer, Gabrielle. "Kendall Simmons Tackles Diabetes." Diabetes Health. 27 Nov. 2006. 17 Mar. 2009 <http://www.diabeteshealth.com/read/2006/11/27/4920/kendall-simmons-tackles-diabetes/>.

Medley, Joe. "Simmons looks to paint winning picture." *Anniston Star* 23 Aug. 2001.

75. Have a Sip of Toomer's Legendary Lemonade

"Drug store still turns lemons into lemonade." *Plainsman [Auburn]* 6 Nov. 2008. The Plainsman. 10 Jan. 2009 <www.theplainsman.com/campus/2008/nov06/drugstore_still_turns_lemons_lemonade>.

Marshall, Phillip. *Stadium Stories Auburn Tigers (Stadium Stories Series)*. Guilford: Globe Pequot, 2005. p. 13.

""Rolling" Toomer's Corner." Rocky Mountain Auburn Club. 17 Mar. 2009<http://www.coloradotigers.com/concourse/traditions_toomers.htm>.

"Toomers Drugs and the Haisten Family." DFW Auburn Club. 17 Mar. 2009 <http://www.dfwauburn.com/html/Archive.htm?article_id=693>.

"Toomer's Drugs, Auburn, Alabama." ChoppedOnion.com. 17 Mar. 2009 <http://www.choppedonion.com/id116.html>.

Weaver, Amy. "Auburn University building names, namesakes." *Opelika-Auburn News* 10 Feb. 2008.

77. Terry Bowden

Perrin, Mike. "Passion for the game leads Terry Bowden back to sidelines as UNA head coach." *Birmingham News* 2 Jan. 2009.

"Terry's Long Bio." The Official Web Site for Terry Bowden. 17 Mar. 2009 <http://www.terrybowden.com/long_bio.html>.

78. Doug Barfield: Following a Legend

Handwerger, Bradley. "Ex-AU coach Barfield still on the job at 69." *Decatur Daily* 13 May 2005.

Marshall, Phillip. *The Auburn Experience.* 2004. p. 70.

79. How Auburn Snagged Carnell Williams

Woodbery, Evan. "A Show of Force: That's what it took to get Carnell Williams to Auburn, and what it'll take to win Tennessee showdown." *Mobile Register* 29 Sept. 2004.

80. The Coldest Game Ever in Alabama? The 2000 Iron Bowl

Medley, Joe. "Tigers Win West!" *Anniston Star* 19 Nov. 2000.

81. Fob James

Webb, Samuel L., and Margaret E. Armbrester. *Alabama Governors.* Tuscaloosa: University of Alabama Press, 2001.

82. Auburn: The "Loveliest Village on the Plains"

"Eagle Over All." *Sports Illustrated* 21 Sept. 1964.

Goldsmith, Oliver, and Arthur Barrett. *The Traveller and The Deserted Village.* Ed. London: Macmillan, 1899.

Rousseau, G. S. *Oliver Goldsmith: The Critical Heritage. The critical heritage series.* London: Routledge, 1995.

Standard Classics with Biographical Sketches and Helpful Notes. Arranged and Edited for Use in the Higher Grades of the Common Schools. A Fifth Reader. Boston, etc: Educational Pub. Co., 1910.

83. Auburn's Athletic Facilities

Woodbery, Evan. "Stadium gets a new look." *Press-Register [Mobile]* 13 July 2007.

84. Dameyune Craig

"Dameyune Craig." USAJaguars.com. 17 Mar. 2009 <http://www.usajaguars.com/ViewArticle.dbml?SPSID=99699& SPID=12275&DB_OEM_ID=8300&ATCLID=1419905&Q_S EASON=2008>.

Marshall, Phillip. *The Auburn Experience.* 2004. p. 81–82.

85. Topping Florida in 2001

Medley, Joe. "Hero-making victory." *Anniston Star* 14 Oct. 2001.

Tutor, Phillip. "Sometimes desire trumps imperfection." *Anniston Star* 14 Oct. 2001.

86. Alabama-Auburn Freshman Game of 1968

Bolton, Clyde. *War Eagle.* Strode Pub, 1979. p. 260-261, 268-269.

87. Al Del Greco and Other Great Kickers in Auburn History

"Biography of Al Del Greco." All-American Speakers Bureau. 17 Mar. 2009<http://www.allamericanspeakers.com/celebritytalentbios/Al -Del-Greco>.

88. The Legend of War Eagle

"War Eagle, Tigers and Plainsmen, oh my." Plainsman [Auburn] 6 Nov. 2008. 10 Jan. 2009 <http://www.theplainsman.com/ campus/2008/nov06/war_eagle_tigers_and_plainsmen_oh_my>.

Windham, Kathryn Tucker. Alabama: one big front porch. Tuscaloosa: University of Alabama, 1991.

89. Carlos Rogers

"Carlos Rogers." Carlos Rogers Official Website. 17 Mar. 2009 <http://www.carlosrogers.com/ssp/biography/>.

"Carlos Rogers." NFL.com. 17 Mar. 2009 <http://www.nfl.com/ players/carlosrogers/profile?id=ROG136198>.

"Carlos Rogers." Personal interview. 15 Dec. 2008.

Woodbery, Evan. "Rogers anchors defense; Cornerback comeback aids Auburn." *Mobile Register* 1 Dec. 2004.

90. Jay Jacobs

"Jay Jacobs." Personal interview. 15 Dec. 2008.

Woodbery, Evan. "Jacobs part of a team as AD at Auburn." *Mobile Register* 17 July 2005.

91. Auburn players in the Hall of Fame
"Procedure Guide and Criteria." College Football Hall of Fame. 17
Mar. 2009 <http://www.collegefootball.org/famerguides.php>.

92. Auburn in the NFL: The Well-Known and Not-So-Well-Known
Pro-Football-Reference.com. 17 Mar. 2009 <http://www.pro-football-
reference.com/>.

93. Al Borges
Woodbery, Evan. "Borges makes impression." *Mobile Register* 7 Oct.
2004.

94. Know Where to Eat in Town
"Dining." The Official Visitor Guide for Auburn-Opelika. 17 Mar.
2009<http://www.aotourism.com/visitors/dining/frmDining.asp
x>.

95. Know the Story of Team Chaplain Chette Williams
Marshall, Phillip. "AU keeping the faith: Thanks to team chaplain,
Tigers find their focus." *Huntsville Times* 2 Dec. 2004.

96. Fear the Thumb
Woodbery, Evan. "Braggin' Rights: Auburn seniors leave without
losing to Alabama." *Press-Register [Mobile]* 19 Nov. 2006.

Woodbery, Evan. "Streak is still alive, but AU staying quiet." *Press-
Register [Mobile]* 20 Nov. 2007.

Woodbery, Evan. "Tuberville playing down 'fear the thumb' motto."
Press-Register [Mobile] 14 Nov. 2006.

97. Bowden's First and Last Seasons
Housel, David. *Auburn University Football Vault.* Grand Rapids:
Whitman, 2007.

98. Know Where to Grab a Cold One
"Dining." The Official Visitor Guide for Auburn-Opelika. 17 Mar.
2009<http://www.aotourism.com/visitors/dining/frmDining.asp
x>.

99. Tony Franklin and Gus Malzahn
Woodbery, Evan. "Ex-coordinator thinks his gamble backfired." *Press-
Register [Mobile]* 23 Oct. 2008.

Woodbery, Evan. "Malzahn ready to run with Auburn." *Press-Register [Mobile]* 30 Dec. 2008.

100. The Story of the 1987 Sugar Bowl

Alfano, Peter. "Dye's Tie Still Ugly In Syracuse's View." *New York Times* 3 Jan. 1988.

Buchanan, Olin. "Auburn's Dye has no regrets about tie." Rivals.com. 13 June 2006. 17 Mar. 2009 <http://collegefootball.rivals.com/content.asp?CID=552251>.

About the Author

Evan Woodbery has covered Auburn University sports for the *Press-Register* since 2004. He previously worked for *The State* newspaper in Columbia, South Carolina, and the *Anniston* (Alabama) *Star*. Woodbery grew up in Bay Village, Ohio, and Germantown, Tennessee. He lives in Auburn.